THE BEGINNER'S
Crossword
DICTIONARY

THE BEGINNER'S Crossword DICTIONARY

Everything you need to know to start solving crosswords with confidence

THE **1,001** MOST COMMON CROSSWORD ANSWERS

STANLEY NEWMAN

PUZZLE
WRIGHT
PRESS

New York

**PUZZLE
WRIGHT
PRESS**

New York

An Imprint of Sterling Publishing Co., Inc.
1166 Avenue of the Americas
New York, NY 10036

This edition is a revised and updated version of
Stanley Newman's Crossword Shortcuts by Stanley Newman

ISBN 978-1-4549-2668-9

Distributed in Canada by Sterling Publishing Co., Inc.
C/o Canadian Manda Group, 664 Annette Street
Toronto, Ontario M6S 2C8, Canada
Distributed in the United Kingdom by GMC Distribution Services
Castle Place, 166 High Street, Lewes, East Sussex BN7 1XU, England
Distributed in Australia by NewSouth Books
University of New South Wales, Sydney, NSW 2052, Australia

For information about custom editions, special sales, and premium
and corporate purchases, please contact Sterling Special Sales at
800-805-5489 or specialsales@sterlingpublishing.com.

Manufactured in Canada

2   4   6   8   10   9   7   5   3   1

sterlingpublishing.com
puzzlewright.com

Cover design by Igor Satanovsky
Cover image: Losswen / Shutterstock.com
For additional photo credits, see page 336

CONTENTS

Crosswords 101

INTRODUCTION

Welcome to *The Beginner's Crossword Dictionary*, your comprehensive guide to the 1,001 words that appear most often as the answers to American crosswords.

As anyone who regularly solves crosswords knows, certain answer words seem to pop up all the time. They're usually three- and four-letter words that are spelled with lots of vowels and common consonants, like ARIA, EAT, and ISLE. As a 35-year veteran of the puzzle biz as crossword author and editor, I know why this is so.

If you think of a completed crossword diagram as a house, short words with common letters are the necessary "mortar" that makes the longer, more interesting "brick" words in a puzzle possible. In other words, it's simply not possible to create crosswords without using these dependable little words.

The specific 1,001 words that are profiled here were selected based on computer analysis of thousands of recent crosswords from numerous American newspapers, including the puzzles I edit for the Long Island, New York, newspaper *Newsday* and the venerable *New York Times* crossword.

Just how frequently do these 1,001 words appear in crosswords? About 25% of the answers in a typical crossword will be one of the 1,001. How do we know this? We tested puzzles from sources not used to create our list, and consistently found more than a quarter of the answers matched the entries in this dictionary.

Clearly then, knowing these words and their meanings is a key for crossword success, perhaps *the* key. If you're just starting out as a crossword solver, *The Beginner's Crossword Dictionary* will truly live up to its name for you. Under each of the 1,001 words, you'll find the most frequently seen clues for that word, categorized by meaning. For example, the clues for ERA are grouped under its "significant period," "baseball statistic," "Constitutional amendment," and "detergent brand" meanings. If the prospect of learning 1,001 words seems daunting to you, keep in mind that many of these words and their meanings will already be familiar—like ADORE, ERASE, NET, and TEST.

Even solvers who are more seasoned will find a lot of good information within these pages. From a list of the world nations that use the PESO, to all the famous people named EMMA from real life and fiction, you're bound to find lots of things to add to your puzzle-solving arsenal.

In addition to the 1,001 words, scattered throughout the book you'll find three other categories of entries that I know you'll find useful:

Not So Fast!: These are common crossword clues that can have two different answers with similar spellings, like "Thin opening," for which SLIT and SLOT are both correct. I've accumulated these "two-way" clues over many years, and hope you'll save yourself a lot of "eraser time" by remembering them. This is the only book I know of that includes them.

Insider's Tip: Helpful hints on some of the 1,001 words. For example, ERIE is the only Great Lake spelled with four letters.

"Crosswords 101" Sidebars: Groups of words from particular categories, such as French words commonly seen in crosswords, Greek goddesses, and OPEC members.

Your comments on any aspect of this book are most welcome. You can reach me via regular mail at P.O. Box 69, Massapequa Park, NY 11762, or electronically through my Web site: www.StanXwords.com.

Best wishes for crossword success!

—Stan Newman

A

Front entrance of the Alamo, San Antonio, Texas, c. 1922.

▶·◆·◆·◆·◀ **AAA** ▶·◆·◆·◆·◀

THE AUTO CLUB
Formerly known as the American Automobile Association, AAA is known for its travel services, such as roadside assistance, maps, and tour books.

THE BOND RATING
AAA is typically the highest rating of creditworthiness that bond-rating services such as Standard & Poor's assign to corporate and municipal bonds.

THE POWER SOURCE
AAA is a standard size of dry-cell batteries, typically used in small electronic devices such as TV remote controls and digital cameras.

THE SHOE WIDTH
Though not commonly seen today, AAA is the narrowest of the standard widths of men's and women's shoes in the United States.

▶·◆·◆·◆·◀ **AAH** ▶·◆·◆·◆·◀

THE EXCLAMATION
Commonly seen clues include "Sound of satisfaction," "Backrub response," "Ooh and ___," and "Open wide and say ___."

▶·◆·◆·◆·◀ **AARON** ▶·◆·◆·◆·◀

THE BASEBALL GREAT
At the time of his 1976 retirement, baseball Hall of Famer Henry "Hank" Aaron held many major-league records, including lifetime home runs and runs batted in.

THE BIBLICAL BROTHER
In the Old Testament, Aaron is the older brother of Moses and Miriam. He speaks for Moses in his dealings with the Egyptian royal court, and creates the "golden calf" idol during Moses's long absence on Mount Sinai. He is portrayed in the epic 1956 film *The Ten Commandments* by John Carradine.

THE COMPOSER

The best-known works of Brooklyn-born classical composer Aaron Copland include "Fanfare for the Common Man" and the ballet scores *Appalachian Spring, Billy the Kid,* and *Rodeo.*

THE DUELER

Revolutionary War hero and third vice president of the United States (under Jefferson), Aaron Burr is most remembered today for his duel with Alexander Hamilton in 1804.

THE MEDIA MOGUL

TV and film producer Aaron Spelling was responsible for many hit series, including *Charlie's Angels, The Love Boat,* and *Dynasty.* His daughter Tori appeared on another of his series, *Beverly Hills 90210.*

▷·◆·◆·◆·◁ **ABA** ▷·◆·◆·◆·◁

THE LAWYERS

ABA is short for the American Bar Association, which sets academic standards for law schools and ethical standards for attorneys.

THE HOOPSTERS

ABA is also short for the American Basketball Association, a professional basketball league founded in the late 1960s. It eventually merged with the NBA (National Basketball Association) in the 1970s.

THE NONSENSE SONG

The 1914 tune "The Aba Daba Honeymoon" concerns an amorous pair of primates. A 1950 recording of the tune by Debbie Reynolds sold over a million copies.

▷·◆·◆·◆·◁ **ABATE** ▷·◆·◆·◆·◁

THE VERB

Commonly seen clues: "Die down," "Diminish," "Ease off," "Lessen," and "Recede."

11

►•◆•◆•◆•◄ **ABBA** ►•◆•◆•◆•◄

THE STATESMAN

South African–born Abba Eban was Israel's ambassador to the United Nations and the United States in the 1940s and 1950s, its deputy prime minister in the 1960s, and its foreign minister in the 1960s and 1970s. His books include *Voice of Israel* and *Diplomacy for a New Century*. He is a member of the very exclusive club of celebrities whose first and last names are crossword regulars (actor Alan Alda is another).

THE POP GROUP

The 1970s–1980s Swedish music pop quartet ABBA was named for the first letters in the first names of its members. Its hits include "Fernando," "Dancing Queen," and "Waterloo." The Broadway musical *Mamma Mia!* and its 2008 film adaptation are based on the songs of ABBA.

THE RHYME SCHEME

In an ABBA rhyme scheme, the first and fourth lines rhyme, as do the second and third.

►•◆•◆•◆•◄ **ABC** ►•◆•◆•◆•◄

THE NETWORK

Crossword clues for the ABC television network, bought by Disney in 1996, may be as up-to-date as the newest prime-time series. Historically, its most popular series have included *Leave It to Beaver*; *Marcus Welby, M.D.*; *Happy Days*; and *NYPD Blue*. More recent shows are *Grey's Anatomy* and *Dancing With the Stars*.

THE SONG

The 1970 Jackson 5 tune "ABC" reached number 1 on the U.S. Billboard Hot 100 charts.

IT'S SIMPLE

The sense of the clues "Exemplar of simplicity" and "Easy as ___."

▶•◆•◆•◆•◀ ABE ▶•◆•◆•◆•◀

THE PRESIDENT
Nickname of Abraham Lincoln, a.k.a. "Honest Abe," whose portrait can be found on a penny and a $5 bill.

THE TOON
Abe Simpson, Homer's father and Bart's grandfather, is a character on the animated sitcom *The Simpsons*.

THE ACTOR
Abe Vigoda portrayed detective Phil Fish on the sitcom *Barney Miller*.

THE JURIST
Appointed by Lyndon Johnson, Abe Fortas served on the U.S. Supreme Court from 1965 to 1969.

THE PRIME MINISTER
Shinzō Abe has served multiple terms as prime minister of Japan.

THE BROADWAY WRITER/PRODUCER
Abe Burrows was involved with such shows as *Silk Stockings* and *Breakfast at Tiffany's*. He won a Pulitzer Prize for *How to Succeed in Business Without Really Trying*.

▶•◆•◆•◆•◀ ABEL ▶•◆•◆•◆•◀

THE SHEPHERD
Abel, son of Adam and Eve, was slain by his brother Cain. Abel's other brother was Seth.

THE EXPLORER
Dutch-born Abel Tasman led the first European expedition to New Zealand and the island named for him, Tasmania, in the 1640s.

THE JUNGLE GUY
Abel is the hero of the W.H. Hudson novel *Green Mansions*, set in South America. He is portrayed in the 1959 film adaptation by Anthony Perkins.

▶·◆·◆·◆·◀ **ABET** ▶·◆·◆·◆·◀

THE VERB
Commonly seen clues: "Assist in a crime," "Drive the getaway car," and "Aid partner" (as in the legal phrase "aid and abet").

THE TWO-WORDER
"Not on a bet!" is a colloquial term for "Never!"

▶·◆·◆·◆·◀ **ABLE** ▶·◆·◆·◆·◀

THE ADJECTIVE
Commonly seen clues: "Competent," "Up to the task," "Well-qualified," and "Having the wherewithal."

NOT SO FAST!

"Greek god": ___ **R** ___ **S**

EROS was the Greek god of love; ARES the Greek god of war. If the clue is "Greek goddess," the answer could be ERIS, goddess of discord, or IRIS, goddess of the rainbow. If the clue is "Greek deity," the answer could be any of the four.

▶·◆·◆·◆·◀ **ABS** ▶·◆·◆·◆·◀

THE MUSCLES
Short for "abdominal muscles," commonly seen clues include "Tummy muscles," "Bodybuilder's pride," "Exercise target," and "Crunch targets" ("crunches" being a popular gym exercise that work the abs).

▸•◆•◆•◆•◂ ABUT ▸•◆•◆•◆•◂

THE VERB
Commonly seen clues: "Be adjacent to," "Border on," "Lie next to," "Adjoin," and "Bump up against."

▸•◆•◆•◆•◂ ACE ▸•◆•◆•◆•◂

THE SPORTS TERMS
In tennis, an ace is an unreturned serve. In golf, it's a hole-in-one. In baseball, a star pitcher.

THE CARD
The highest-ranking card in a standard deck of 52. In the game blackjack, an ace is worth either 1 or 11 points.

THE ADJECTIVE AND NOUN
Meaning "expert," in both the adjective and noun senses, and often specifically meaning an expert pilot. Similar clues: "Adept," "Crackerjack," "Champion," and "Top-notch."

▸•◆•◆•◆•◂ ACH ▸•◆•◆•◆•◂

IN GERMANY
The exclamation "*Ach!*" is the German word for "Oh!," for which commonly seen clues include "German exclamation," "Otto's exclamation," and "Alas, in Munich."

▸•◆•◆•◆•◂ ACHE ▸•◆•◆•◆•◂

THE NOUN AND VERB
The pain of an ache may be physical or psychological, as in "Yearn," "Feel sore," "Need liniment," "Flu symptom," "Charley horse," and "Feel sympathy for."

▶·◆·◆·◆·◀ ACID ▶·◆·◆·◆·◀

THE CHEMICAL
Often clued by example, such as "Boric or acetic." Other acids include amino, hydrochloric, sulfuric, nitric, citric, and folic. In the lab, it's a low-pH chemical that turns litmus paper red. An acid's opposite is an alkali, a.k.a. base. It's the "A" in DNA (deoxyribonucleic acid) and RNA (ribonucleic acid). It may also be clued by its practical usage, like "Etcher's chemical" and "Battery fluid."

THE ADJECTIVE
Meaning "sharp" or "biting"—taken literally, as to the taste; figuratively, as criticism.

▶·◆·◆·◆·◀ ACME ▶·◆·◆·◆·◀

THE NOUN
Commonly seen clues: "Apex," "Highest point," "Summit," "Zenith," and "Pinnacle."

THE CARTOON CONNECTION
Acme is the mail-order company from which Warner Bros. toon Wile E. Coyote purchases all sorts of outlandish devices, in his eternally unsuccessful attempts to do in the Road Runner.

▶·◆·◆·◆·◀ ACRE ▶·◆·◆·◆·◀

THE MEASURE
As a unit of land area, an acre equals 43,560 square feet, or $\frac{1}{640}$ of a square mile. Milne bear Winnie-the-Pooh lives in the Hundred Acre Wood. *God's Little Acre* is a novel by Erskine Caldwell.

ON THE MAP
Acre is a city in Israel, near Haifa. It is also the name of a state in the northwest part of Brazil, bordering Bolivia and Peru.

▶•◆•◆•◆•◀ ACT ▶•◆•◆•◆•◀

THE VERB

Commonly seen clues: "Create a role," "Do something," "Perform," "Play a part," and "Take steps." To "act up" is to misbehave.

THE NOUN

An act may be a part of a stage play or opera, a performer's routine, or a pretense. It may also be a piece of legislation or a royal decree.

▶•◆•◆•◆•◀ ACTI ▶•◆•◆•◆•◀

THEATRICALLY SPEAKING

ACT I, short for "Act One," is the start of a theatrical performance, for which typical clues include "Start of a play," "Overture follower," and "Beginning of a musical."

▶•◆•◆•◆•◀ ADA ▶•◆•◆•◆•◀

THE ABBREVIATIONS

ADA stands for the American Dental Association, whose endorsement can often be seen on boxes of toothpaste. Another organizational ADA is Americans for Democratic Action, a group that advocates liberal policies. ADA can also stand for "assistant district attorney."

THE BOOK

Ada is a 1969 novel by *Lolita* author Vladimir Nabokov.

ON THE MAP

Ada is a city in Oklahoma, as well as a county in Idaho, whose seat and largest city is Boise.

THE WOMEN

Ada Louise Huxtable was a Pulitzer Prize–winning architecture critic. Ada Lovelace was a British mathematician and the daughter of Lord Byron. In the movies, characters named Ada are portrayed by Holly Hunter in *The Piano* and Nicole Kidman in *Cold Mountain*.

▶·◆·◆·◆·◀ ADAGE ▶·◆·◆·◆·◀

JUST SAYING

An adage is a traditional saying, synonym clues for which include "Maxim," "Proverb," and "Wise saying."

▶·◆·◆·◆·◀ ADAM ▶·◆·◆·◆·◀

FIRST OF ALL

In the book of Genesis, Adam is the partner of Eve, and father of Cain, Abel, and Seth. The Michelangelo fresco *The Creation of Adam* is on the ceiling of the Vatican's Sistine Chapel. He's also a character in Milton's *Paradise Lost*.

REAL MEN

There's British economist Smith who wrote *The Wealth of Nations*; actors Sandler, Arkin (son of Alan), and West (TV Batman of the 1960s); and British rock singer Adam Ant.

UNREAL MEN

Adam is a servant character in Shakespeare's *As You Like It*. Adam Cartwright is the brother of Joe and Hoss in the TV western series *Bonanza*. Adam Schiff is the district attorney portrayed by Steven Hill in the series *Law & Order*.

NOT SO FAST!

"Leslie Caron film": ___ I ___ I

The answer can be GIGI or LILI.

▶·◆·◆·◆·◀ ADD ▶·◆·◆·◆·◀

THE VERB

Commonly seen clues: "Contribute," "Do sums," "Interject," "Tack on," and "Throw in."

▶·◆·◆·◆·◄ ADE ▶·◆·◆·◆·◄

THE DRINK

A soft drink with citrus flavoring, such as lemon, lime, or orange. There's also the brand-name drinks Gatorade and Powerade.

THE WRITER

The best-known work of Indiana-born author/humorist George Ade is *Fables in Slang*.

THE SUFFIX

Besides the citrus fruits, words to which -ade can be added as a suffix include block, cannon, and chiffon.

▶·◆·◆·◆·◄ ADIEU ▶·◆·◆·◆·◄

THE PARTING WORD

Commonly seen clues: "French farewell," "Good-bye," and "It may be bid" (as in to "bid adieu").

▶·◆·◆·◆·◄ ADO ▶·◆·◆·◆·◄

THE FUSS

Commonly seen clues: "Commotion," "Excitement," "Hoo-ha," "Hoopla," "Hubbub," and "Ruckus."

ON THE STAGE

Ado Annie is a character in the Rodgers and Hammerstein musical *Oklahoma!*, and let us not forget the Shakespeare comedy *Much Ado About Nothing*.

▶·◆·◆·◆·◄ ADORE ▶·◆·◆·◆·◄

THE VERB

Commonly seen clues: "Be gaga over," "Cherish," "Hold dear," "Like a lot," "Love," "Venerate," and "Worship."

▶•◆•◆•◆•◀ ADS ▶•◆•◆•◆•◀

WORDS FROM THE SPONSOR

Short, of course, for "advertisements" (in Britain it's "adverts," by the way), you're likely to see clues such as "Classifieds, for example," "Paid notices," "Web page pop-ups," and "TV program breaks."

▶•◆•◆•◆•◀ AERO ▶•◆•◆•◆•◀

THE ADJECTIVE

It can mean "pertaining to aircraft," and is also a shortened form of "aerodynamic," especially when it pertains to the design of a vehicle.

THE PREFIX

In addition to "dynamic," aero- can precede words such as ballistic, biology, marine, nautical, and space.

THE PROPER NAMES

Aero is the graphical user interface of the Windows Vista computer operating system. The Akron Aeros are a minor-league baseball team.

▶•◆•◆•◆•◀ AESOP ▶•◆•◆•◆•◀

THE MAN

Aesop was the legendary ancient Greek storyteller credited with numerous fables, the best known of which include "The Tortoise and the Hare," "The Boy Who Cried Wolf," "The Fox and the Grapes," and "The Ant and the Grasshopper. Clues often include "moral" (the traditional conclusion of fables) or "fabulist" (teller of fables).

▶•◆•◆•◆•◀ AFAR ▶•◆•◆•◆•◀

THE ADVERB

Commonly seen clues: "In the distance," "Miles away," "Way off," "Worship from ___," and "Yonder."

20

▶•◆•◆•◆•◀ AFRO ▶•◆•◆•◆•◀

THE HAIR

The spherical hairstyle popular in the 1960s and 1970s was worn by African Americans such as Jesse Jackson and Jimi Hendrix, and more recently by pop singer Beyoncé.

▶•◆•◆•◆•◀ AFT ▶•◆•◆•◆•◀

AT SEA

On a ship, "aft" means "to the rear," for which clues include "Nautical direction," "Toward the stern," "Back, on a boat."

THE ABBREVIATION

Occasionally, AFT will be defined as the abbreviation for "afternoon," with a clue such as "P.M. period."

▶•◆•◆•◆•◀ AGAIN ▶•◆•◆•◆•◀

THE ADVERB

Commonly seen clues: "Another time," "From the top," and "Once more." It is also the last word of the "Humpty Dumpty" nursery rhyme.

▶•◆•◆•◆•◀ AGE ▶•◆•◆•◆•◀

THE VERB

Commonly seen clues: "Get older," "Improve, as wine," "Mature," "Mellow," and "Ripen."

THE NOUN

Commonly seen clues: "Candle count" (as in birthday candles), "Era," "Generation," "Historical period," "Retirement factor," and "Time of one's life."

▷·◆·◆·◆·◁ AGENT ▷·◆·◆·◆·◁

IN GENERAL

Commonly seen clues: "Actor's representative," "Contract negotiator," "FBI employee," "Go-between," "Intermediary," and "Operative."

SPECIFICALLY

Fictional agents often seen in "clues by example" include James Bond (a.k.a. 007), Mulder and Scully from the TV series *The X-Files*, Austin Powers (portrayed by Mike Myers in films), Maxwell Smart (portrayed by Don Adams on TV and Steve Carell in a 2008 film), and the John le Carré novel character George Smiley.

▷·◆·◆·◆·◁ AGILE ▷·◆·◆·◆·◁

MOVING IT

Clues for "agile" are almost always direct synonyms, such as "Nimble," "Spry," "Limber," and sometimes "Mentally quick."

▷·◆·◆·◆·◁ AGO ▷·◆·◆·◆·◁

THE ADJECTIVE

Commonly seen clues: "Back in time," "Gone by," "In the past," "Long, long ___," "Many moons ___," and "Years ___."

THE TWO-WORDER

"Give it ___" and "Have ___ at," both colloquial terms for "try," are common clues for A GO.

▷·◆·◆·◆·◁ AGOG ▷·◆·◆·◆·◁

THE ADJECTIVE

Virtually always clued synonymously, clues you'll often see include "Enthusiastic," "Enthralled," "Highly excited," "All worked up," and "Gung-ho."

22

▶·◆·◆·◆·◄ **AGRA** ▶·◆·◆·◆·◄

ON THE MAP

This city in the Uttar Pradesh state of northern India, on the Yamuna River, is most famous as the site of the Taj Mahal. The Pearl Mosque is another popular tourist attraction in the city. Agra was the capital of the Mogul Empire in the 16th and 17th centuries.

▶·◆·◆·◆·◄ **AGREE** ▶·◆·◆·◆·◄

THE VERB

Commonly seen clues: "Coincide," "Come to terms," "Concur," "Go along," "Match," "See eye to eye," and "Think alike."

NOT SO FAST!

"Haw partner": H E ___

The answer can be either HEM (as in "hem and haw") or HEE (as in the hee-haw sound of a donkey).

▶·◆·◆·◆·◄ **AHA** ▶·◆·◆·◆·◄

THE EXCLAMATION

Commonly seen clues: "Cry of discovery," "Eureka!," "Gotcha!," "I understand now!," and "So that's it!" OHO is very similar in meaning and has many of the same clues.

THE ROCK GROUP

The Norwegian rock band a-ha had a #1 tune in 1985 with "Take On Me."

▶•◆•◆•◆•◀ AHAB ▶•◆•◆•◆•◀

IN LITERATURE

The obsessed Captain Ahab is the skipper of the whaler *Pequod* in the Herman Melville novel *Moby-Dick*. His subordinates include Ishmael, Queequeg, and Starbuck. Ahab was portrayed by Gregory Peck in the 1956 film adaptation.

IN THE BIBLE

In the Old Testament, Ahab is a king of ancient Israel. He is the son and successor of Omri and the husband of Jezebel.

IN SONG

"Ahab the Arab" is a 1962 novelty song by Ray Stevens.

▶•◆•◆•◆•◀ AHEM ▶•◆•◆•◆•◀

THE EXCLAMATION

Commonly seen clues: "Attention-getter," "Excuse me!," "I beg your pardon," and "Throat-clearing sound."

▶•◆•◆•◆•◀ AHOY ▶•◆•◆•◆•◀

AT SEA

Clues for the nautical greeting are variations of "Sailor's shout," "Captain's cry," and "Hail on the ocean."

▶•◆•◆•◆•◀ AID ▶•◆•◆•◆•◀

THE VERB

As a verb, synonym clues include "Assist," "Help out," "Lend a hand," and "Support."

THE NOUN

As a noun, there's "Assistance," "Helping hand," and, once again, "Support."

AIDA

THE OPERA

Aida is the title character in the opera of the same name by Giuseppe Verdi. She is an Ethiopian princess who is captured and brought into slavery in Egypt. Her love is Radames, captain of the guard. A 1953 Italian film adaptation stars Sophia Loren in the title role.

THE PLAY

The Disney-produced musical drama based on the opera, with music by Elton John and lyrics by Tim Rice, had a 2000–04 run on Broadway.

THE ACTRESS

Aida Turturro, cousin of John, portrayed Janice Soprano (sister of Tony) in the HBO series *The Sopranos*.

AIDE

THE HELPER

Commonly seen clues: "Assistant," "Deputy," "Gofer," "Right-hand person," "Subordinate," and "White House worker."

NOT SO FAST!

"In the know": **H ___ P**

The answer can be HIP or HEP.

AIL

THE VERB

Commonly seen clues: "Be under the weather," "Feel poorly," "Have a bug," and other very similar colloquial synonyms.

CROSSWORDS 101
Lesson 1: The Simpsons

These characters from the animated sitcom "The Simpsons" appear frequently as crossword answers:

ABE (grandfather)
APU Nahasapeemapetilon (Kwik-E-Mart clerk)
BART (son)
EDNA Krabappel (schoolteacher)
HOMER (father)
LISA (daughter, saxophone player)
MOE Szyslak (bartender)
NED Flanders (neighbor)
OTTO Mann (bus driver)
Disco **STU** (lover of disco music)

▶•◀•▶•◀•▶•◀ **AIM** ▶•◀•▶•◀•▶•◀

THE VERB

Commonly seen verb clues: "Draw a bead," "Point at the target," "Set one's sights," "Prepare to shoot," and "We ___ to please." Referring to "Ready, aim, fire," you may also see "Ready follower" and "Fire preceder."

THE NOUN

Commonly seen noun clues: "Ambition," "Goal," "Intention," "Purpose," and "Sharpshooter's asset."

THE TOOTHPASTE BRAND

In this sense, usually clued in terms of its competitors, which include Aquafresh, Colgate, Crest, and Rembrandt.

▶•◆•◆•◆•◀ AINT ▶•◆•◆•◆•◀

BLANKETY-BLANKS

Commonly seen colloquialisms include "If it ___ broke ...," "It ___ over till it's over," "___ it the truth," and "Say it ___ so."

BLANKLESS

Commonly seen clues: "Isn't, informally" and "Nonstandard contraction."

IN SONGS

Popular song titles that include the word: "Ain't Misbehavin'," "Ain't No Sunshine," "Ain't She Sweet," "Ain't That a Shame," "Ain't We Got Fun," and "It Ain't Necessarily So."

▶•◆•◆•◆•◀ AIR ▶•◆•◆•◆•◀

THE NOUN

Commonly seen atmospheric clues: "Balloon filler," "Football filler," "Former gas station freebie," and "Vacuum's lack." The word may also refer to the appearance and bearing of a person, or to a melody.

THE VERB

Commonly seen clues: "Broadcast," "Expose," "Publicize," "Televise," and "Ventilate."

▶•◆•◆•◆•◀ AISLE ▶•◆•◆•◆•◀

THE NOUN

The aisles seen in crosswords are usually in airplanes, churches, supermarkets, or theaters. Other related clues: "Narrow walkway," "Seat selection," and "Usher's domain."

▶•◆•◆•◆•◀ AJAR ▶•◆•◆•◆•◀

THE ADJECTIVE/ADVERB

Commonly seen clues: "Admitting a draft," "Barely open," "Not quite shut," and "Open a crack."

▶•◆•◆•◆•◀ **AKA** ▶•◆•◆•◆•◀

THE ABBREVIATION
Standing for "also known as," commonly seen clues include "Alias: Abbr.," "Rap sheet letters," "Sometimes called," and "Wanted poster initials."

▶•◆•◆•◆•◀ **AKIN** ▶•◆•◆•◆•◀

THE ADJECTIVE
Commonly seen clues: "Analogous," "Comparable," "Related," and "Similar."

▶•◆•◆•◆•◀ **ALA** ▶•◆•◆•◆•◀

ON THE MAP
As an abbreviation for Alabama, it'll be worth your while to know the state's nickname ("Heart of Dixie"), neighbors (Florida, Georgia, Mississippi, and Tennessee), major cities (Birmingham, Huntsville, Mobile, Montgomery, and Tuscaloosa), and universities (Auburn, Tuskegee, and the University of Alabama, whose sports teams are known as the Crimson Tide).

ON THE MENU
The two-word A LA means "like" or "in the style of," as in the menu phrases "À la carte," "Chicken à la king," and "Pie à la mode."

▶•◆•◆•◆•◀ **ALAI** ▶•◆•◆•◆•◀

THE GAME
Nearly always clued these days as "Jai ___." The game of jai alai, literally "merry festival" in the Basque language, originated in Spain. Similar to handball, it is played on a court called a fronton. Players catch and propel the ball with a basketlike device called a cesta.

ON THE MAP
When not part of the game, Alai is a mountain range is located in Kyrgyzstan and Tajikistan.

►•◆•◆•◆•◄ ALAMO ►•◆•◆•◆•◄

THE SHRINE
This San Antonio museum, once a mission, was the site of the 1836 battle between the forces of the Republic of Texas (which included Jim Bowie and Davy Crockett) and Mexico (led by Santa Anna).

THE RENT-A-CAR COMPANY
In this sense, usually clued in terms of its competitors, which include Avis, Budget, Dollar, and Hertz.

►•◆•◆•◆•◄ ALAN ►•◆•◆•◆•◄

THE ASTRONAUTS
Alan Shepard was the first American in space, and later commanded the Apollo 14 mission to the moon. Alan Bean was the fourth man to walk on the moon.

IN ENTERTAINMENT
There's Alda (of *M*A*S*H*), Arkin (Oscar winner for *Little Miss Sunshine*), Ayckbourn (knighted British playwright), Bates (knighted British actor), Freed (pioneering rock-and-roll DJ), Hale (of *Gilligan's Island*), King (comedian), Ladd (of *Shane*), Paton (South African author), Rickman (the villain in *Die Hard* and wizard Severus Snape in the Harry Potter films), Thicke (of *Growing Pains*), and Young (of *Mister Ed*). Lyricist Alan Jay Lerner collaborated with Frederick Loewe on many memorable musicals.

IN GOVERNMENT
Chester Alan Arthur was the 21st president of the United States. Economist Alan Greenspan served as head of the Federal Reserve from 1987 to 2006.

NOT SO FAST!

"Type of tree": ___ **L D E R**

The answer can be ALDER or ELDER.

▶•◆•◆•◆•◀ ALARM ▶•◆•◆•◆•◀

AS A VERB

Synonym clues include "Frighten," "Scare," "Unnerve," "Startle," and "Dismay."

AS A NOUN

As a tangible sound or device, there's "Clock radio feature," "Warning signal," "Elevator button," and "Security device." Intangibly speaking, there's "Sudden fear," "Trepidation," "Anxiety," and "Fright."

▶•◆•◆•◆•◀ ALAS ▶•◆•◆•◆•◀

THE EXCLAMATION

Commonly seen clues: "So sorry!," "Too bad!," "Woe is me!," and "Word of regret." Hamlet says "Alas, poor Yorick ..." in Shakespeare's play.

▶•◆•◆•◆•◀ ALDA ▶•◆•◆•◆•◀

THE SON

By virtue of his conveniently spelled first and last names, Alan Alda is definitely someone you want as a draft pick in your fantasy crossword league. Best known for his starring role as Hawkeye Pierce in the sitcom *M*A*S*H*, his other television credits include *Scientific American Frontiers* and *The West Wing*. He has directed such films as *Betsy's Wedding* and *The Four Seasons*.

THE DAD

Alan's father Robert originated the role of Sky Masterson in the musical *Guys and Dolls*, and portrayed George Gershwin in the 1945 biopic *Rhapsody in Blue*.

►·◆·◆·◆·◄ ALE ►·◆·◆·◆·◄

THE DRINK

Commonly seen clues: "British brew," "Pub serving," "Stein filler," and "Stout relative" (stout is a malt beverage). Popular brands of ale include Ballantine, Bass, Guinness, and McSorley's. *Cakes and Ale* is a novel by Somerset Maugham. And of course, there's the nonalcoholic ginger ale.

►·◆·◆·◆·◄ ALEC ►·◆·◆·◆·◄

THE AMERICAN

Actor Alec Baldwin has appeared in many films, as well as on the sitcom *30 Rock* and, recently, as host of *Match Game*. His acting brothers are Daniel, Stephen, and William. He was formerly married to actress Kim Basinger.

THE BRITS

Actor Alec Guinness portrays Obi-Wan Kenobi in the film *Star Wars*. Alec Douglas-Home (pronounced "Hume") served as British prime minister in the 1960s. Novelist Alec Waugh was the elder brother of novelist Evelyn Waugh. Pianist Alec Templeton had his own U.S. radio show in the 1940s.

►·◆·◆·◆·◄ ALERT ►·◆·◆·◆·◄

THE ADJECTIVE

Commonly seen adjective clues: "Attentive," "On one's toes," "Vigilant," "Watchful," and "Wide awake."

THE VERB

Commonly seen verb clues: "Give notice to," "Tip off," and "Warn."

THE NOUN

Commonly seen noun clues: "Heads-up," "Siren, for example," and "State of readiness."

▶•◆•◆•◆•◀ ALI ▶•◆•◆•◆•◀

THE BOXER

Born Cassius Clay, Muhammad Ali was world heavyweight boxing champ for three separate periods in the 1960s and 1970s. Nicknamed "the Greatest," Ali was named "Sportsman of the Century" by *Sports Illustrated* in 1999. His daughter Laila Ali was also a professional boxer. Will Smith portrays him in the 2001 biopic *Ali*.

THE WOODCUTTER

Ali Baba is the poor woodcutter who outwits the Forty Thieves in the Arabian Nights tale.

THE ACTRESSES

Former fashion model Ali (short for Alison) Larter is a star of the sci-fi TV series *Heroes*. Ali (short for Alice) MacGraw is best known for her Oscar-nominated role in the 1970 film *Love Story*.

▶•◆•◆•◆•◀ ALIBI ▶•◆•◆•◆•◀

THIS WAY OUT

A common plot element in detective stories, you're likely to see clues that are variations of "Suspect's story," "Whodunit excuse," "Defendant's explanation," and "Courtroom ploy."

▶•◆•◆•◆•◀ ALIEN ▶•◆•◆•◆•◀

FROM ANOTHER COUNTRY

Commonly seen clues: "Foreigner," "Green-card holder," and "Non-native."

FROM ANOTHER PLANET

Commonly seen clues: "Extraterrestrial," "Martian," "Sci-fi character," "Superman, e.g.," and "UFO pilot." The 1979 film *Alien* stars Sigourney Weaver.

THE ADJECTIVE

Commonly seen clues: "Otherworldly," "Strange," and "Unfamiliar."

▶•◆•◆•◆•◀ ALIT ▶•◆•◆•◆•◀

THE VERB
The past tense of "alight." Commonly seen clues: "Dismounted," "Got off," "Landed," "Returned to earth," "Stepped off," and "Touched down."

▶•◆•◆•◆•◀ ALL ▶•◆•◆•◆•◀

THE ADJECTIVE
Commonly seen clues: "100%," "Completely," "Everyone," "Nothing but," "Solely," and "Totally."

THE DETERGENT
In this sense, usually clued in terms of its competitors, which include Era, Fab, Surf, and Tide.

▶•◆•◆•◆•◀ ALOE ▶•◆•◆•◆•◀

THE PLANT AND ITS USES
Native to Africa, aloes are succulent plants often seen in gardens and on windowsills. The most popular of the hundreds of species is aloe vera. The gel from its leaves is used as an emollient (soother), and is often an ingredient in skin creams, moisturizers, and other lotions.

▶•◆•◆•◆•◀ ALOHA ▶•◆•◆•◆•◀

ON THE ISLANDS
In Hawaiian, the word can mean "hello" or "good-bye." The NFL's annual post-season Pro Bowl is held annually at Hawaii's Aloha Stadium. "Aloha Oe" is a Hawaiian farewell song.

▶•◆•◆•◆•◀ ALONE ▶•◆•◆•◆•◀

THE ADJECTIVE
Commonly seen clues: "By oneself," "Isolated," "Solo," "Stag," "Unassisted," and "Unaccompanied."

▶•◆•◆•◆•◄ **ALOT** ▶•◆•◆•◆•◄

THE PHRASAL ADVERB

Clues for A LOT are almost always synonyms, such as "Frequently," "Very much," "All the time," "Greatly," and "Often." Once in a while, you might see "Thanks ___!"

▶•◆•◆•◆•◄ **ALP** ▶•◆•◆•◆•◄

WAY UP HIGH

While the dictionary says "alp" means "any high mountain," in crosswords it is almost always taken to mean one of the Alps, the European mountain chain, which runs through France, Switzerland, Germany, Italy, and several other countries not usually cited in puzzle clues. Specific Alps often seen in clues include Mount Blanc, the Matterhorn, and Jungfrau. Numerous Winter Olympics have taken place in the Alps, most recently Turin, Italy, in 2006.

▶•◆•◆•◆•◄ **ALSO** ▶•◆•◆•◆•◄

THE ADVERB

Commonly seen clues: "Additionally," "As well," "Furthermore," "In addition," "Likewise," "Moreover," "Plus," and "Too."

▶•◆•◆•◆•◄ **ALT** ▶•◆•◆•◆•◄

THE ABBREVIATIONS

"Substitute: Abbr." clues the shortened form of "alternate." "Hgt." and "Cockpit abbr." indicate the shortened form of "altitude."

THE KEY

The PC-keyboard Alt key is usually located in the bottom row, adjacent to the space bar.

THE MODEL

Supermodel Carol Alt appeared on over 500 magazine covers in the 1980s.

▶•◆•◆•◆•◀ ALTAR ▶•◆•◆•◆•◀

THE RELIGIOUS PLACE
Commonly seen clues: "Church platform," "Rite place," "Vow venue," and "Wedding site."

▶•◆•◆•◆•◀ ALTO ▶•◆•◆•◆•◀

MUSICALLY SPEAKING
The alto voice range is lower than soprano, but higher than tenor. It is also the range of some musical instruments, such as the saxophone and flute.

ON THE MAP
Palo Alto, literally "high stick" in Spanish, is located in California's Silicon Valley, and is the headquarters of Hewlett-Packard.

▶•◆•◆•◆•◀ ALUM ▶•◆•◆•◆•◀

OUT OF SCHOOL
As a short form of "alumnus," commonly seen clues include "Grad," "Homecoming attendee," and "Reunion goer."

IN THE MEDICINE CHEST
This alum, known chemically as aluminum potassium sulfate, is an astringent (tissue-contracting agent), often used in styptic pencils to stop the bleeding from minor cuts.

▶•◆•◆•◆•◀ AMA ▶•◆•◆•◆•◀

THE DOC BLOC
As an abbreviation for American Medical Association, commonly seen clues are usually variations of "Drs.' org." and "Physicians' gp."

THE TITLES
"I Am a Rock" is a 1960s song by Simon and Garfunkel. *I Am a Camera* is a 1955 film based on the Christopher Isherwood novel *Goodbye to Berlin*, which was also the source for the musical play and film *Cabaret*.

▶·◆·◆·◆·◀ AMANA ▶·◆·◆·◆·◀

IN THE KITCHEN AND LAUNDRY ROOM

Household appliance brand Amana is perhaps best known for its Radarange brand of microwave ovens, and is now a subsidiary of the Whirlpool Corporation. You're most likely to see clues based either on the various types of appliances they make (refrigerators, washing machines, etc.), or competitive brands (Hotpoint, Maytag, KitchenAid, Frigidaire, etc.).

▶·◆·◆·◆·◀ AMASS ▶·◆·◆·◆·◀

THE VERB

Commonly seen clues: "Accumulate," "Collect," "Gather," and "Pile up."

▶·◆·◆·◆·◀ AMEN ▶·◆·◆·◆·◀

RELIGIOUSLY SPEAKING

Commonly seen clues: "Grace finale," "Hymn ending," and "Prayer conclusion." It is the last word of the New Testament.

THE SECULAR EXCLAMATION

As an expression of agreement, AMEN is usually clued colloquially with variations on "I agree!," "Right on!," and "You said it!"

ON TV

The sitcom *Amen* ran from 1986 to 1991, starring Sherman Hemsley as a Philadelphia deacon.

▶·◆·◆·◆·◀ AMES ▶·◆·◆·◆·◀

ON THE MAP

The city of Ames, on the Skunk River, is the home of Iowa State University.

THE SURNAME

In the 1960s, Ed Ames appeared on the TV series *Daniel Boone* and had a Top 10 song, "My Cup Runneth Over." Aldrich Ames was a former CIA agent convicted in 1994 of spying for Russia.

▶·◆·◆·◆·◀ **AMI** ▶·◆·◆·◆·◀

IN FRENCH

As the French word for "friend," commonly seen clues are variations of "Buddy in Bordeaux" and "Parisian pal."

BLANKETY-BLANKS

Cluing the two words AM I, commonly seen colloquialisms include "What ___, chopped liver?" and "Who ___ to argue?" From Genesis, there's "___ my brother's keeper?" And let's not forget the immortal words of Little Jack Horner, "What a good boy ___."

▶·◆·◆·◆·◀ **AMID** ▶·◆·◆·◆·◀

THE PREPOSITION

Commonly seen clues: "During," "In the center of," and "Surrounded by."

▶·◆·◆·◆·◀ **AMMO** ▶·◆·◆·◆·◀

IN WEAPONS

As the short form of "ammunition," commonly seen clues include "Arsenal contents," "Bullets," "Military stockpile," and "Sharpshooter's need."

▶·◆·◆·◆·◀ **AMOK** ▶·◆·◆·◆·◀

THE ADVERB

Commonly seen clues: "In a frenzy," "Out of control," "Run ___," and "Wildly."

▶·◆·◆·◆·◆·◀ **AMOR** ▶·◆·◆·◆·◆·◀

FOR LOVERS

"*Amor*" is the word for "love" in Latin and Spanish. Amor was another name for the Roman love god Cupid, the son of Venus. The Latin expression "*Omnia vincit amor*" means "Love conquers all."

▶·◆·◆·◆·◆·◀ **AMOS** ▶·◆·◆·◆·◆·◀

IN THE BIBLE

Amos is a book of the Old Testament, named for a minor prophet.

LAST NAMES

Tori Amos is a pop singer/pianist. Actor John Amos appeared in the miniseries *Roots* and was a regular on the 1970s sitcom *Good Times*. Cookie entrepreneur Wally Amos gave his name to the Famous Amos brand.

FIRST NAMES

Amos Oz is an Israeli author. Amos Alonzo Stagg had a 56-year career as a college football coach. *Amos 'n' Andy* was a long-running sitcom on old-time radio.

▶·◆·◆·◆·◆·◀ **AMP** ▶·◆·◆·◆·◆·◀

IN PHYSICS

Short for "ampere," the amp is a unit of current.

IN SOUND

As a shortened form of "amplifier," commonly seen clues include "Guitarist gear," "Roadie's burden," "Rock concert equipment," "Sound booster," and "Stereo component."

►·◄·◄·◄·◄ ANA ►·◄·◄·◄·◄

THE PLACES

Santa Ana, California, is the largest city in Orange County. Santa Ana winds sweep through southern California in late fall and winter. ANA can also be clued with references to Anaheim sports teams, such as "Scoreboard abbr. for the NHL's Ducks."

THE PEOPLE

Ana Ivanovic is a retired tennis pro from Serbia, Ana Gasteyer was once a regular on *Saturday Night Live*, and actress Ana-Alicia is best known for her starring role in the TV series *Falcon Crest*. The narrator of the *Fifty Shades* books, Anastasia Steele, is called Ana for short.

IN THE AIR

ANA, short for All Nippon Airways, is Japan's largest airline.

IN THE DICTIONARY

An ana is a collection of miscellaneous information on a particular subject.

ON TV

Contestants on the game show *Wheel of Fortune* can "buy" any vowel for $250. Thus the answer to "Wheel of Fortune purchase" may be AN A (as well as AN E, AN I, and AN O).

COLLOQUIALLY

As in the phrase "Get an A for effort." But be careful on this one, because "Get an E for effort" is also a common phrase, so the answer to "Get ___ for effort" may be either ANA or ANE.

►·◄·◄·◄·◄ AND ►·◄·◄·◄·◄

THE CONJUNCTION

Commonly seen clues: "As well as," "Furthermore," "In addition," "Moreover," and "Plus."

NOT SO FAST!

"Bird home": C ___ ___ E

The answer can be CAGE (at home or in a zoo)
as well as COTE (as for pigeons or doves).

▶·◆·◆·◆·◀ **ANEW** ▶·◆·◆·◆·◀

THE ADVERB

Commonly seen clues: "All over again," "Another time," "From
scratch," "From the top," and "Once more."

▶·◆·◆·◆·◀ **ANITA** ▶·◆·◆·◆·◀

THE SINGERS

There's soul singer Anita Baker, pop singer Anita Bryant, jazz
singer Anita O'Day, and Anita Pointer, one of the Pointer Sisters.
In *West Side Story*, the character of Anita (played by Rita Moreno
in the film version) sings "America" and "A Boy Like That."

OTHER CELEBRITIES

Writer Anita Loos is best known for *Gentlemen Prefer Blondes*.
Other Anita authors are Shreve and Brookner. Actress Anita
Ekberg starred in the Fellini film *La Dolce Vita*.

▶·◆·◆·◆·◀ **ANKA** ▶·◆·◆·◆·◀

THE SINGER/SONGWRITER

The hits of Canadian singer-songwriter Paul Anka include "Diana,"
"Times of Your Life," "Puppy Love," and "My Way." He composed
"Johnny's Theme," the theme music for *The Tonight Show* when
Johnny Carson was the host.

►•●•●•●•◄ **ANN** ►•●•●•●•◄

IN THE MOVIES

There are actresses Blyth, Jillian, Miller, Reinking, Sheridan, and Sothern. Ann Darrow is the lead female role in the original *King Kong* film (portrayed originally by Fay Wray, and in remakes by Jessica Lange and Naomi Watts).

OTHER CELEBRITIES

Writers named Ann include Beattie, Coulter, Patchett, and Rule. Ann Compton and Ann Curry are TV journalists. Ann Lee founded the Shakers religious sect. Advice columnist Ann Landers was the twin sister of advice columnist Dear Abby. Ann Richards was governor of Texas in the 1990s.

UNREAL ANNS

Ann Taylor is the name of a chain of women's clothing stores, but the name was made up and isn't the name of a real person. Rag doll Raggedy Ann is the sister of Raggedy Andy in a series of children's books.

ANN IN THE MIDDLE

Lee Ann Womack is a country singer, Penelope Ann Miller is an actress, Mary Ann Evans was the real name of British writer George Eliot, and "Barbara Ann" is a Beach Boys tune.

ON THE MAP

Ann Arbor, Michigan, is near Detroit. Cape Ann is in eastern Massachusetts.

►•●•●•●•◄ **ANNA** ►•●•●•●•◄

FOR REAL

Authors named Anna include Sewell and Quindlen. Actress Annas include Faris, Magnani, and Paquin. First lady Eleanor Roosevelt's full name was Anna Eleanor Roosevelt. Anna Kournikova is a Russian tennis pro. Anna Pavlova was a Russian ballerina. Anna Moffo was an opera star. Anna Freud, daughter of psychologist Sigmund, was also a psychologist.

IN FICTION

She's the title character in Eugene O'Neill's play *Anna Christie*, the Tolstoy novel *Anna Karenina*, and the "I" in the Rodgers and Hammerstein musical *The King and I.*

▶•◆•◆•◆•◀ **ANNE** ▶•◆•◆•◆•◀

WRITERS AND WRITINGS

Anne Frank wrote a famous World War II–era diary. Anne Brontë was the sister of Charlotte and Emily. Anne Rice is best known for her vampire novels, Anne Tyler for *The Accidental Tourist.* *Anne of Green Gables* is a novel by Canadian author Lucy Maud Montgomery.

THE ACTRESSES

There's Archer, Bancroft, Baxter, Francis, Hathaway, Heche, Jackson, and Meara (mother of actor Ben Stiller).

THE BRITS

Princess Anne is the daughter of Queen Elizabeth II. Queen Anne succeeded her father James II to the throne of England in 1702, and two of Henry VIII's six wives were Annes: Anne Boleyn and Anne of Cleves. Anne was the name of William Shakespeare's wife.

OTHER CELEBRITIES

Anne Klein is a fashion designer, Anne Murray is a Canadian pop singer, and Anne Lindbergh was the wife of aviator Charles.

▶•◆•◆•◆•◀ **ANNIE** ▶•◆•◆•◆•◀

FOR REAL

The life of sharpshooter Annie Oakley was the basis of the musical *Annie Get Your Gun.* There's also singer Lennox, photographer Leibovitz, and actress Potts.

IN FICTION

The comic strip "Little Orphan Annie" was turned into the musical *Annie*, in which the title character sings "Tomorrow." Annie's dog is named Sandy and her guardian is Daddy Warbucks. The title character in the Woody Allen film *Annie Hall* was portrayed by Diane Keaton.

▶·◆·◆·◆·◀ **ANNO** ▶·◆·◆·◆·◀

IN LATIN

All you need to know about "*anno*" is that it's Latin for "in the year of," seen today almost always as part of the phrase *anno Domini*, "A.D." for short.

▶·◆·◆·◆·◀ **ANON** ▶·◆·◆·◆·◀

THE ABBREVIATION

As a short form of "anonymous," commonly seen clues include variations of "Quote book abbr." and "Unknown auth."

THE ADVERB

As a synonym for "soon" often seen in poems, commonly seen clues include "Before long," "In a while," "Presently," and "Shortly, to Shakespeare."

▶·◆·◆·◆·◀ **ANT** ▶·◆·◆·◆·◀

THE INSECT

Commonly seen clues: "Aardvark snack," "Hill builder," "Pantry invader," "Picnic pest," "Queen's subject," and "Tiny colonist." Paul Rudd plays the superhero Ant-Man in several Marvel movies. The main character of Pixar's *A Bug's Life* is an ant named Flik.

▶•◆•◆•◆•◀ ANTE ▶•◆•◆•◆•◀

CARDWISE

In the sense of an initial payment in poker, commonly seen clues include "Chip in a chip," "Deal preceder," "Pay to play," "Penny, perhaps," and "Start the pot."

FROM THE LATIN

"*Ante*" is the Latin word for "before," and the "A" in the timely abbreviation "A.M."

▶•◆•◆•◆•◀ ANTI ▶•◆•◆•◆•◀

FOR STARTERS

As a prefix meaning "against," commonly seen clues include "Contra- relative," "Part of ABM" (as in "antiballistic missile"), and clues that start with "Prefix for" and usually end with "freeze," "social," or "virus."

THE NOUN

Although it's in the dictionary as a person who is against something, it's commonly seen with this meaning only in crosswords, with clues like "Dissenter," "Naysayer," "Opponent," and "Pro foe."

▶•◆•◆•◆•◀ ANY ▶•◆•◆•◆•◀

THE ADJECTIVE

Commonly seen clues: "Even one," "One or more," and "Whichever."

IN TITLES

"Any" films include *Any Given Sunday* (directed by Oliver Stone), *Any Wednesday* (starring Jane Fonda and Jason Robards), and *Any Which Way You Can* (with Clint Eastwood). *Unsafe at Any Speed* is Ralph Nader's book on auto safety.

OTHER BLANKETY-BLANKS

Common colloquialism clues: "___ luck?," "___ objections?," "___ questions?," and "___ takers?" There's also the excerpt from the "Baa Baa Black Sheep" nursery rhyme, "Have you ___ wool?"

▶•◆•◆•◆•◀ **AOL** ▶•◆•◆•◆•◀

ON THE WEB

Short for the internet service provider (ISP) originally known as America Online, AOL purchased media conglomerate Time Warner at the height of its popularity in 2001. It was later spun off as a separate company, which merged with Verizon in 2015. It's known for its Buddy List, instant messaging service (AIM), and its "You've got mail" announcement to users, although all of those things have been retired.

▶•◆•◆•◆•◀ **AONE** ▶•◆•◆•◆•◀

GREAT STUFF

Commonly seen A-ONE clues: "Excellent," "First-class," "Superb," and "Top-notch."

▶•◆•◆•◆•◀ **AORTA** ▶•◆•◆•◆•◀

HEARTY

The aorta is the largest artery in the human body. Commonly seen clues are variations of "Blood line," "It comes from the heart," and "Major artery."

▶•◆•◆•◆•◀ **APART** ▶•◆•◆•◆•◀

THE ADVERB

Commonly seen clues: "Independently," "In pieces," "Isolated," "Not together," and "Separated."

▶•◆•◆•◆•◀ **APE** ▶•◆•◆•◆•◀

LITERALLY SPEAKING

Apes are nonhuman primates without tails, which distinguishes them from monkeys. The adjective "simian" can refer to either monkeys or apes. Apes seen in crossword clues include the chimpanzee, gibbon, gorilla, and orangutan, and filmdom's King Kong.

FIGURATIVELY SPEAKING

As a clumsy person, commonly seen clues include "Big lug," "Bruiser," "Galoot," and "Lummox."

THE VERB

As a synonym for "mimic," commonly seen clues include "Copy," "Emulate," "Imitate," and "Parrot."

▶•◆•◆•◆•◄ **APOP** ▶•◆•◆•◆•◄

INFORMALLY SPEAKING

As a slang term for "each," clues you'll see most often for A POP will be variations of "Apiece," "Individually," and "Per unit."

▶•◆•◆•◆•◄ **APR** ▶•◆•◆•◆•◄

ON THE CALENDAR

As an abbreviation for the month of April, clues for "Apr." will usually contain, in addition to "mo." ("month" abbreviated), one of these keywords: spring, 30 days, IRS, CPA, or showery.

IN ADS

This is also an abbreviation for "annual percentage rate," which, per the Truth in Lending Act, is required to be posted in ads for mortgages, auto loans, and so on.

▶•◆•◆•◆•◄ **APT** ▶•◆•◆•◆•◄

THE ADJECTIVE

As a synonym for "prone," commonly seen clues include "Disposed," "Inclined," and "Likely." Meaning "appropriate": "Fitting," "Suitable," and "Well-put." Meaning "intelligent": "Quick to learn" and "Very smart."

THE ABBREVIATION

As a short form of "apartment," commonly seen clues include "Envelope abbr.," "It may have an EIK" (short for "eat-in kitchen"), and "Rental dwelling: Abbr."

▶•◆•◆•◆•◀ AQUA ▶•◆•◆•◆•◀

THE COLOR

The Latin word for "water," aqua is almost always a color when seen in crosswords. Sometimes called a "greenish blue," sometimes a "bluish green," and often referred to as a "pastel shade."

▶•◆•◆•◆•◀ ARAB ▶•◆•◆•◆•◀

THE PERSON

Arabs are the majority in the Middle Eastern nations of Abu Dhabi, Bahrain, Egypt, Iraq, Jordan, Kuwait, Oman, Qatar, Saudi Arabia, and Yemen. Arab men's traditional garb includes a burnoose (cloak) and kaffiyeh (headdress).

THE BEAST

The Arab (or Arabian) breed of horse is known for its intelligence, grace, and speed.

▶•◆•◆•◆•◀ ARC ▶•◆•◆•◆•◀

THE LINE

Commonly seen clues: "Circle section," "Curved line," "Eyebrow shape," "Fly ball trajectory," and "Orbital path." The "line" of an arc can also be a figurative one, as in a temporary storyline of a TV soap opera.

▶•◆•◆•◆•◀ ARCH ▶•◆•◆•◆•◀

THE NOUN

An arch may be a curved architectural feature, such as the famous ones in Paris and St. Louis, or a part of the foot or a shoe.

THE ADJECTIVE

As a synonym for "sly," commonly seen clues include "Crafty," "Cunning," and "Roguish."

▶•◆•◆•◆•◀ ARE ▶•◆•◆•◆•◀

THE VERB

Commonly seen clues: "Exist," "Have being," and "Live and breathe."

IN TITLES

There's "All the Things You Are" (Jerome Kern tune), "Chances Are" (Johnny Mathis tune), *Diamonds Are Forever* (James Bond film), and "Where the Boys Are" (Connie Francis tune).

COLLOQUIALLY SPEAKING

Often seen phrases include "Are we there yet?," "Are you serious?," "Who do you think you are?," and "You are here."

▶•◆•◆•◆•◀ AREA ▶•◆•◆•◆•◀

GENERIC

Commonly seen clues include "Neck of the woods," "Neighborhood," "Region," "Sector," and "Vicinity." The word can also mean one's field of expertise or specialty.

MATHEMATICALLY SPEAKING

As it relates to a two-dimensional measure: "Carpet calculation," "Geographical stat," "Geometry finding," and "Square footage."

▶•◆•◆•◆•◀ ARENA ▶•◆•◆•◆•◀

THE NOUN

Commonly seen clues: "Battleground," "Field of conflict," "Sports stadium," and "Where the action is."

NOT SO FAST!

"Modify": ___ M E N D

The answer can be AMEND or the similar EMEND.

▶•◆•◆•◆•◀ ARES ▶•◆•◆•◆•◀

THE GOD

The Greek god Ares was the god of war, equivalent to the Romans' Mars. The son of Zeus and Hera, his children include the Amazons and Romulus and Remus.

▶•◆•◆•◆•◀ ARF ▶•◆•◆•◆•◀

BY THE POUND

"Arf!" is the sound of a dog's bark, popularized by the comic strip "Little Orphan Annie" as coming from Annie's dog Sandy.

▶•◆•◆•◆•◀ ARGO ▶•◆•◆•◆•◀

THE MOVIE

The 2012 film *Argo*, starring and directed by Ben Affleck, won three Oscars, including Best Picture.

THE SHIP

In Greek mythology, the *Argo* carried Jason and his Argonauts in search of the Golden Fleece.

▶•◆•◆•◆•◀ ARI ▶•◆•◆•◆•◀

PEOPLE

Ari Shapiro is an NPR host and reporter. Ari was the nickname of Greek shipping magnate Aristotle Onassis, second husband of Jacqueline Kennedy. Ari Fleischer is a former presidential press secretary. Actress Ari Meyers appeared on the sitcom *Kate & Allie*. Ari Ben Canaan is the main character in the Leon Uris novel *Exodus*, portrayed by Paul Newman in the film adaptation of the same name. Ariana Grande's nickname (and perfume) is Ari.

IN SPORTS

"ARI" is the abbreviation for the Arizona Diamondbacks major-league baseball team, as it often appears on scoreboards. As such, "N.L. West team" will often be seen as part of the clue.

▶•◆•◆•◆•◀ ARIA ▶•◆•◆•◆•◀

IN MUSIC

An aria is a voice solo in an opera or oratorio. Clues will usually refer to well-known operas (such as *Carmen, Otello, Rigoletto,* and *Tosca*), opera singers (such as Kiri Te Kanawa, Luciano Pavarotti, Leontyne Price, and Beverly Sills), opera houses (such as the Met and La Scala), opera composers (such as Puccini and Verdi) or the arias themselves (such as "Caro nome," "Summertime," and "Vesti la giubba").

▶•◆•◆•◆•◀ ARID ▶•◆•◆•◆•◀

LITERALLY SPEAKING

As a synonym for "dry" as in "parched," commonly seen clues include "Desertlike," "Lacking water," "Like the Gobi," and "Saharan."

FIGURATIVELY SPEAKING

As a synonym for "dry" as in "uninteresting," commonly seen clues include "Jejune," "Uninspired," and "Vapid."

▶•◆•◆•◆•◀ ARIEL ▶•◆•◆•◆•◀

REAL PEOPLE

Ariel Sharon was prime minister of Israel from 2001 to 2006. Historian Ariel Durant collaborated with her husband Will on *The Story of Civilization*.

UNREAL PEOPLE, ETC.

Ariel is the title character of the Disney film *The Little Mermaid* and the sprite in Shakespeare's *The Tempest*. Ariel is also one of the moons of the planet Uranus.

▶•◆•◆•◆•◀ ARIES ▶•◆•◆•◆•◀

UP IN THE SKY

Aries is the constellation of the ram, and a sign of the zodiac (after Pisces and before Taurus), covering the period from March 20 to April 19.

▶•◆•◆•◆•◀ ARISE ▶•◆•◆•◆•◀

AS PEOPLE DO

Commonly seen clues: "Get out of bed," "Greet the day," and "Stand up."

AS THINGS DO

Ideas and events may arise also. Commonly seen clues in this sense: "Become evident," "Come to mind," "Crop up," and "Originate."

The past tense, "arose," actually appears in crosswords somewhat more often than "arise." Due, no doubt, to the letter "O" being more useful for puzzle authors than "I."

▶•◆•◆•◆•◀ ARK ▶•◆•◆•◆•◀

BIBLICALLY, ETC.

Human passengers on Noah's Ark included Noah, his wife, and his three sons (Ham, Shem, and Japheth) and their wives; the Ark landed on Mount Ararat. Indiana Jones finds the Ark of the Covenant in *Raiders of the Lost Ark*. An ark is built by Steve Carell's character under the direction of the Supreme Being in the 2007 film *Evan Almighty*.

ON THE MAP

As an abbreviation for Arkansas, clues will most often refer either to the state's neighbors (Louisiana, Texas, Tennessee, Oklahoma, Missouri, Mississippi), its cities (Little Rock, Pine Bluff), or as it being the birthplace of president Bill Clinton.

▶•◆•◆•◆•◀ ARLO ▶•◆•◆•◆•◀

IN MUSIC

Folk singer Arlo Guthrie, son of balladeer Woody Guthrie, is best known for his 1967 song "Alice's Restaurant."

IN THE PAPER

"Arlo and Janis" is a comic strip about a baby-boomer couple.

▶·◆·◆·◆·◀ ARM ▶·◆·◆·◆·◀

ON THE BODY
Commonly seen clues in this sense may reference arm bones (such as the ulna, humerus, and radius), arm muscles and joints (such as the biceps and elbow), or be more evocative (such as "Escort's offering," "Part of a shirt," "Pitcher's pride," and "Tattoo site").

ELSEWHERE
Other things with arms to keep in mind: chairs, phonographs, slot machines, sofas, and starfish.

THE VERB
Commonly seen clues in this sense include "Give guns to," "Prepare for battle," and "Provide with weapons."

▶·◆·◆·◆·◀ ARNE ▶·◆·◆·◆·◀

IN MUSIC
English composer Thomas Arne is best known for writing the anthem "Rule, Britannia!"

IN THE CABINET
Arne Duncan served as secretary of education for Barack Obama from 2009 to 2015.

▶·◆·◆·◆·◀ AROMA ▶·◆·◆·◆·◀

IN YOUR NOSE
Synonym clues include "Odor," "Scent," "Bouquet," and "Fragrance." More evocative clues will mention places known for their pleasant aromas, such as bakeries, kitchens, and coffeehouses. Less pleasant aromas are referred to now and then.

▶·◆·◆·◆·◀ AROSE ▶·◆·◆·◆·◀

THE VERB
See ARISE for common clues that refer to the past tense verb.

NOT THE VERB

The partial phrase "a rose" sometimes appears in clues like "End of a Gertrude Stein line" ("Rose is a rose is a rose"), or in excerpts from the famous *Romeo and Juliet* quotation ("'That which we call ___ ...': Shakespeare" or "'___ / By any other name ...': Shakespeare").

▶·◆·◈·◆·◀ ART ▶·◆·◈·◆·◀

THE NOUN

Commonly seen clues in this sense include "Creative skill," "Critic's specialty," "Gallery display," "Illustrations," and "Painting or sculpture."

THE VERB

In this sense, it's the old-style form of "are." Juliet says "Wherefore art thou Romeo?" in Shakespeare's *Romeo and Juliet*, and the word is used in the Lord's Prayer.

THE PEOPLE

Celebrities named Art include columnist Buchwald, actor Carney, TV hosts Fleming and Linkletter, and jazz musicians Blakey and Tatum.

▶·◆·◈·◆·◀ ASA ▶·◆·◈·◆·◀

SIMILES

"Cool ___ cucumber," "Fit ___ fiddle," "Flat ___ pancake," "Hard ___ rock," "High ___ kite," and "Smart ___ whip" all clue AS A. "Simile center" hints at these without a fill-in-the-blank.

TO START WITH

Common phrases that start with "as a" are "as a matter of fact" and "as a rule."

THE PEOPLE

Asa Hutchinson is a former Arkansas congressman, Asa Gray was an American botanist, and Asa was the original first name of entertainer Al Jolson.

▶•◆•◆•◆•◄ ASAP ▶•◆•◆•◆•◄

THE ACRONYM
Short for "as soon as possible," commonly seen clues include "Letters of urgency," "Memo directive," "PDQ," and "Pronto, in the office."

▶•◆•◆•◆•◄ ASEA ▶•◆•◆•◆•◄

ONE WORD
In the sense of "On the ocean," commonly seen clues are variants of "Between ports," "On the briny," "Sailing," and "Taking a cruise."

TWO WORDS
"Or to take arms against a sea of troubles" is part of the title character's famous "To be or not to be" soliloquy in Shakespeare's *Hamlet.*

▶•◆•◆•◆•◄ ASH ▶•◆•◆•◆•◄

THE TREE
Ash is a hardwood, used in the manufacture of baseball bats and hockey sticks.

THE RESIDUE
In this sense, ash is the powdery remains of burning, such as from volcanoes or fireplaces. Ash Wednesday is the first day of Lent.

THE COLORS
Ash can be a grayish blond or a silvery gray color.

▶•◆•◆•◆•◄ ASHE ▶•◆•◆•◆•◄

THE COURT GREAT
Tennis great Arthur Ashe, contemporary of Jimmy Connors and Björn Borg, won the men's Wimbledon title in 1975. The New York tennis stadium that is the site of the annual U.S. Open is named for him. Ashe's books include *Off the Court, A Hard Road to Glory,* and *Days of Grace.*

54

CROSSWORDS 101
Lesson 2: French

These French words appear frequently as crossword answers (accent and diacritical marks, if any, are omitted):

ADIEU (goodbye)	MER (sea)
AMI/AMIE (male/female friend)	MLLE (Miss or Ms.)
BON (good)	MME (Mrs.)
EAU (water)	MOI (my)
ENTRE (between)	MOT (word)
EST (is)	NEE (born)
ETAT (state)	NOIR (black)
ETE (summer)	OUI (yes)
ETES (are, summers)	PERE (father)
ETRE (to be)	ROI (king)
ICI (here)	SEL (salt)
IDEE (idea)	STE (female saint)
ILE (island)	TETE (head)
LAIT (milk)	TRES (very)
LES (the)	UNE (one)

▸•◆•◆•◆•◂ **ASI** ▸•◆•◆•◆•◂

BLANKETY-BLANKS

"___ was saying ...," "___ live and breathe!," and "___ recall ..." can all clue AS I. *As I Lay Dying* is a novel by William Faulkner, and "A Fool Such as I" is an Elvis Presley tune.

▶·◆·◆·◆·◀ ASIA ▶·◆·◆·◆·◀

ON THE MAP

The world's largest and most populous continent, Asia is often clued by a country within it, such as China, India, Japan, South Korea, Laos, and Thailand. The Himalayas, Siberia, and the Gobi Desert are all in Asia. The Ural Mountains mark part of the border between Europe and Asia. In the game of Risk, occupying Asia earns a player the most bonus troops.

ON THE RADIO

The band Asia's hits include "Heat of the Moment" and "Only Time Will Tell."

▶·◆·◆·◆·◀ ASIDE ▶·◆·◆·◆·◀

THE NOUN

An aside is a "stage whisper," a comment that is addressed to the audience by a character in a play, and which is not heard by any other characters on stage. Off the stage, an aside can be any short digression.

THE ADVERB

Commonly seen clues in this sense: "In reserve," "Notwithstanding," "Out of the way," and "All kidding ___."

▶·◆·◆·◆·◀ ASIS ▶·◆·◆·◆·◀

THE CAVEAT

As a warning to potential buyers, commonly seen clues for AS IS include "Auction proviso," "Not guaranteed," "Sales condition," "Warts and all," and "Without a warranty."

▶·◆·◆·◆·◀ ASK ▶·◆·◆·◆·◀

THE VERB

Commonly seen clues include "Inquire," "Invite," "One way to learn," "Pop the question," "Query," and "Show curiosity."

56

▶•◆•◆•◆•◀ ASOF ▶•◆•◆•◆•◀

FOR STARTERS

The phrase AS OF is often seen before dates to indicate when a certain something is to begin. Typical clues include "Starting from," "Up until," "Ever since" and "___ now (so far)."

▶•◆•◆•◆•◀ ASONE ▶•◆•◆•◆•◀

INDIVISIBLE

"As one" is synonymous with "all together." Clues in that vein: "In unison," "Acting in concert," "En masse," and "United."

▶•◆•◆•◆•◀ ASP ▶•◆•◆•◆•◀

MAN AND BEAST

The venomous snake that was reputedly the undoing of Cleopatra, it is also known as the Egyptian cobra and the horned viper. The Asp is a henchman of Daddy Warbucks in the "Little Orphan Annie" comic strip.

▶•◆•◆•◆•◀ ASS ▶•◆•◆•◆•◀

THE BEAST

Commonly seen clues include "Beast of burden," "Brayer," "Pack animal," and "Wild equine."

THE PERSON

In this sense, commonly seen clues include "Buffoon," "Bozo," "Dolt," "Knucklehead," "Ninny," "Obstinate cuss," and "Pompous one."

▶•◆•◆•◆•◀ ASSET ▶•◆•◆•◆•◀

LITERALLY SPEAKING

In the accounting sense, commonly seen clues include "Balance sheet listing," "Item of value," "Liability's opposite," and "Stock or bond."

FIGURATIVELY SPEAKING

Less tangible assets include intelligence, poise, wisdom, and diplomacy, for example.

▶·◆·◆·◆·◆·◀ **ASSN** ▶·◆·◆·◆·◆·◀

THE ABBREVIATION

As a short form of "association," it is part of the names of the ABA, AMA, NAACP, NBA, NEA, PGA, PTA, and YMCA. Clued more synonymously, there's "Professional org.," "Special-interest gp.," and "Trade org."

▶·◆·◆·◆·◆·◀ **ASST** ▶·◆·◆·◆·◆·◀

THE ABBREVIATION

As a short form of "assistant," commonly seen clues include "Aide: Abbr.," "CEO's helper," "Deputy: Abbr.," "Prof.'s rank," and "Type of D.A."

▶·◆·◆·◆·◆·◀ **ASTI** ▶·◆·◆·◆·◆·◀

ON THE MAP

The Italian province of Asti, in the Piedmont region, is famous for its wines. In particular, the sparkling wine known as Asti spumante originated there.

▶·◆·◆·◆·◆·◀ **ASTO** ▶·◆·◆·◆·◆·◀

IN LEGALESE

"As to" appears at the beginning of legal memos, where it is synonymous with "about," "concerning," "in the matter of," "in re," and "regarding."

►•◆•◆•◆•◄ ASTRO ►•◆•◆•◆•◄

IN SPORTS

Houston's major-league baseball team is the Astros. The Astros switched their big-league affiliation in 2013 from the National League to the American League.

IN TOONDOM

Astro is the dog of the title family in the futuristic animated series *The Jetsons*.

TO START WITH

As a prefix, "astro" can precede "physics" and "nautical."

►•◆•◆•◆•◄ ATAD ►•◆•◆•◆•◄

NOT SO GREAT

Clues for A TAD are almost always synonyms, such as "Slightly," "Not much," "Hardly any," and "The merest bit."

►•◆•◆•◆•◄ ATARI ►•◆•◆•◆•◄

THE COMPANY

Atari introduced the first commercially successful video game, Pong, in 1972. Its other successful games include Asteroids, Breakout, Centipede, Gauntlet, Missile Command, and Tempest.

►•◆•◆•◆•◄ ATIT ►•◆•◆•◆•◄

COLLOQUIALLY SPEAKING

In the sense of "fighting," commonly seen clues for AT IT include "Arguing," "Bickering," and "Squabbling." In the sense of "busy": "Buckling down," "Hard at work," and "Plugging away."

BLANKETY-BLANKS

To "Have at it" is to fight, to "take a crack at it" is to try, and to "keep at it" is to persist.

►•◆•◆•◆•◄ ATL ►•◆•◆•◆•◄

IN THE WATER

"Atl." is an abbreviation for "Atlantic," for which you'll see clues such as "Part of NATO: Abbr." (North Atlantic Treaty Organization), and "It's east of Fla."

ON LAND

It's also an abbreviation for "Atlanta," with clues such as "Home of the Braves: Abbr.," "N.L. East team," and "Capital of Ga."

►•◆•◆•◆•◄ ATLAS ►•◆•◆•◆•◄

THE LIFTER

Atlas, brother of Prometheus, was the mythical Titan who was condemned to support the sky on his shoulders.

THE BOOK

The book of maps gets its name from the mythical Atlas.

THE MISSILE

Atlas was the first U.S. intercontinental ballistic missile.

►•◆•◆•◆•◄ ATM ►•◆•◆•◆•◄

IN THE MONEY

The ATM (automated teller machine) was embraced by crossword authors about as rapidly as by bank customers. Typical clues: "S&L convenience," "$ dispenser," and "24-hr. bank feature." NCR (formerly called National Cash Register) is one of the largest manufacturers of ATMs.

►•◆•◆•◆•◄ ATOM ►•◆•◆•◆•◄

IN SCIENCE

As it relates to chemistry or physics, commonly seen clues include "Building block of matter," "Energy source," "Fission subject," and "Molecule part."

THINKING SMALL
In the sense of something very small: "Little bit," "Scintilla," and "Tiny quantity."

▶·◆·◆·◆·◀ **ATONE** ▶·◆·◆·◆·◀

THE VERB
Commonly seen clues: "Expiate," "Do penance," "Make amends," and "Observe Yom Kippur" (the Jewish annual day of atonement).

▶·◆·◆·◆·◀ **ATOP** ▶·◆·◆·◆·◀

THE PREPOSITION
Commonly seen clues: "At the summit," "On the crest of," "Perched on," and "Surmounting."

▶·◆·◆·◆·◀ **ATSEA** ▶·◆·◆·◆·◀

COLLOQUIALLY SPEAKING
Although dictionaries tell us that both "asea" and "at sea" can mean "confused," "asea" is rarely clued this way in puzzles, while "at sea" is clued in this sense most of the time, with clues such as "Baffled," "Befuddled," "Clueless," and "Perplexed."

LITERALLY SPEAKING
Commonly seen clues in this sense are similar to those for "asea," such as "Between ports," "On the briny," "Sailing," and "Taking a cruise."

▶·◆·◆·◆·◀ **ATT** ▶·◆·◆·◆·◀

LEGALLY SPEAKING
As a short form of "attorney," commonly seen clues include "ABA member" (American Bar Association), "Courtroom fig.," and "Lawyer: Abbr."

61

MA BELL

Though the large telephone company is properly known as AT&T, you'll sometimes see telephonic clues for ATT like "Long-distance letters."

▶•◆•◆•◆•◀ **ATTN** ▶•◆•◆•◆•◀

ON CORRESPONDENCE

Short for "attention," ATTN is seen on business correspondence, to direct a piece of mail to a particular person or department. Clues will always be something like: "Memo abbr.," "Letters on an envelope," or "Mail-routing abbr."

▶•◆•◆•◆•◀ **AUDI** ▶•◆•◆•◆•◀

ON THE ROAD

Audi is a make of German automobile, a subsidiary of the Volkswagen Group. Typical clues: "German car," "BMW competitor," "Mercedes rival," and "Autobahn auto" (an autobahn is a German highway).

▶•◆•◆•◆•◀ **AURA** ▶•◆•◆•◆•◀

THE ATMOSPHERE

Commonly seen clues: "Ambiance," "Distinctive air," "New Age glow," and "Subtle quality."

▶•◆•◆•◆•◀ **AUTO** ▶•◆•◆•◆•◀

ON THE ROAD

Clues in the vehicle sense are usually by example, listing auto makes (Chevrolet, Toyota, etc.), or body styles (coupe, convertible, etc.).

FOR STARTERS

As a prefix, "auto" can precede words such as "graph," "biography," and "pilot."

FOR SHORT

As a shortened form for "automatic," the most commonly seen clues are variations on "Camera setting" and "Opposite of manual."

▶•◆•◆•◆•◀ AVE ▶•◆•◆•◆•◀

THE ABBREVIATION

As a short form of "avenue," generic clues include "City map abbr.," "St. crosser," and "Urban rd." Specific avenues often seen are New York City's Madison and Lexington, and Washington, D.C.'s Pennsylvania and Constitution.

IN LATIN

As an old Roman word of greeting meaning "hail," clues are variations of "Forum welcome" and "Greeting to Galba." "Ave Maria" is a Roman Catholic prayer.

▶•◆•◆•◆•◀ AVER ▶•◆•◆•◆•◀

THE VERB

Commonly seen clues: "Assert," "Declare," "Maintain," "Profess," and "State confidently."

INSIDER'S TIP: "Aver" and "avow" are nearly synonymous, and the same clues are often seen for both words. That's why experienced puzzlers always wait for crossing-clue verification before filling in the last two letters of "**A V __ __**."

▶•◆•◆•◆•◀ AVID ▶•◆•◆•◆•◀

GETTING EMOTIONAL

Clues for AVID are almost always synonyms, such as "Enthusiastic," "Ardent," "Zealous," and "Raring to go."

▶·◆·◆·◆·◀ AVIS ▶·◆·◆·◆·◀

THE COMPANY

Avis Rent-a-Car, founded in 1946, has been using the slogan "We try harder" since the 1960s. It is often defined as an "alternative" to other car rental companies, such as Alamo, Budget, Dollar, Enterprise, Hertz, and National.

IN LATIN

"*Avis*" is the Latin word for "bird." The Latin idiom *rara avis* means "rare bird," or anything out of the ordinary.

▶·◆·◆·◆·◀ AVON ▶·◆·◆·◆·◀

THE RIVER

Avon is the name of at least four different rivers in Great Britain, but in crosswords it's always the one that flows through the town of Stratford-Upon-Avon, home of William Shakespeare, a.k.a. "the Bard."

THE COMPANY

Avon Products is primarily in the perfume and cosmetics business, its memorable "Avon calling" TV commercials featuring a salesperson ringing a homeowner's doorbell. Its competitors include Revlon and Mary Kay.

▶·◆·◆·◆·◀ AWARE ▶·◆·◆·◆·◀

THE ADJECTIVE

Commonly seen clues: "Clued in," "Cognizant," "Conscious," "In the know," "Mindful," and "With it."

NOT SO FAST!

"Open-eyed": **A W A ___ E**

The answer can be AWAKE or AWARE.

►·•·•·•·◄ AWE ►·•·•·•·◄

THE NOUN

Commonly seen noun clues: "Amazement," "Reverence," "Veneration," and "Wonderment."

THE VERB

As a verb, there's "Blow away," "Bowl over," "Flabbergast," "Impress greatly," and "Wow."

►·•·•·•·◄ AWOL ►·•·•·•·◄

THE ACRONYM

The military term AWOL is short for "absent without leave," and may be used as an adjective, adverb (as in "go AWOL"), or noun (for the soldier guilty of the offense). Commonly seen clues: "Army no-show," "GI's offense," "Mil. truant," and "MP's quarry."

►·•·•·•·◄ AXE ►·•·•·•·◄

THE TOOL

People using axes include firefighters, loggers, lumberjacks (the legendary Paul Bunyan, notably), and the Tin Woodman from *The Wizard of Oz*. Tomahawks and hatchets are two kinds of axes. As a verb meaning "to wield an axe," clues are variations of "Chop down."

THE JOB VERB

As a synonym for "dismiss from a job," commonly seen clues include "Can," "Fire," "Let go," and "Pink-slip."

►·•·•·•·◄ AXLE ►·•·•·•·◄

ON A VEHICLE

An axle is the bar that connects two wheels of an automobile, covered wagon, etc. Vehicle charges on toll roads are often based on the number of axles that the vehicle has.

THAT'S O.K.

"Aye" is the traditional assent spoken by sailors and Scots, and by legislators in parliamentary roll calls, for whom "nay" is the opposite.

INSIDER'S TIP: Other than the sailor and Scots senses, clues for AYE are also applicable to YEA, and both words are regularly seen in crosswords. You've been warned.

B–C

West Indies boa

▶·◆·◆·◆·◀ BAA ▶·◆·◆·◆·◀

IN THE FIELD

As the bleat or sound made by a sheep, commonly seen clues include "Cote call," "Lamb's cry," "Ram's remark," and the immortal "Ewe said it."

▶·◆·◆·◆·◀ BAD ▶·◆·◆·◆·◀

NOT SO NICE

Clues for BAD are almost always synonyms, such as "Evil," "Villainous," "Atrocious," "Loathsome," "Counterfeit," and "Naughty." "Bad" is also the title of a Michael Jackson song and album.

▶·◆·◆·◆·◀ BAH ▶·◆·◆·◆·◀

THE EXCLAMATION

This old-timey interjection of disgust is particularly associated with the miserly Ebenezer Scrooge in the Charles Dickens story *A Christmas Carol*, in which he memorably says, "Bah! Humbug!" You might also see the word defined as another similar interjection, such as "Pshaw!" or "Fiddlesticks!"

▶·◆·◆·◆·◀ BAR ▶·◆·◆·◆·◀

THE VERB

As a synonym for "prevent," commonly seen clues include "Block," "Eliminate," "Keep out," and "Prohibit."

EATING AND DRINKING PLACES

As a place to drink, commonly seen clues include "Grill partner," "Pub," and "Tavern." There are also salad bars, sushi bars, and piano bars.

THE SHAPE

Bar-shaped things include candy and chocolate, soap, certain graphs, slot machine symbols, and gold ingots.

IN LAW

"The bar" is a symbol for the legal profession.

NOT SO FAST!

"Prohibit": **B A** ___

The answer can be BAR or BAN.

▶◆◆◆◆◀ BAT ▶◆◆◆◆◀

IN SPORTS

Bats are used in cricket as well as baseball. The best-known brand of baseball bat is the Louisville Slugger.

THE BEAST

Bats are flying mammals that live in caves. Vampires, Count Dracula in particular, can take the form of a bat.

▶◆◆◆◆◀ BEE ▶◆◆◆◆◀

THE GATHERINGS

There are spelling bees, quilting bees, and husking bees.

THE INSECT

"Apiary resident," "Buzzer," "Honey handler," "Nectar collector," and "Stinger" all clue the insect directly. Jerry Seinfeld provided the voice of bee Barry B. Benson in the 2007 animated film *Bee Movie*.

IN THE NEWS

Sacramento and Fresno both have daily newspapers known as the *Bee*.

▶·◆·◆·◆·◀ BET ▶·◆·◆·◆·◀

THE VERB

There's "Take a chance," "Speculate with cash," "Put at risk," "Play the horses," and "Do some gambling."

THE NOUN

Clues like "Amount wagered" and "Casino action" clue the noun sense.

NOUN OR VERB

Many synonymous clues work in both the noun and verb senses, such as "Wager," "Gamble," and "Venture."

▶·◆·◆·◆·◀ BIO ▶·◆·◆·◆·◀

IN PRINT

As a short form of "biography," there is "Life story," "Book jacket write-up," and synonymous variants, usually ending "..., for short."

IN THE CLASSROOM

As a short form of "biology," you'll see "College major" and "Science class," also usually ending "..., for short."

THE PREFIX

"Bio" can serve as a prefix for such words as physics, hazard, and chemistry.

▶·◆·◆·◆·◀ BLT ▶·◆·◆·◆·◀

FOR LUNCH

BLT is short for the bacon, lettuce, and tomato sandwich, with "sandwich" and "for short" usually appearing in the clue, often accompanied by "diner," "lunch," or "crunchy."

THE SNAKE

Commonly seen clues in this sense: "Amazon squeezer,"
"___ constrictor," and "Snake with a squeeze."

WHAT TO WEAR

A boa can also be a scarf or stole made of feathers, fur, or fabric.

NOT SO FAST!

"String tie": **B O L** ___

Both BOLO and BOLA are correct.

▶·◆·◆·◆·◀ **BRA** ▶·◆·◆·◆·◀

WHAT TO WEAR

Commonly seen clues in this sense: "Bikini part," "Lingerie item,"
and "Victoria's Secret buy." Other well-known bra manufacturers
include Bali, Olga, and Maidenform.

ON A CAR

A bra may also be a removable cover for an automobile that
protects the grille from road debris.

▶·◆·◆·◆·◀ **BRO** ▶·◆·◆·◆·◀

IN THE FAMILY

As a short form of "brother," you'll often see "Family nickname" or
"Sis's counterpart."

IN SLANG

As contemporary slang for "friend," common clues include "Dude,"
"Homeboy," and "Pal."

▶·◆·◆·◆·◀ CAN ▶·◆·◆·◆·◀

THE NOUN

As a container, clues will often mention these items commonly found in cans: coffee, corn, soup, soda pop, and paint. As a slang term for "jail," clues will usually be other slang terms, such as "Slammer," "Cooler," and "Hoosegow,"

THE VERB

Not often clued as a verb meaning "Keep in a can," it's usually either a rather straight "Is able to" or a slang term for "discharge from a job," such as "Send packing" or "Give the boot to."

▶·◆·◆·◆·◀ CAR ▶·◆·◆·◆·◀

ON THE ROAD

Any make or model of automobile is fair game as a clue. They can be tricky to figure out when they're also the names of other things, like Lincoln and Jaguar.

OFF THE ROAD

Elevators, trains, and roller coasters also have cars.

▶·◆·◆·◆·◀ CASE ▶·◆·◆·◆·◀

AT WORK

Lawyers and detectives are often seen for clues in this sense.

HOLD IT

As a container, common clues include items found in cases, such as a violin or beer.

AS A VERB

The informal verb "case" means "to survey before planning a crime."

▶•◆•◆•◆•◀ CAT ▶•◆•◆•◆•◀

TYPES

Breeds of house cat often seen include the Abyssinian, Burmese, Persian, and Siamese. Other house cat categories are the calico and tabby. Any type of wild feline, such as the leopard or tiger, may also clue CAT.

FELINE CELEBRITIES

In cartoons, there's Felix, Garfield, Heathcliff, and Stimpy, and there's Morris in TV commercials. The title characters in the Andrew Lloyd Webber musical *Cats* include Grizabella, Macavity, and Rum Tum Tugger.

THE PERSON

A "cat" may also be a "cool" person, particularly a lover of jazz music.

▶•◆•◆•◆•◀ CBS ▶•◆•◆•◆•◀

THE NETWORK

CBS comes from the initials of the television network's former name, the Columbia Broadcasting System, known for its eye logo. It's usually clued by its longtime rivals (NBC, ABC, or Fox), its best-remembered shows of the past (such as *Gunsmoke* or *I Love Lucy*), or its current popular shows (such as *60 Minutes* or *The Big Bang Theory*).

▶•◆•◆•◆•◀ CDS ▶•◆•◆•◆•◀

THE DISCS

Short for "compact discs," CDs may hold data or music. Clues in this sense often mention DJs (who play them), PCs (which can hold them), or LPs (which preceded them).

THE DOLLARS

As a shortened form of "certificates of deposit," clues in this sense will often mention S&Ls, IRAs, or similar investment-related terms.

▶•◈•◈•◈•◀ CEDE ▶•◈•◈•◈•◀

THE VERB

Meaning "to formally relinquish," CEDE is always clued synonymously, with clues like "Give up legally" and "Surrender claims to."

▶•◈•◈•◈•◀ CEO ▶•◈•◈•◈•◀

IN CHARGE

Short for "chief executive officer," CEO will usually have a generic clue such as "Boardroom VIP" or "Corporate bigwig."

INSIDER'S TIP: While generic clues such as these will almost always be correctly answered as CEO, they also can be clues for CFO (short for "chief financial officer"), though CFO appears in crosswords far less often.

▶•◈•◈•◈•◀ CIA ▶•◈•◈•◈•◀

THE SPIES

Based in Langley, Virginia, and nicknamed "The Company," the Central Intelligence Agency handles foreign intelligence gathering. Its directors have included George H.W. Bush, Robert Gates, George Tenet, Leon Panetta, and Mike Pompeo. Its World War II–era predecessor was the OSS (Office of Strategic Services). Its Cold War–era Soviet counterpart was the KGB.

▶•◈•◈•◈•◀ CIAO ▶•◈•◈•◈•◀

COMING OR GOING

Pronounced "chow," CIAO is an informal interjection from Italian which, not unlike "aloha" and "shalom," can mean "hello" or "goodbye." Though in crosswords it's almost always defined as the latter, with clues like "See ya," "So long," or "Arrivederci."

▶·◆·◆·◆·◀ **CNN** ▶·◆·◆·◆·◀

ON THE AIR

Short for "Cable News Network," CNN was founded by media mogul Ted Turner in 1980. It's usually defined in terms of either its cable TV competitors (such as Fox News or MSNBC), its reporters (such as Wolf Blitzer, Erin Burnett, and Anderson Cooper), or its programs (such as *The Situation Room* and *Inside Politics*).

▶·◆·◆·◆·◀ **COLA** ▶·◆·◆·◆·◀

THE CARBONATED SOFT DRINK

Colas are served at fast-food restaurants and vending machines. The most popular brands are Coke, Pepsi, RC, and Jolt. Cola is an ingredient in the rum cocktail known as the Cuba libre.

NOT SO FAST!

"Fizzy drink": ___ O ___ A

The answer can be COLA or SODA.

▶·◆·◆·◆·◀ **CON** ▶·◆·◆·◆·◀

THE SCAM

As a synonym for "swindle" as a noun or verb, typical clues include (as a verb) "Deceive," "Flimflam," and "Take in," and (as a noun) "Racket" and "Shell game."

THE PERSON

As a slang term for "prisoner," you'll often see "Cell occupant," "Jailbird," and "One in the cooler."

BLANKETY-BLANKS

In various senses of the word, there's "Pro and ___," "Chile ___ carne," "Arroz ___ pollo," and "Allegro ___ brio" (a fast tempo seen on musical scores).

CROSSWORDS 101
Lesson 3: German

These German words appear
frequently as crossword answers
(diacritical marks, if any, are omitted):

ACH (oh)
DAS (the)
DREI (three)
EINE (a)
EINS (one)
HERR (mister)
ICH (I)
OST (east)
SIE (you)
UBER (above)

▶•◆•◆•◆•◀ **COO** ▶•◆•◆•◆•◀

FOR THE BIRDS

As a noun or verb, "coo" is the soft sound made by doves and pigeons.

FOR THE PEOPLE

With a meaning derived from the above, when people coo, they are murmuring fondly.

▶•◆•◆•◆•◀ CPA ▶•◆•◆•◆•◀

BY THE BOOKS

Short for "certified public accountant," CPA will usually have clues with such keywords as "taxes," "IRS," "auditor," and "e-file" (the electronic filing of tax returns).

▶•◆•◆•◆•◀ CUE ▶•◆•◆•◆•◀

AT THE POOL HALL

In the related games of pool and billiards, a cue is the stick with which players strike a ball.

AT THE PERFORMANCE

As a noun, a cue given to a performer as a signal to begin speaking, or a reminder of one's next line. As a verb, it is to provide such a signal.

D

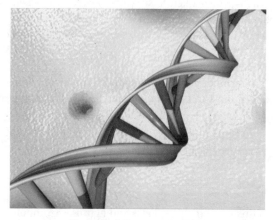

The double helix structure of DNA

▶·◆·◆·◆·◆·◀ **DAD** ▶·◆·◆·◆·◆·◀

ALL IN THE FAMILY

Clues will usually be variants of "Family man," "Father," "Patriarch," and "June honoree."

▶·◆·◆·◆·◆·◀ **DAM** ▶·◆·◆·◆·◆·◀

IN THE WATER

As the barrier, you're likely to see clues like "River blocker," "Flood controller," "Beaver construction," and "Hydroelectric power source." Less often, it'll be clued in the verb sense, as "Stop the flow of."

IN THE STABLE

"Dam" is a term for a female parent of a four-footed domestic animal, seen most frequently in crosswords as the mother of a horse.

▶·◆·◆·◆·◆·◀ **DATA** ▶·◆·◆·◆·◆·◀

THE NUMBERS

Clues in this sense include "Facts and figures," "Computer input," "Spreadsheet contents," and "Numerical details."

THE CHARACTER

Data is the android character portrayed by Brent Spiner in the TV series *Star Trek: The Next Generation*.

INSIDER'S TIP: The word "data" can be correctly used as a singular or plural noun, so its clues can take either form.

NOT SO FAST!

"Type of flower": ___ A ___ S Y

The answer can be DAISY, PANSY, or TANSY.

DATE

FOR ESCORTING
As a verb there's "Go out with" and "See socially," with similar noun clues like "Prom partner" and "Romantic outing."

FOR ENTERING
Related to the above, a date may be found on a check, an appointment book, or on a envelope's postmark.

FOR EATING
In this sense, a date is a tropical fruit that grows on certain palm trees.

DDE

HAIL TO THE CHIEF
DDE was the monogram of Dwight David "Ike" Eisenhower, 34th U.S. president, and a five-star general during World War II, where he oversaw the European Theater of Operations, or ETO (which is why you will sometimes see DDE clued as "ETO commander"), including the Allied invasion of mainland Europe which commenced on D-Day. Presidentially, he followed HST (Harry S. Truman) and preceded JFK (John F. Kennedy).

DEAN

IN GENERAL
A dean can be the head of an administrative division of a school, or the senior member of a group.

SPECIFICALLY
Celebrities with that first name include singer Martin (of "Rat Pack" fame) and actor Stockwell. Those with that last name include actor James and baseball great Dizzy.

►·◆·◆·◆·◄ DEE ►·◆·◆·◆·◄

THE LETTER
As the spelled-out version of the letter D, you'll see academic references like "Barely passing" and "Poor grade."

THE LAST NAME
There are actresses Ruby and Sandra (Gidget portrayer in the movies), and singers Kiki and Joey.

FIRST AND MIDDLE NAMES
There's actress Dee Wallace and actor Billy Dee Williams.

ON THE MAP
Scotland's River Dee flows through the city of Aberdeen and near Balmoral Castle.

►·◆·◆·◆·◄ DEER ►·◆·◆·◆·◄

THE BEAST
Commonly seen clues: "Antlered animal," "Moose relative," "Timid creature," "Venison source," and "Woodland beast."

INSIDER'S TIP: Keep in mind that the plural of "deer" is also "deer," so the plural forms of all the previous clues are also correct for DEER.

►·◆·◆·◆·◄ DEERE ►·◆·◆·◆·◄

THE MAN AND HIS MACHINES
Illinois blacksmith John Deere founded the farm equipment company named for him in 1837, the same year that he invented the first commercially successful steel plow. Today, the company's many products include everything from excavators to lawn mowers. Caterpillar is its principal competitor, at least as seen in crosswords.

▶•◆•◆•◆•◀ DELI ▶•◆•◆•◆•◀

THE STORE

A deli, short for "delicatessen," is a neighborhood store where sandwiches, cold cuts, etc., are sold. By extension, it is also the department of a supermarket where these items are found.

▶•◆•◆•◆•◀ DEN ▶•◆•◆•◆•◀

FOR ANIMALS

A den is a lair for wild animals, such as lions and bears.

FOR PEOPLE

The den of a home (a.k.a. "study" or "family room") is usually thought of as a cozy place for relaxation. A den is also a group of Cub Scouts.

▶•◆•◆•◆•◀ DENT ▶•◆•◆•◆•◀

ON A CAR

Usually defined in this sense as a variation of "Body shop repair" and "Fender damage."

FIGURATIVELY SPEAKING

One makes a dent in a project if there has been small but noticeable progress made toward completing it.

▶•◆•◆•◆•◀ DES ▶•◆•◆•◆•◀

ON THE MAP

"___ Moines, Iowa" and "___ Plaines, Illinois" (a suburb of Chicago) are by far the two most popular clues for DES.

▶·◆·◆·◆·◀ **DIE** ▶·◆·◆·◆·◀

AT THE GAMES

As the singular form of "dice," a die can be found in casinos, and in home games such as Monopoly, Trivial Pursuit, and Yahtzee.

AT FACTORIES

In this sense, a die is a device that cuts or stamps material, often seen in the phrase "tool and die company."

AT LAST

As a verb, cars and other machines are the most likely things to die, with clues like "Stop functioning" and "Conk out." There traditionally isn't all that much corporeal dying in crosswords, but you may see synonyms for this sense of the word in certain puzzles.

▶·◆·◆·◆·◀ **DNA** ▶·◆·◆·◆·◀

THAT'S LIFE

Common clues such as "Genetic material" and "Substance in cells" can define RNA as well as DNA. "Chromosome component," "Double-helix molecule," and "High-tech fingerprint" are unique to DNA.

▶·◆·◆·◆·◀ **DOE** ▶·◆·◆·◆·◀

THE ANIMAL

A doe is a female deer, rabbit, or kangaroo.

THE SURNAME

The names John Doe and Jane Doe are used for unidentified men and women in legal proceedings.

▶•◆•◆•◆•◀ DRAT ▶•◆•◆•◆•◀

THE MILD OATH

Commonly seen clues are variations of "Darn it!," "Fiddlesticks!," and "Phooey!" It was uttered by W.C. Fields more than once in his films.

▶•◆•◆•◆•◀ DRS ▶•◆•◆•◆•◀

THE HEALERS

Although anyone with a doctorate degree may be addressed as "Doctor," in crosswords doctors are almost always physicians. So clues for DRS usually contain abbreviations to signal the abbreviated answer, such as "AMA members," "ICU workers," "Hospital VIPs," and "ER personnel."

INSIDER'S TIP: Many clues for DRS, such as the latter three above, can also clue RNS (registered nurses), another common crossword entry.

▶•◆•◆•◆•◀ DUO ▶•◆•◆•◆•◀

MORE THAN ONE

Commonly seen clues: "Twosome," "Couple," and "Performing pair."

▶•◆•◆•◆•◀ DYE ▶•◆•◆•◆•◀

AS A NOUN

In the noun sense, you'll see variations of "Hair coloring," "Food additive," "Salon bottle," and "Easter egg decoration."

AS A VERB

There's "Change the color of," "Use indigo or henna on," etc.

E

An emu

▶·◆·◆·◆·◀ EACH ▶·◆·◆·◆·◀

NOT TOGETHER

Almost always clued synonymously, there's "Apiece," "Per unit," "Purchased separately," and the informal "A pop."

▶·◆·◆·◆·◀ EAGLE ▶·◆·◆·◆·◀

IN THE AIR

Straightforwardly speaking, an eagle is a bird of prey, a relative of the hawk.

ON THE COURSE

"Eagle" is the term for a score of two under par on a particular golf hole, or one stroke better than a birdie.

SYMBOLICALLY

The bald eagle is the national bird of the U.S., appearing on the back of a U.S. quarter, and it's a symbol of the U.S. Postal Service. "Eagle" is also the highest rank that a Boy Scout can attain.

NOT SO FAST!

"Praise highly": E X __ __ __

The answer can be EXALT or the nearly synonymous EXTOL.

▶·◆·◆·◆·◀ EAR ▶·◆·◆·◆·◀

THE NOUN

In addition to the organ of hearing, it is a portion of corn on the cob, a handle of a jug or large pitcher, as well as musical discernment. The anvil, hammer, and stirrup are three small bones located inside the ear.

▶·◆·◆·◆·◀ **EARL** ▶·◆·◆·◆·◀

THE TITLE
Earl is a British title of nobility, below a marquis and above a viscount. The wife of an earl is a countess. Earl Grey is a variety of tea.

THE FIRST NAME
Bowler Anthony, jazz pianist Hines, banjoist Scruggs, Supreme Court justice Warren, basketball great Monroe and baseball manager Weaver are well-known Earls. Jason Lee played the title character on the sitcom *My Name Is Earl.*

THE MIDDLE NAME
Earl is the middle name of president Jimmy Carter and actor James Earl Jones.

▶·◆·◆·◆·◀ **EARN** ▶·◆·◆·◆·◀

THE VERB
Commonly seen clues: "Bring home," "Deserve," "Have coming," and "Merit."

▶·◆·◆·◆·◀ **EASE** ▶·◆·◆·◆·◀

THE VERB
Commonly seen verb clues include "Alleviate," "Facilitate," "Lighten," and "Simplify."

THE NOUN
As a synonym for "freedom from concern" or "freedom from difficulty," there's "Comfort," "Fluency," "Naturalness," and "Relaxation."

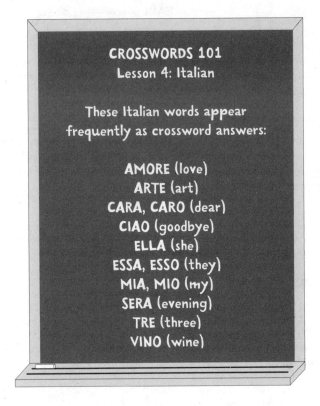

CROSSWORDS 101
Lesson 4: Italian

These Italian words appear
frequently as crossword answers:

AMORE (love)
ARTE (art)
CARA, CARO (dear)
CIAO (goodbye)
ELLA (she)
ESSA, ESSO (they)
MIA, MIO (my)
SERA (evening)
TRE (three)
VINO (wine)

▶·◆·◆·◆·◀ **EAST** ▶·◆·◆·◆·◀

THE DIRECTION

"Compass point," "Right, on a map," "Sunrise direction," and
"Toward the dawn" all commonly clue EAST. East is also one of the
four players in the game of bridge.

ON THE MAP

"The East" may denote the eastern part of the U.S., or the Asian
region a.k.a. "the Orient." "Down East" is a nickname for the state
of Maine. The East River separates the island of Manhattan from
the other New York City boroughs of Brooklyn and Queens.

IN SPORTS

The Big East is a college football conference, and the major
professional sports leagues have East (or Eastern) divisions.

▶·◆·◆·◆·◀ EASY ▶·◆·◆·◆·◀

THE ADJECTIVE
Commonly seen clues: "Effortless," "Elementary," "Lenient," "Not difficult," and "Simple."

THE EXCLAMATION
"Calm down!," "No problem!," and "Piece of cake!" can clue EASY used as an interjection.

▶·◆·◆·◆·◀ EAT ▶·◆·◆·◆·◀

FOODWISE
Commonly seen clues are variations of "Consume," "Dig in!," "Have dinner," and "Mother's directive."

OTHER MEANINGS
"Eat" may also be a synonym for "erode" or "corrode," and is a slang term meaning "absorb, as a financial loss."
The past tense, "ate," also appears frequently in crosswords.

PLURALIZED PARLANCE
Separate from the meanings of EAT mentioned above, EATS is a slang term for "food," which is supposedly seen on signs for informal eateries such as diners.

▶·◆·◆·◆·◀ EAVE ▶·◆·◆·◆·◀

ON THE HOUSE
An eave is an overhanging lower edge of a roof, where icicles may form in the winter.

▶·◆·◆·◆·◀ EAU ▶·◆·◆·◆·◀

LE NOUN
"*Eau*" is the French word for "water," which is its literal meaning in "Eau de Cologne" and "eau de vie" (a French brandy). Eau Claire is a city in Wisconsin.

▶•◆•◆•◆•◀ EBAY ▶•◆•◆•◆•◀

SOLD!

Clues for this highly popular internet site are usually variations of "Online auctioneer" and "Cyberbidding locale."

▶•◆•◆•◆•◀ EBB ▶•◆•◆•◆•◀

THE VERB

Commonly seen clues: "Diminish," "Flow's partner," "Recede," "Slacken," and "Withdraw."

THE MAN

Lyricist Fred Ebb collaborated with composer John Kander on the musicals *Cabaret*, *Chicago*, and *New York, New York*.

▶•◆•◆•◆•◀ ECHO ▶•◆•◆•◆•◀

THROUGH THE AIR

Commonly seen clues: "Canyon sound effect," "Resound," "Reverberate," and "Sonic bounce."

TO THE GREEKS

In Greek mythology, Echo was a nymph who had an unrequited love for Narcissus.

▶•◆•◆•◆•◀ ECO ▶•◆•◆•◆•◀

THE MAN

The books of Italian author Umberto Eco include *Baudolino*, *Foucault's Pendulum*, and *The Name of the Rose*.

THE PREFIX

"Eco-friendly," "ecosystem," and "ecotourism" all start with the "green" prefix "eco-."

INSIDER'S TIP: Though it may seem as if it should be, "eco." is not an abbreviation for "economics." That would be "econ." (See below.)

ECOL

FOR SHORT

As an abbreviation for "ecology," typical clues include "Earth sci.," "EPA concern," and "Environmental subj."

ECON

FOR SHORT

As an abbreviation for "economics," you'll see clues like "Supply-and-demand subj.," "MBA's course," "Nobel Prize field: Abbr.," and "A social science."

ECRU

THE COLOR

Ecru is a light brown, often the color of curtains, hosiery, linen, and silk.

EDAM

THE CHEESE

Edam is a mild yellow cheese named for the Dutch town where it is made. It is typically sold in spheres, coated with red wax.

EDDY

THE WATER

Commonly seen clues: "Countercurrent," "Sea swirl," "Vortex," and "Whirlpool."

THE PEOPLE

Mary Baker Eddy founded the religion of Christian Science. Actor Nelson Eddy costarred with Jeanette MacDonald in a series of film musicals in the 1930s and 1940s. Duane Eddy is a Grammy-winning rock guitarist.

▶•◆•◆•◆•◀ EDEN ▶•◆•◆•◆•◀

THE PARADISE

In Genesis, Eden was the garden paradise where Adam and Eve lived. The word can also refer to any blissful or delightful place.

THE PEOPLE

Anthony Eden was a 1950s British prime minister, whose title was Earl of Avon. Actress Barbara Eden is best known for her title role in the sitcom *I Dream of Jeannie*.

▶•◆•◆•◆•◀ EDGE ▶•◆•◆•◆•◀

THE NOUN

In the literal sense, commonly seen clues include "Border," "Brink," "Fringe," "Margin," and "Rim." Meaning "competitive advantage," there's "Head start" and "Upper hand."

THE VERB

As a verb, it can mean to sharpen or to defeat by a narrow margin.

NOT SO FAST!

"Within: Prefix": **E N ___ O**

The answer can be ENDO or ENTO.

▶•◆•◆•◆•◀ EDIT ▶•◆•◆•◆•◀

THE VERB

Commonly seen clues: "Blue-pencil," "Do newspaper work," "Improve prose," "Revise," and "Work on galleys." "Edit" is also a command in word-processing programs.

▶•◀•▶•◀•▶•◀ EDNA ▶•◀•▶•◀•▶•◀

REAL

There are authors Buchanan, Ferber, and O'Brien, and poet St. Vincent Millay.

FICTIONAL

Edna Krabappel was Bart's teacher in the animated sitcom *The Simpsons*. Dame Edna Everage is the alter ego of Australian comedian Barry Humphries. Edna, portrayed by John Travolta, is the mother of Tracy Turnblad in the 2007 film *Hairspray*.

▶•◀•▶•◀•▶•◀ EDS ▶•◀•▶•◀•▶•◀

THE PEOPLE

Men named Ed who are often paired to get EDS include author McBain; former New York City mayor Koch; TV personalities Bradley, McMahon, and Sullivan; and actors Asner, Begley, and O'Neill.

THE ABBREVIATION

As a short form for "editors," commonly seen clues are variations of "Mag. workers," "Masthead figs.," and "Newspaper execs."

▶•◀•▶•◀•▶•◀ EDSEL ▶•◀•▶•◀•▶•◀

THE CAR

Edsel was an unsuccessful model of Ford automobile that was sold from 1958 to 1960. It was named for Edsel Ford, the only son of company founder Henry Ford.

▶•◀•▶•◀•▶•◀ EDU ▶•◀•▶•◀•▶•◀

ON THE WEB

".edu" is the suffix for websites of higher-education institutions. In addition to variations on this definition, you'll often see fill-in-the-blank clues with well-known colleges and universities, such as "www.ucla.____."

▷•◆•◆•◆•◁ **EEE** ▷•◆•◆•◆•◁

THE SHOE SPECIFICATION

EEE in a shoe or on a shoebox indicates a very wide shoe of a particular size.

▷•◆•◆•◆•◁ **EEK** ▷•◆•◆•◆•◁

THE EXCLAMATION

A cry of fright seen in comic strips, often at the sight of a mouse.

▷•◆•◆•◆•◁ **EEL** ▷•◆•◆•◆•◁

THE FISH

A snakelike fish, a.k.a. "conger" or "moray," some of which carry an electrical charge. Eels are proverbially slippery fish, hence the simile "slippery as an eel." A sniggler is a fisherman who catches eels. The Japanese word for eel is "*unagi*," often seen in sushi bars where eels are served; *anago* is another kind of eel also used in Japanese cuisine. In Disney's *The Little Mermaid*, the villainess Ursula is attended by two moray eels, Flotsam and Jetsam.

INSIDER'S TIP: The plural of "eel" can be either "eels" or "eel."

▷•◆•◆•◆•◁ **EEN** ▷•◆•◆•◆•◁

THE ADVERB

"E'en" is a poetical term for "evening," and may be clued with "Dusk," "Nightfall," or "Twilight."

THE SUFFIX

The words "velvet" and "hallow" may have the suffix "-een" added to form new words.

▶•◆•◆•◆•◀ EER ▶•◆•◆•◆•◀

THE ADVERB
"E'er" is a poetical term for "ever" or "always."

THE SUFFIX
As an "occupational" suffix, "-eer" can be added to words such as "auction," "chariot," "mountain," and "musket."

▶•◆•◆•◆•◀ EERIE ▶•◆•◆•◆•◀

THE ADJECTIVE
Commonly seen clues: "Creepy," "Like a haunted house," "Spooky," "Strange," "Uncanny," and "Weird."

▶•◆•◆•◆•◀ EGAD ▶•◆•◆•◆•◀

THE OLD-TIME EXCLAMATION
Commonly seen clues: "Mild oath," "My goodness!," "Yikes!," and "Zounds!" Fictional characters Dr. Watson (Sherlock Holmes's pal) and Major Hoople (from the old comic strip "Our Boarding House") were known to utter it.

▶•◆•◆•◆•◀ EGG ▶•◆•◆•◆•◀

THE EDIBLE
Commonly seen clues: "Heckler's missile," "Omelet ingredient," and "Poultry product." Sometimes you'll see the old slang term "Cackleberry."

THE INEDIBLES
Silly Putty comes in a plastic egg. In the sitcom *Mork and Mindy*, Robin Williams's alien character comes to Earth in an egg-shaped spaceship. Fabergé eggs are highly prized collectibles.

THE VERB
To "egg on" is to prod or provoke.

▶•◆•◆•◆•◀ EGO ▶•◆•◆•◆•◀

IN PSYCHOLOGY

Derived from the Latin word for "I," the ego is the part of the psyche that experiences and reacts to the outside world. In common usage, "Conceit," "Self-esteem," and "Swelled head" all clue EGO.

▶•◆•◆•◆•◀ EGRET ▶•◆•◆•◆•◀

THE FEATHERED FRIEND

An egret is a wading bird and type of heron, usually white in color. Often seen in marshy areas, egrets are known for their long plumes.

▶•◆•◆•◆•◀ EIRE ▶•◆•◆•◆•◀

ON THE MAP

Eire is the Irish name for the island of Ireland (a.k.a. "Hibernia" and "the Emerald Isle") as well as for the Republic of Ireland, whose major cities include Dublin, Cork, Galway, and Limerick. "Eire" may be seen on euro coins that originate in the Republic of Ireland.

▶•◆•◆•◆•◀ EKE ▶•◆•◆•◆•◀

THE VERB

To "eke out" is to supplement or to achieve with difficulty, as in "eke out a living" or "eke out a win" (in sports).

▶•◆•◆•◆•◀ ELAL ▶•◆•◆•◆•◀

THE CARRIER

El Al is the national airline of Israel. Its hub is Ben Gurion Airport, outside of Tel Aviv.

►·◆·◆·◆·◄ ELAN ►·◆·◆·◆·◄

THE FEELING

As a synonym for "enthusiasm," commonly seen clues for "élan" include "Gusto," "Joie de vivre," "Pizzazz," "Verve," "Zest," and "Zing."

►·◆·◆·◆·◄ ELATE ►·◆·◆·◆·◄

THE VERB

Commonly seen clues: "Cheer up," "Delight," "Gladden," "Overjoy," and "Tickle pink."

►·◆·◆·◆·◄ ELENA ►·◆·◆·◆·◄

THE NAME

Elena Kagan was appointed to the Supreme Court by Barack Obama in 2010. Elena Dementieva is a Russian-born tennis pro. Spain's Princess Elena is the daughter of former king Juan Carlos. Actress Elena Verdugo appeared on the TV series *Marcus Welby, M.D.* "Maria Elena" is a 1940s tune popularized by Jimmy Dorsey and his orchestra.

►·◆·◆·◆·◄ ELF ►·◆·◆·◆·◄

FOR SHORT

Elves are creatures in the *Lord of the Rings* books of J.R.R. Tolkien (major elf characters include Arwen, Legolas, Elrond, and Galadriel), and are also assistants to Santa Claus at the North Pole. The Keebler Elves, well-known from television commercials, make cookies instead of toys. Synonyms for "elf" include "sprite" and "pixie." The word can also refer to a mischievous child. The Will Ferrell movie *Elf* was adapted into a Broadway musical.

▶•◆•◆•◆•◀ ELI ▶•◆•◆•◆•◀

THE NAME

There's pro quarterback Manning, actor Wallach, and cotton gin inventor Whitney. In the Old Testament, Eli is a Hebrew priest who trained the young prophet Samuel. The middle name of pioneer automaker Ransom Olds was Eli.

SCHOLASTICALLY SPEAKING

An Eli is any student of Yale University, coined for the school's benefactor, Elihu Yale. So any celebrity who attended Yale might be seen in a crossword clue similar to "Meryl Streep, once." Other Yalies: Bill and Hillary Clinton, actress Jodie Foster, and composer Cole Porter.

▶•◆•◆•◆•◀ ELIE ▶•◆•◆•◆•◀

THE FIRST NAME

Author and political activist Elie Wiesel received the 1986 Nobel Peace Prize. There's also Lebanese fashion designer Saab and composer Siegmeister.

▶•◆•◆•◆•◀ ELIOT ▶•◆•◆•◆•◀

THE LAST NAME

The works of writer T.S. Eliot (recipient of the 1948 Nobel Prize in Literature) include *Ash Wednesday*, *The Waste Land*, "The Love Song of J. Alfred Prufrock," and a collection of light verse that was the basis for the Andrew Lloyd Webber musical *Cats*. George Eliot was the pen name of 19th-century British novelist Mary Ann Evans, whose best-known works include *Adam Bede*, *Middlemarch*, and *Silas Marner*.

THE FIRST NAME

Eliot Ness led the Chicago team of law-enforcement agents known as "the Untouchables," who were responsible for sending gangster Al Capone to prison. Ness was portrayed by Robert Stack in the TV series *The Untouchables*, and by Kevin Costner in the film of the same name. Eliot Janeway was an American economist.

►·◄·◄·◄·◄ ELITE ►·◄·◄·◄·◄

THE SELECT

As a synonym for "high-class," commonly seen adjective clues include "Aristocratic," "Choice," "Posh," "Ritzy," and "Top drawer." In the noun form: "A-list," "Bluebloods," "Cream of the crop," "Influential group," "Upper crust," and "Who's who."

THE TYPEFACE

Elite and pica were two popular typewriter typefaces.

►·◄·◄·◄·◄ ELK ►·◄·◄·◄·◄

THE BEAST

The antlered American elk (a.k.a. wapiti) is a member of the deer family (thus a cousin to the caribou and moose) native to the western part of the U.S., including Yellowstone National Park.

THE MAN

An Elk is any member of the Benevolent and Protective Order of Elks fraternal lodge, BPOE for short.

►·◄·◄·◄·◄ ELL ►·◄·◄·◄·◄

THE SHAPE

L-shaped items known as ells include wings, annexes of buildings (often clued as "Building extension"), plumbing pipes, and halves of rectangles or squares (which might be clued simply as "Right-angled shape").

THE LETTER

"Ell" may also be defined as the spelled-out version of the letter itself, in clues like "Kay follower" or "Em preceder."

▶•◆•◆•◆•◀ ELLA ▶•◆•◆•◆•◀

THE NAME

Jazz singer Fitzgerald is by far the most frequently seen Ella in crossword clues. There are also onetime Connecticut governor Grasso, actress Raines, and poet Ella Wheeler Wilcox.

THE FOREIGN WORD

"*Ella*" is the Spanish and Italian word for "she."

NOT SO FAST!

"Born first": ___ L D E R

The answer can be OLDER or the nearly synonymous ELDER.

▶•◆•◆•◆•◀ ELLE ▶•◆•◆•◆•◀

IN FRANCE

"*Elle*" is the French word for "she" or "her." It is also the name of a French fashion magazine, which has an American edition, for which *Vogue* and *Glamour* are competitors.

THE NAME

There's Elle Macpherson (Australian model and television host) and actress Elle Fanning. And Elle Woods is the Harvard law student portrayed by Reese Witherspoon in the film *Legally Blonde*.

▶•◆•◆•◆•◀ ELM ▶•◆•◆•◆•◀

THE SHADE TREE

The American elm is the state tree of Massachusetts. Dutch elm disease is a fungal ailment of elms. The "slippery elm" variety gets its name from its inner bark.

THE STREET

Elm is a popular street name nationwide. In particular, it is the setting of the *Nightmare on Elm Street* film series, whose evil main character is Freddy Krueger.

▶·◆·◆·◆·◆·◀ **ELMO** ▶·◆·◆·◆·◆·◀

THE NAME

Elmo is the name of a red Muppet; the Tickle Me Elmo doll was America's top fad toy of 1996. Elmo is the patron saint of sailors, from whose name is derived "St. Elmo's fire." Elmo Tuttle is the bratty neighbor of the Bumsteads in the comic strip *Blondie*.

▶·◆·◆·◆·◆·◀ **ELOPE** ▶·◆·◆·◆·◆·◀

THE VERB

Commonly seen clues are variations of "Avoid a big wedding," "Marry in haste," and "Run off for romance." Romeo and Juliet elope in the Shakespeare play.

▶·◆·◆·◆·◆·◀ **ELS** ▶·◆·◆·◆·◆·◀

THE GOLFER

South African pro Ernie Els (pronounced "else") is nicknamed "The Big Easy" for his height and seemingly effortless swing.

THE TRAINS

This "els" is short for "elevated railways," part of the public transportation system of Chicago.

THE LETTERS

"Els" may (like "ell" and "ells") also be defined as the spelled-out version of the letter itself, in clues like "Kay followers" or "Em preceders."

►·◆·◆·◆·◄ ELSE ►·◆·◆·◆·◄

THE ADVERB
Commonly seen clues: "Alternatively," "If not," "Otherwise," and "Ultimatum ender" (as in "... or else!").

THE ADJECTIVE
As an adjective, "else" is synonymous with "additional" or "more," as in "What else is new?"

►·◆·◆·◆·◄ EMAIL ►·◆·◆·◆·◄

YOU SEND ME
Commonly seen clues are variations of "Online message," "Internet letter," "Source of some spam," and "Paperless correspondence."

►·◆·◆·◆·◄ EMCEE ►·◆·◆·◆·◄

THE NOUN/VERB
Commonly seen clues: "Game show host," "Intro giver," "Officiate at a banquet," and "Toastmaster."

►·◆·◆·◆·◄ EMIT ►·◆·◆·◆·◄

THE VERB
Commonly seen clues: "Discharge," "Give off," "Radiate," and "Send out."

►·◆·◆·◆·◄ EMMA ►·◆·◆·◆·◄

FOR REAL
There's poet Lazarus (who wrote "The New Colossus," inscribed at the base of the Statue of Liberty), TV actress Samms (of *Dynasty*), and film actresses Watson, Stone, and Thompson.

IN FICTION

Emma is a novel by Jane Austen; the title character was portrayed by Gwyneth Paltrow in the film version. Emma is the first name of the title character of the Flaubert novel *Madame Bovary*. Emma Peel is a character in the TV series *The Avengers*, portrayed by Diana Rigg. Uma Thurman portrayed Ms. Peel in the film adaptation.

▶•◆•◆•◆•◀ EMOTE ▶•◆•◆•◆•◀

THE VERB

Although "emote" has a neutral meaning of expressing emotion while acting, it is usually clued in the sense of overemoting. Commonly seen clues: "Act poorly," "Chew the scenery," "Ham it up," and "Overact." The dictionary says that the word can also mean "to feign emotion," but that sense is almost never cited in crosswords.

▶•◆•◆•◆•◀ EMS ▶•◆•◆•◆•◀

ON THE PAGE

Ems are measures of width in printing and typesetting, derived from the width of the letter "m." An em dash is thus longer than an en dash.

THE ABBREVIATION

The letters EMS, short for "emergency medical service," may be seen on ambulances.

ON THE MAP

Bad Ems is a spa city in Germany. The Ems River flows through Germany and the Netherlands.

▶•◆•◆•◆•◀ EMT ▶•◆•◆•◆•◀

ON CALL

EMT is short for "emergency medical technician" (a.k.a. "paramedic"). EMTs respond to 911 calls in ambulances, and are experts in CPR (cardiopulmonary resuscitation).

▶·◆·◆·◆·◀ EMU ▶·◆·◆·◆·◀

THE BIRD

The emu, related to the ostrich, is a large flightless bird native to Australia. It lays green eggs, and can reach speeds of up to 35 miles per hour.

▶·◆·◆·◆·◀ END ▶·◆·◆·◆·◀

TO CONCLUDE

Commonly seen verb clues: "Cease," "Finish," "Stop," and "Wrap up."

THE CONCLUSION

Commonly seen noun clues: "Finale," "Goal," "Outcome," "Swan song," and "Terminal."

IN SPORTS

An end is a position on a football team, as well as a wicket in the game of cricket.

▶·◆·◆·◆·◀ ENE ▶·◆·◆·◆·◀

THE ABBREVIATION

ENE stands for the direction of east-northeast, which is the point opposite west-southwest (WSW) on a compass. You'll often see city clues like "Toronto-to-Montreal dir.," where the second city is located east-northeast of the first. ENE and all the other compass points can be seen in weather reports (referring to wind direction) and on the screens of GPS devices.

THE SUFFIX

-ENE is a suffix for the name of organic compounds such as ethylene and butylene.

▶•◆•◆•◆•◀ ENEMY ▶•◆•◆•◆•◀

THE OPPOSITION

Synonymous clues include "Foe," "Adversary," "Nemesis," and "Antagonist." Also often seen are well-known pairs of fictional adversaries, as in "The Joker, to Batman" and "Moriarty, to Holmes."

▶•◆•◆•◆•◀ ENG ▶•◆•◆•◆•◀

THE ABBREVIATIONS

As a short form of "England," commonly seen clues include "London's loc.," "Neighbor of Scot.," and "Part of the U.K." As a short form of "English": "College dept.," "H.S. course," and "Part of ESL: Abbr." (English as a second language).

THE NAME

Eng Bunker and his brother Chang were the original Siamese twins, from whom the term (now called "conjoined twins") was derived.

▶•◆•◆•◆•◀ ENID ▶•◆•◆•◆•◀

ON THE MAP

The city of Enid, Oklahoma, on the Chisholm Trail, is the site of Phillips University and Vance Air Force Base.

THE NAME

Enid Bagnold and Enid Blyton were both British writers. Enid, the wife of Sir Geraint in the legendary tales of King Arthur, is a character in Tennyson's *Idylls of the King*.

▶·◆·◆·◆·◀ ENOS ▶·◆·◆·◆·◀

THE NAME
In the book of Genesis, Enos is the son of Seth and grandson of Adam and Eve. Enos Slaughter is a member of the Baseball Hall of Fame. Enos is a deputy sheriff in the TV series *The Dukes of Hazzard*; the series *Enos* was spun off from it. A chimpanzee named Enos was launched into space by NASA in 1961.

▶·◆·◆·◆·◀ ENS ▶·◆·◆·◆·◀

ON THE PAGE
Ens are a measure of width in printing and typesetting, derived from the width of the letter "n." An en dash is thus shorter than an em dash.

THE ABBREVIATION
"Ens." is the short form for "ensign," the lowest rank of commissioned officer in the U.S. Navy and Coast Guard. Graduates of the U.S. Naval Academy (USNA) and Coast Guard Academy (USCGA) are commissioned as ensigns.

▶·◆·◆·◆·◀ ENTER ▶·◆·◆·◆·◀

THE VERB
Commonly seen clues: "Come in," "Gain access to," "Go on stage," "Maze marking," and "Type in."

THE KEY WORD
"Enter" is a key on computer keyboards, located near the Shift key.

▶·◆·◆·◆·◀ ENYA ▶·◆·◆·◆·◀

THE ARTIST
Enya is an Irish singer and songwriter in the New Age genre.

▶•◆•◆•◆•◀ EON ▶•◆•◆•◆•◀

A LONG TIME

In astronomy, an eon is one billion years. It is also a nonspecific unit of geologic time. Unscientifically, it is an extremely long period of time, with clues similar to "Many millennia," "Seemingly forever," and "Zillions of years."

▶•◆•◆•◆•◀ EPA ▶•◆•◆•◆•◀

THE AGENCY

EPA is short for the U.S. government's Environmental Protection Agency, established in 1970, and responsible for protecting public health and the environment. It disseminates fuel economy stats (measured in miles per gallon, or MPG) for new automobiles, and administers the Superfund and Clean Air Act.

▶•◆•◆•◆•◀ EPEE ▶•◆•◆•◆•◀

THE WEAPON

An épée is a fencing sword, used in Olympic competition as part of the modern pentathlon.

▶•◆•◆•◆•◀ EPIC ▶•◆•◆•◆•◀

THE BIG DEAL

Clued as an adjective, you'll see "Grand-scale," "Heroic," "Larger-than-life," and "Monumental." As a noun, it's a grand-scale novel, film, etc. Director Cecil B. DeMille was noted for his film epics. Homer's *Iliad* and *Odyssey*, Dante's *Divine Comedy*, and Tolkien's *Lord of the Rings* are all considered epics.

▶•◆•◆•◆•◀ ERA ▶•◆•◆•◆•◀

THE TIME

As a synonym for "significant period," commonly seen clues include "Chapter of history," "Epoch," and "Noteworthy time." You'll see specific historical eras as fill-in-the-blanks such as "Big Band ___" and "Elizabethan ___." An era is also a unit of geologic time, such as the Mesozoic or Paleozoic.

THE STAT

In baseball, ERA is short for "earned run average," an important statistic in gauging a pitcher's effectiveness.

THE AMENDMENT

ERA, short for Equal Rights Amendment, is a proposed amendment to the U.S. Constitution, intended to give equal rights to men and women, that has never been ratified.

IN THE WASH

Era is a Procter & Gamble brand of laundry detergent. It's usually clued in terms of other detergents, which include All, Fab, Surf, and Tide.

▶•◆•◆•◆•◀ ERASE ▶•◆•◆•◆•◀

THE VERB

Commonly seen clues: "Clear, as a blackboard," "Delete," "Expunge," "Obliterate," "Rub out," and "Wipe clean."

▶•◆•◆•◆•◀ ERE ▶•◆•◆•◆•◀

THE PREPOSITION

"Ere" is a poetic synonym of "before." It's a palindrome, since it is spelled the same in either direction. "Afore" is a poetic synonym.

▶•◆•◆•◆•◀ ERECT ▶•◆•◆•◆•◀

THE VERB

Commonly seen verb clues: "Build," "Construct," "Raise," and "Set up."

THE ADJECTIVE

In this sense, there's "At attention," "Not slouching," "Standing," and "Upright."

▶•◆•◆•◆•◀ ERGO ▶•◆•◆•◆•◀

SO WHAT

"Ergo" is a fancy word for "therefore." Other synonyms: "Thus," "Hence," "Consequently," and "As a result."

▶•◆•◆•◆•◀ ERIC ▶•◆•◆•◆•◀

THE PEOPLE

There's author Ambler, actor Bana, rock guitarist Clapton, Olympic skater Heiden, comic Idle, lexicographer Partridge, television newsman Sevareid, and ancient explorer Eric the Red (father of Leif Ericson). Eric Cartman is one of the main characters in the animated series *South Park*; his friends are Stan, Kyle, and Kenny.

NOT SO FAST!

"Norse explorer": **E R I ___**

There are two acceptable ways to spell his name:
ERIC and ERIK.

THE LAKE

Erie is the world's 10th-largest lake. Of the five Great Lakes, Erie is the shallowest, southernmost, warmest, the last discovered by the French explorers in the 17th century, and the smallest by volume. Cities on its shores include Buffalo, New York; Erie, Pennsylvania (see below); and Toledo, Sandusky, and Cleveland, Ohio. It was the site of an 1813 battle (in the War of 1812) in which a U.S. Navy fleet led by Commodore Oliver Perry defeated six vessels of the British Royal Navy. It is also frequently clued as "Part of HOMES," referring to the mnemonic for the names of the Great Lakes.

THE PENNSYLVANIA CONNECTION

The city of Erie, seat of Erie County, is located in the northwest corner of the state on the southern shore of Lake Erie. The 1996 film *That Thing You Do!*, the first feature film directed by Tom Hanks, is set in Erie.

THE CANAL

The 1825 completion of New York's Erie Canal, linking the Great Lakes with the Atlantic Ocean, was instrumental in earning New York its "Empire State" nickname. It was pejoratively dubbed "Clinton's Big Ditch," after New York governor DeWitt Clinton, who supported the funding of its construction.

THE NATIVE AMERICANS

All of the above Eries are ultimately named for the Erie Indians, who once inhabited the southern shore of Lake Erie. The tribe was exterminated by and absorbed into the Iroquois circa 1600, for aiding the Hurons, an enemy of the Iroquois League.

INSIDER'S TIP: ERIE is the only Great Lake whose name has four letters, and HURON is the only five-letter Great Lake, so you can safely ignore the rest of any other four-letter or five-letter "Great Lake" clue and fill in the answer PDQ (or ASAP, if you prefer).

▶·◆·◆·◆·◆·◀ ERIN ▶·◆·◆·◆·◆·◀

THE COUNTRY

"Erin" is a literary synonym for Ireland, a.k.a. "Hibernia" and "the Emerald Isle." It's the homeland of writers James Joyce and William Yeats. The patriotic phrase "Erin go bragh" means "Ireland forever."

THE NAME

Erin Burnett hosts the CNN program *OutFront*. Actress Erin Moran appeared on the sitcom *Happy Days*. Julia Roberts won an Oscar for portraying the title character in the film *Erin Brockovich*. Erin is also the name of one of the daughters in the TV series *The Waltons*.

▶·◆·◆·◆·◆·◀ ERNIE ▶·◆·◆·◆·◆·◀

REAL

There's baseball Hall of Famer Banks, golf pro Els, singer "Tennessee" Ernie Ford, comedian Kovacs, and World War II correspondent Pyle.

FICTIONAL

Muppet Ernie is Bert's friend on the kids' TV series *Sesame Street*. Ernie is one of the elves seen in commercials for Keebler cookies. It's the first name of Sergeant Bilko, the conniving character in the 1950s sitcom *The Phil Silvers Show*, portrayed by Silvers. And Ernie is one of the sons on the 1960s sitcom *My Three Sons*.

▶·◆·◆·◆·◆·◀ ERODE ▶·◆·◆·◆·◆·◀

THE VERB

Commonly seen clues are variations on "Eat into," "Undermine," and "Wear away."

113

▶•◆•◆•◆•◀ EROS ▶•◆•◆•◆•◀

THE GOD

Youngest of the Greek gods, winged archer Eros was the son of Aphrodite and Zeus, and the god of love. His Roman equivalent is Cupid, a.k.a. Amor.

THE STATUE

Atop the memorial fountain in London's Piccadilly Circus is the statue formally named *The Angel of Christian Charity*, but popularly called *Eros*.

THE ASTEROID

Discovered in 1898, this Eros is the second largest of the near-Earth asteroids.

▶•◆•◆•◆•◀ ERR ▶•◆•◆•◆•◀

THE VERB

Commonly seen clues: "Flub," "Go wrong," "Goof," "Make a mistake," "Mess up," and "Slip." "To err is human" is a line from English writer Alexander Pope.

▶•◆•◆•◆•◀ ERROR ▶•◆•◆•◆•◀

THE NOUN

Commonly seen clues: "Baseball blunder," "Boo-boo," "Glitch," "Goof," "Miscue," and "Mistake."

▶•◆•◆•◆•◀ ERS ▶•◆•◆•◆•◀

THE ABBREVIATION

As a short form of "emergency rooms," commonly seen clues are variations of "Hosp. areas," "Trauma ctrs.," and "Where MDs work."

THE SOUNDS

As the sounds made by a hesitant speaker, there's "Pause fillers," "Speech stumbles," and "Verbal uncertainties."

NOT SO FAST!

"Hospital areas, for short": ___ R S

The answer could be ERS (emergency rooms) or ORS (operating rooms).

▸•◂•◂•◂•◂ **ERTE** ▸•◂•◂•◂•◂

THE ARTIST

Russian-born artist Erté is remembered for his Art Deco works, including many illustrations for the magazine *Harper's Bazaar*. His real name was Romain de Tirtoff.

▸•◂•◂•◂•◂ **ESAU** ▸•◂•◂•◂•◂

IN THE BIBLE

In the book of Genesis, Esau was the son of Isaac and the twin brother of Jacob. Clues may reference the Biblical story in which Esau sold his birthright to his brother.

▸•◂•◂•◂•◂ **ESC** ▸•◂•◂•◂•◂

ON THE BOARD

Short for "escape," the ESC key on computer keyboards, usually found in the upper-left corner, is a "stop doing this" key.

►·◆·◆·◆·◄ **ESE** ►·◆·◆·◆·◄

THE ABBREVIATION

ESE stands for the direction of east-southeast, which is the point opposite west-northwest (WNW) on a compass. You'll often see city clues like "Pittsburgh-to-Baltimore dir.," where the second city is located east-southeast of the first. ESE and all the other compass points can be seen in weather reports (referring to wind direction) and on the screens of GPS devices.

THE SUFFIX

Words ending in "-ese" are usually either real languages/nationalities (like Japanese and Portuguese) or the jargon/accent of a particular region (such as Brooklynese) or profession (such as legalese).

►·◆·◆·◆·◄ **ESL** ►·◆·◆·◆·◄

THE ABBREVIATION

ESL, short for "English as a second language," is a course often taken by new immigrants to the United States who don't speak the language.

►·◆·◆·◆·◄ **ESP** ►·◆·◆·◆·◄

THE POWER

As a short form of "extrasensory perception," commonly seen clues include "Clairvoyance, for short," "Mentalist's claim," "Paranormal power," "Psychic's skill," "Sixth sense," and "Uncommon sense."

THE ABBREVIATION

"Esp." is also an abbreviation for "especially," so you may sometimes see a clue like "Particularly: Abbr."

▶•◆•◆•◆•◀ ESPN ▶•◆•◆•◆•◀

ON THE AIR

ESPN, originally short for "Entertainment and Sports Programming Network," is a sports cable channel owned and operated by the Walt Disney Company. It broadcasts live games in many professional and college sports. Its regular programs include *SportsCenter*, *Monday Night Football*, and *Baseball Tonight*.

▶•◆•◆•◆•◀ ESS ▶•◆•◆•◆•◀

THE SHAPE

Commonly seen clues: "Part of a winding road," "Pothook shape," "Serpentine shape," and "Slalom curve."

THE LETTER

"Double-curve letter," "Superman's insignia," "Tee preceder," and "The first of September" all clue the spelled-out version of the letter S.

THE SUFFIX

While "-ess" is a feminine suffix, it is not exactly politically correct these days in terms for people and so is clued that way less frequently.

▶•◆•◆•◆•◀ ESSAY ▶•◆•◆•◆•◀

THE NOUN

As a noun, it's a relatively short literary prose piece. An essay may appear on a newspaper editorial (a.k.a. op-ed) page, or may be a student's homework assignment or part of a written exam.

THE VERB

In this sense, it's a synonym of "attempt."

▶•◆•◆•◆•◀ ESSO ▶•◆•◆•◆•◀

THE BRAND

Esso, short for "Standard Oil," is the former name of the Exxon oil company, and the brand of gasoline it sold. The Esso brand is still used at Canadian gas stations. It is often defined as the competitor of other defunct U.S. gasoline brand names, such as Flying "A."

▶•◆•◆•◆•◀ EST ▶•◆•◆•◆•◀

THE ABBREVIATIONS

As a short form for "estimate," you'll see clues like "Approx." and "Ballpark fig." When it stands for "Eastern Standard Time," the clue will usually have an abbreviated state or city name, like "D.C. clock setting" or "N.C. winter hours." If it's short for "established," there's "Cornerstone abbr." and "Founded, for short."

THE SUFFIXES

As a suffix, "-est" is a superlative suffix for adjectives as well as an archaic or Biblical ending for verbs.

THE FOREIGN WORDS

"*Est*" means "is" in both French (as in "*C'est la vie*") and Latin (as in "*id est*," the spelled-out version of "i.e.," which means "that is").

THE SELF-HELP TREND

In the 1970s, Werner Erhard's EST (short for Erhard Seminars Training) was a popular series of self-help seminars.

▶•◆•◆•◆•◀ ESTA ▶•◆•◆•◆•◀

IN SPANISH

Spelled "*está*," it means "is" or "are," as in "*¿Cómo está usted?*" ("How are you?"). Without the accent mark, it means "this." Either meaning may be seen in crosswords, since accent marks are omitted from the answers in American crosswords.

▶•◆•◆•◆•◀ ESTATE ▶•◆•◆•◆•◀

THE NOUN

An estate may be bequeathed property, or a large property with an elaborate house.

▶•◆•◆•◆•◀ ESTEE ▶•◆•◆•◆•◀

THE NAME

Estée Lauder founded the cosmetics company that bears her name.

▶•◆•◆•◆•◀ ETA ▶•◆•◆•◆•◀

THE LETTER

The vowel eta is the seventh letter of the Greek alphabet, preceded by zeta and followed by theta. An uppercase eta resembles the letter "H." Bear in mind that any letter of the Greek alphabet can be defined as "Frat letter," though ETA is by far the most common Greek letter seen in crosswords.

THE ABBREVIATION

As a short form of "estimated time of arrival," commonly seen clues are variations of "Airport stat.," "LAX posting" (LAX is the symbol for Los Angeles International Airport), or "Pilot's announcement."

INSIDER'S TIP: ETD (short for "estimated time of departure") may also be a possible answer to many of the clues for ETA, although the latter appears much more often in crosswords.

▶•◆•◆•◆•◀ ETAL ▶•◆•◆•◆•◀

THE ABBREVIATION

"Et al." is a short form for the Latin *et alii* or *et alia* ("and others"). It is frequently used in footnotes and bibliographies to shorten a long list of names.

▶·◆·◆·◆·◀ ETAT ▶·◆·◆·◆·◀

IN FRANCE

"*État*" is the French word for "state." A coup d'état is a sudden overthrow of a government. French king Louis XIV once said, "*L'état, c'est moi*" ("I am the state"). ÉTAT is also often clued by example with French translations of U.S. states, such as "Californie, e.g."

▶·◆·◆·◀ ETC ▶·◆·◆·◆·◀

THE ABBREVIATION

Commonly seen clues for "etc." are variations of "And so on: Abbr.," "Catchall abbr.," and "List-shortening abbr."

▶·◆·◆·◆·◀ ETCH ▶·◆·◆·◆·◀

THE VERB

Commonly seen clues: "Draw on glass," "Engrave deeply," "Outline clearly," and "Work with acid."

▶·◆·◆·◆·◀ ETHER ▶·◆·◆·◆·◀

THE NOUN

Ether is a former anesthetic, as well as a synonym for the clear sky.

▶·◆·◆·◆·◀ ETNA ▶·◆·◆·◆·◀

THE SPEWER

Italy's Mount Etna is an active volcano on the island of Sicily. Sicilians call the peak "Mongibello."

THE EQUIPMENT

An etna is a piece of equipment formerly used in laboratories to heat liquids, similar to a Bunsen burner. This definition is used much less often, but it does appear in clues now and then.

120

▶·◆·◆·◆·◀ ETO ▶·◆·◆·◆·◀

THE ABBREVIATION

ETO is short for "European Theater of Operations," the Allies' term for the World War II section of Europe north of Italy and the Mediterranean coast. The ETO's commander was General Dwight D. Eisenhower, whose initials (DDE) are often used to clue it.

▶·◆·◆·◆·◀ ETON ▶·◆·◆·◆·◀

THE SCHOOL

Eton College is a British prep school on the Thames, founded by Henry VI in 1440. Notable people who attended Eton include Princes William and Harry, George Orwell, Percy Shelley, Ian Fleming, and Fleming's spy James Bond. Eton's rival school is Harrow.

▶·◆·◆·◆·◀ ETRE ▶·◆·◆·◆·◀

IN FRANCE

"*Être*" is the French infinitive verb for "to be." "*Raison d'être*" is an idiom for "justification" (literally "reason to be").

▶·◆·◆·◆·◀ ETS ▶·◆·◆·◆·◀

IN SCI-FI

As an abbreviation for "extraterrestrials," commonly seen clues are variations of "Aliens," "Little green men," "Martians, for example," and "UFO pilots."

IN SCHOOL

ETS, or Educational Testing Service, is the company that develops and administers standardized tests such as the SAT.

▶•◆•◆•◆•◀ ETTA ▶•◆•◆•◆•◀

REAL
There are singers Etta James and Etta Jones, and Etta Place, girlfriend of the Sundance Kid, partner in crime of Butch Cassidy. Place was portrayed by Katharine Ross in the film *Butch Cassidy and the Sundance Kid*.

FICTIONAL
The old comic strip "Etta Kett" was designed to teach good manners to children ("etiquette," get it?).

▶•◆•◆•◆•◀ ETTE ▶•◆•◆•◆•◀

THE SUFFIX
The suffix "-ette" can denote miniaturization (as in "kitchenette"), feminization (as in "bachelorette"), or imitation (as in "leatherette"). Other "Suffix for" words often seen in clues are disk, luncheon, major, and novel.

▶•◆•◆•◆•◀ ETTU ▶•◆•◆•◆•◀

THE ACCUSATION
In the Shakespeare play *Julius Caesar*, "Et tu, Brute?" (Latin for "You too, Brutus?") are among the last words spoken by the title character to Brutus, one of his assassins.

▶•◆•◆•◆•◀ EURO ▶•◆•◆•◆•◀

IN THE BANK
Though also a prefix for the European continent, "euro" is almost always clued as the money used by about 20 European nations. Most frequently seen in crossword clues: Spain (where it replaced the peseta), France (where it replaced the franc) and Italy (where it replaced the lira), as well as major cities in each of these nations.

▶•◆•◆•◆•◀ EVA ▶•◆•◆•◆•◀

THE ACTRESSES

There's Gabor (sister of Zsa Zsa) of the 1960s sitcom *Green Acres*, Longoria of the TV series *Desperate Housewives*, Mendes of *Training Day*, Green of the 2006 James Bond film *Casino Royale* and the TV series *Penny Dreadful*, and Eva Marie Saint of the Hitchcock film *North by Northwest* and the Elia Kazan film *On the Waterfront*.

OTHER PEOPLE

Argentine first lady Eva (a.k.a. Evita) Perón, wife of Juan, was portrayed by Madonna in the film version of the Andrew Lloyd Webber musical *Evita*. Little Eva is a character in the Harriet Beecher Stowe novel *Uncle Tom's Cabin*. And Eva is the heroine of the Richard Wagner opera *Die Meistersinger*.

THE ACRONYM

To NASA, EVA stands for "extravehicular activity," its term for a spacewalk.

▶•◆•◆•◆•◀ EVADE ▶•◆•◆•◆•◀

THE VERB

Typical synonym clues: "Steer clear of," "Sidestep," "Avoid," and "Circumvent."

NOT SO FAST!

"Get away from": **E** ___ ___ **D E**

The answer can be EVADE as well as the nearly synonymous ELUDE.

CROSSWORDS 101
Lesson 5: Russian

These Russian words appear
frequently as crossword answers
(diacritical marks, if any, are omitted):

CCCP ("USSR" in the Russian
language; letters on Soviet
spacecrafts)
ERTE (Russian-born Art Deco designer)
IVAN (Russian form of "John")
LENIN (first Soviet Union leader)
NYET (no)
OLGA (gymnast Korbut)
TSAR or **CZAR** (former monarch)
TASS (news agency, formerly part
of **ITAR-TASS**)
URAL (Russian river and
mountain range)

▶•◀•◆•◀•◆•◀ **EVE** ▶•◆•◀•◆•◀•◀

THE DAY BEFORE

Commonly seen clues in this sense: "Celebratory night," "Holiday preceder," and "December 24 or 31, e.g."

THE PEOPLE

Eve is the first woman mentioned in the Bible, mother of Cain, Abel, and Seth, and mate of Adam. Title characters named Eve are portrayed by Anne Baxter in the 1950 film *All About Eve* and Joanne Woodward in the 1957 film *The Three Faces of Eve*. Actress Eve Arden had the title role in the 1950s sitcom *Our Miss Brooks*.

▶·◆·◆·◆·◀ EVEN ▶·◆·◆·◆·◀

IN BALANCE

Usually clued as an adjective, there's "Balanced," "Level," "Neck and neck," "Not odd" (as a number), "Tied," "and "Uniform." When clued as a verb, it's "Equalize" or "Smooth out."

▶·◆·◆·◆·◀ EVENT ▶·◆·◆·◆·◀

THE NOUN

Commonly seen clues: "Happening," "Important occasion," "Occurrence," and "Track meet contest." Olympic events include the 10-event decathlon, high jump, javelin, marathon, and shot put.

▶·◆·◆·◆·◀ EVER ▶·◆·◆·◆·◀

THE ADVERB

Commonly seen clues: "Always," "At any time," "Continuously," "Even once," and "In any way."

▶·◆·◆·◆·◀ EVIL ▶·◆·◆·◆·◀

THE BAD

Commonly seen clues: "Diabolical," "Satanic," "Sinful," and "Wicked." Dr. Evil is one of Mike Myers's roles in the Austin Powers film series.

▶·◆·◆·◆·◀ EWE ▶·◆·◆·◆·◀

THE BEAST

Clues for the female sheep are variations of "Flock member," "Lamb's mother," "Ram's mate," and "Wool source."

125

NOT SO FAST!

"Chilly": **C O** __ __

The answer can be COOL or COLD.

▶•◆•◆•◆•◀ **EXES** ▶•◆•◆•◆•◀

THE EX-COUPLES
Clues in this sense are similar to "Former spouses."

THE LETTERS
The dictionary tells us that "ex" can mean "The letter X," but "exes" is rarely clued that way in crosswords.

▶•◆•◆•◆•◀ **EXIT** ▶•◆•◆•◆•◀

THE VERB
Commonly seen verb clues: "Depart," "Go," "Leave the stage," and "Take off."

THE NOUN
Noun clues: "Door sign," "Escape route," "Highway ramp," and "Way out."

▶•◆•◆•◆•◀ **EYE** ▶•◆•◆•◆•◀

THE VERB
Commonly seen verb clues: "Examine," "Ogle," "Look at," and "Observe."

THE NOUN
Noun clues: "CBS logo," "Hurricane center," "Needle hole," and "Potato part."

▶◆▶◆▶◆◄ **EYRE** ▶◆▶◆▶◆◄

THE CHARACTER

Jane Eyre, title character of the Charlotte Brontë novel, is the governess of Thornfield Hall, the English manor of Edward Rochester, whom she eventually marries.

F-H

Alaskan tundra hare

▷•◆•◆•◆•◁ FEE ▷•◆•◆•◆•◁

THE NOUN
Commonly seen clues: "Commission, for example," "Honorarium," "Professional payment," and "Service charge."

▷•◆•◆•◆•◁ FREE ▷•◆•◆•◆•◁

ON THE HOUSE
Synonym clues in this sense: "Complimentary," "For the asking," "Gratis," and "Without charge."

ON THE LOOSE
As an adjective, there's "Off the leash" and "Unrestrained." As a verb: "Release" and "Let go."

OFF THE SCHEDULE
In this sense, there's "Not busy," "Available," and "Doing nothing."

NOT SO FAST!

"Kitchen device": ___ I C E R

The answer can be DICER or RICER.

▷•◆•◆•◆•◁ FRO ▷•◆•◆•◆•◁

ON THE MOVE
"To and fro" is a back-and-forth movement, such as that of a pendulum.

ON THE HEAD
FRO is a shortened form of the Afro hairdo.

▶•◆•◆•◆•◀ GAS ▶•◆•◆•◆•◀

IN CHEMISTRY

Gaseous chemical elements include argon, helium, hydrogen, krypton, neon, nitrogen, oxygen, radon, and xenon.

IN YOUR CAR

As a short form for "gasoline," there's "Auto fuel," "Driver's need," "Highway sign," and "Tank filler." "Gas" is also a slang term for a car's accelerator pedal.

FIGURATIVELY SPEAKING

As a synonym for "empty talk," commonly seen clues include "Blather," "Hot air," and "Idle chatter." When it means "something entertaining," there's "Loads of fun" and "Swell time."

▶•◆•◆•◆•◀ GEE ▶•◆•◆•◆•◀

THE EXCLAMATION

"Golly!," "That's amazing!," "Wow!," and "You don't say!" are all exclamations of amazement like "gee."

THE LETTER

As the spelled-out version of the letter G, you may see wordplay clues like "Capital of Germany." "Gee" is a slang term for $1,000 (G being short for "grand"), with clues like "Thou" and "10 C-notes."

▶•◆•◆•◆•◀ GEESE ▶•◆•◆•◆•◀

FEATHERED FRIENDS

Typical clues: "Honking birds," "Formation fliers," and "Gaggle members." The idiom "silly goose" means you'll sometimes see a clue like "Silly ones."

▶•◆•◆•◆•◀ GEL ▶•◆•◆•◆•◀

THE NOUN

Clues in the noun sense will usually refer to toothpaste or the goo used to hold hair.

THE VERB

Synonym clues include "Coagulate," "Solidify," and "Harden."

▶•◆•◆•◆•◀ GEM ▶•◆•◆•◆•◀

LITERALLY SPEAKING

"Precious stone," "Jewel," and "Sparkler" clue a gemstone in general. Types of gems include diamond, emerald, opal, ruby, sapphire, topaz, and turquoise.

FIGURATIVELY SPEAKING

As a person or thing that is highly prized, there's "Masterpiece," "Rare find," and "Special person."

▶•◆•◆•◆•◀ GENE ▶•◆•◆•◆•◀

IN SCIENCE

As the unit of heredity, commonly seen clues include "Chromosome component," "Inheritance factor," "Splicer's need," and "Trait transmitter."

THE NAME

There's Oscar-winning actor Hackman, screen dancer Kelly, jazz drummer Krupa, and comic actor Wilder.

▶•◆•◆•◆•◀ GNAT ▶•◆•◆•◆•◀

THE BUG

The pesky, biting insect is actually a small fly.

▶•◆•◆•◆•◀ HAHA ▶•◆•◆•◆•◀

THE EXCLAMATION
Commonly seen "ha-ha" clues are variations of "Reaction to a joke," "Sounds of laughter," and "Very funny!"

▶•◆•◆•◆•◀ HALO ▶•◆•◆•◆•◀

THE LIGHT
A halo can be the circular light above an angel's head as well as the bright circle of light sometimes seen around the sun or moon. A halo is thought to be a symbol of sanctity, saintliness, or virtue.

▶•◆•◆•◆•◀ HAM ▶•◆•◆•◆•◀

ON YOUR PLATE
"Edible" clues include "Omelet ingredient," "Lunch meat," and "Easter entrée."

ON THE STAGE
In the "performer" sense, there's "Bad actor," "Scenery chewer," and "Theatrical showoff."

IN THE BIBLE
Ham was the second son of Noah and one of the passengers on the Ark.

▶•◆•◆•◆•◀ HARE ▶•◆•◆•◆•◀

IN GENERAL
A relative of the rabbit, the hare is part of the order of mammals known as lagomorphs. One may be the quarry of a fox or hound. A young hare is known as a leveret.

SPECIFICALLY
The March Hare is a character in Lewis Carroll's *Alice's Adventures in Wonderland*. A hare lost the race to the tortoise in one of Aesop's fables.

▶·◆·◆·◆·◆·◀ HAS ▶·◆·◆·◆·◆·◀

THE VERB

Commonly seen clues: "Keeps," "Orders for dinner," "Owns," and "Possesses."

▶·◆·◆·◆·◆·◀ HAT ▶·◆·◆·◆·◆·◀

OVER YOUR HEAD

HAT is almost always defined either as a synonym ("Topper" or "Headgear") or with a type of hat, such as a beret, fedora, or derby.

▶·◆·◆·◆·◆·◀ HBO ▶·◆·◆·◆·◆·◀

ON THE AIR

Originally short for "Home Box Office," HBO can be defined generically ("Cable movie channel"), in terms of its direct competitors (such as Showtime or Starz), or with its popular series of the past or present (such as *The Sopranos*, *Veep*, or *Game of Thrones*).

▶·◆·◆·◆·◆·◀ HEN ▶·◆·◆·◆·◆·◀

THE FEMALES

In addition to the egg-laying barnyard animal, a hen can also be a female lobster, octopus, pheasant, or turkey.

▶·◆·◆·◆·◆·◀ HER ▶·◆·◆·◆·◆·◀

THE PRONOUN

Commonly seen clues: "Part of HRH" (Her Royal Highness), "Term for a ship," "That woman," and "Yonder lass." "And I Love Her" is a Beatles tune. In the 1960s, President Lyndon Johnson had pet beagles named Him and Her. The 2013 Spike Jonze movie *Her* stars Joaquin Phoenix and the voice of Scarlett Johansson.

▷•◆•◆•◆•◁ **HERE** ▷•◆•◆•◆•◁

THE ADVERB/EXCLAMATION

Commonly seen adverb clues: "In this place," "Now's partner," "Present," and "Roll call answer." Grammatically speaking, using "Here!" to call a dog makes it an interjection.

▷•◆•◆•◆•◁ **HERO** ▷•◆•◆•◆•◁

THE BRAVE ONE

Commonly seen clues in this sense: "Idolized one," "Life saver," "Medal recipient," and "Protagonist."

THE LUNCH

A hero is a sandwich on a long roll. Other names for it are grinder, hoagie, po'boy, and sub.

IN MYTH

In Greek mythology, Hero was a priestess who loved a young man named Leander.

NOT SO FAST!

"Type of sandwich": ___ ___ **R O**

The answer can be the American HERO or the Greek GYRO.

▷•◆•◆•◆•◁ **HMO** ▷•◆•◆•◆•◁

TO YOUR HEALTH

Short for "health maintenance organization," clues for HMO will be variations of "Health insurance org.," "Medical plan: Abbr.," or "MDs' group."

►·●·●·●·◄ HOE ►·●·●·●·◄

DOWN TO EARTH

A hoe is used by farmers and gardeners to remove weeds and till soil, in preparation for planting.

►·●·●·●·◄ HONE ►·●·●·●·◄

THE VERB

Commonly seen clues: "Fine-tune," "Improve," "Perfect," and "Sharpen."

NOT SO FAST!

"NBA team, in headlines": ___ A V S

The answer can be CAVS or MAVS.

►·●·●·●·◄ HOT ►·●·●·●·◄

FOOD-WISE

"Temperature" clues for HOT include "Sultry," "Steamy," "Sizzling," and "Boiling." "Spicy" clues: "Peppery," "Pungent," and "Like jalapeños."

TEMPER-WISE

There's "Angry," "Steamed," and "Wrathful."

IN DEMAND

Clues in this sense: "Fashionable," "Very popular," and "Best-selling."

GOING GREAT

There's also the "On a winning streak" meaning of "hot."

▶•◆•◆•◆•◀ HRS ▶•◆•◆•◆•◀

ON THE CLOCK
As an abbreviation for "hours," you'll see clues like "Day fractions: Abbr." and "Many mins."

ON THE DIAMOND
As an abbreviation for "home runs," there's "Baseball stat: Abbr.," "Ballpark figs.," and "Slugger's blows: Abbr."

▶•◆•◆•◆•◀ HUE ▶•◆•◆•◆•◀

THE LOOK
Clues like "Color," "Pigment," "Tinge," and "Tint" all can define "hue."

THE SOUND
Less commonly, a "hue" can be a shout, most often seen in the phrase "hue and cry."

I

Lyricist Ira Gershwin, c. 1938

▶•◆•◆•◆•◀ IAGO ▶•◆•◆•◆•◀

THE NAME
The villainous Iago is a character in the Shakespeare play *Othello*, and the Giuseppe Verdi opera based on it, *Otello*. Iago is also the name of the parrot in the Disney animated film *Aladdin*.

▶•◆•◆•◆•◀ IAN ▶•◆•◆•◆•◀

THE NAME
There's James Bond creator Fleming; actors Holm, McKellen, and McShane; and golfer Woosnam. Janis Ian is a pop singer.

▶•◆•◆•◆•◀ IBET ▶•◆•◆•◆•◀

SKEPTICALLY SPEAKING
"I bet!" clues will either describe the phrase (such as "Sarcastic comment") or provide a similar comment (such as "Yeah, right!" or "A likely story!").

▶•◆•◆•◆•◀ ICE ▶•◆•◆•◆•◀

THE HARD STUFF
Ice is a winter road hazard, a drink cooler, the surface for skaters and hockey players, a treatment for sprains, and a slang term for diamonds.

THE VERB
Besides adding icing to a cake, "ice" can mean to "make sure of" or "assure."

▶•◆•◆•◆•◀ ICON ▶•◆•◆•◆•◀

THE SYMBOLS
An icon may be a religious image, a much-admired person, or a graphic image on a computer screen.

►•◆•◆•◆•◄ IDA ►•◆•◆•◆•◄

THE NAME

Ida was the wife of President William McKinley. Ida Tarbell was a "muckracking" author. Ida Lupino was an actress and director. "Ida, Sweet as Apple Cider" is an old song. Fictionally speaking, *Princess Ida* is a Gilbert and Sullivan operetta, and Ida was the title character's mother on the sitcom *Rhoda*.

THE PLACES

Crete's Mount Ida was sacred in Greek mythology. "Ida." is an abbreviation for Idaho (see below).

►•◆•◆•◆•◄ IDAHO ►•◆•◆•◆•◄

THE PLACE

Idaho is usually defined in terms of its neighbors (British Columbia, Montana, Nevada, Oregon, Utah, Washington, and Wyoming), its capital (Boise), or the potatoes for which it is famous.

►•◆•◆•◆•◄ IDEA ►•◆•◆•◆•◄

THE NOUN

Commonly seen clues: "Brainstorm," "Creative thought," "Inspiration," and "Notion."

►•◆•◆•◆•◄ IDEAL ►•◆•◆•◆•◄

AS GOOD AS IT GETS

Commonly seen adjective clues: "Best," "Exemplary," "Perfect," and "Utopian." As a noun: "Paragon," "Role model," and "Standard of perfection."

▶·◆·◆·◆·◀ IDES ▶·◆·◆·◆·◀

THE DAY

In the ancient Roman calendar, the ides was the 15th day of March, May, July, and October, and the 13th day of the other months. The ides of March was the day Julius Caesar was assassinated, as he was warned by a soothsayer in the Shakespeare play.

▶·◆·◆·◆·◀ IDLE ▶·◆·◆·◆·◀

THE ADJECTIVE AND VERB

Commonly seen adjective clues: "Doing nothing," "In neutral," "Just hanging around," and "Not working." In the verb sense, there's "Lounge around" and "Run in neutral."

THE NAME

British comedian Eric Idle was a member of the group Monty Python, whose other members included John Cleese and Michael Palin.

▶·◆·◆·◆·◀ IDO ▶·◆·◆·◆·◀

THE AFFIRMATION

Clued most often as a nuptial response, as variations of "Altar agreement," "Bachelor's last words," "Rite answer," and "Wedding vow." "I do" is also spoken by a witness in a courtroom while being sworn in.

▶·◆·◆·◆·◀ IDOL ▶·◆·◆·◆·◀

THE NOUN

Commonly seen clues referring to a person: "Admired one," "Hero," "Object of adoration," and "One on a pedestal." Referring to an object: "False god," "Golden calf," and "Graven image." There's also the TV series *American Idol*.

THE NAME

Popular songs by singer Billy Idol include "White Wedding," "Mony Mony," and "Rebel Yell."

►·◆·◆·◆·◄ IDS ►·◆·◆·◆·◄

TO DR. FREUD

The id is one of the three components of the psyche, being the source of instinctive impulses. The other two components are the ego and superego.

THE SHORTENED NOUN

As an short form of "identifications," there's "Wallet cards," "Passports, for example," and "Bouncer's requests."

THE SHORTENED VERB

As an informal way to say "identifies," you're likely to see such clues as "Points the finger at" and "Recognizes."

►·◆·◆·◆·◄ IGOR ►·◆·◆·◆·◄

THE NAME

Real Igors include helicopter inventor Sikorsky and composer Stravinsky. Igor is the traditional name of the villain's assistant in horror films, specifically in the Mel Brooks horror film satire *Young Frankenstein* and the 2008 animated film *Igor*. *Prince Igor* is an opera by Alexander Borodin.

►·◆·◆·◆·◄ IHOP ►·◆·◆·◆·◄

LET'S EAT

Originally short for "International House of Pancakes," IHOP is a nationwide restaurant franchise specializing in pancakes (a.k.a. "flapjacks" and "stacks"). Its competitors include Denny's and Waffle House.

►·◆·◆·◆·◄ III ►·◆·◆·◆·◄

TO CAESAR

As the Roman numeral for three, III appears on ancient sundials, at the end of some men's names (meaning "the third"), and at the end of film titles, denoting the second sequel in a series.

143

▶•◆•◆•◆•◆•◀ **IKE** ▶•◆•◆•◆•◆•◀

THE NAME

Ike was the nickname of World War II general and 1950s president Dwight Eisenhower. Ike Turner was a rock musician, ex-husband of Tina. Ike Clanton was one of the bad-guy foes of the Earp brothers at the famous O.K. Corral gunfight. Ike is also the name of one of the boys in the *South Park* animated TV series.

▶•◆•◆•◆•◆•◀ **ILE** ▶•◆•◆•◆•◆•◀

IN FRANCE

"*Île*" is the French word for "island," and may be clued generically in variations of "Seine sight" and "Spot in *la mer*" (French for "the sea"). Islands owned by France include Martinique and Tahiti. Île-de-France is a French region, Île de la Cité is an island in Paris in the river Seine, and Île du Diable is the French name for Devil's Island.

THE SUFFIX

-ILE can be added to words such as "duct," "percent," and "tact."

▶•◆•◆•◆•◆•◀ **ILL** ▶•◆•◆•◆•◆•◀

THE ADJECTIVE/ADVERB

Commonly seen adjective clues: "Below par," "Indisposed," "Under the weather," and "Unwell." As an adverb: "Poorly," "Unfavorably," and "Unsatisfactorily."

THE ABBREVIATION

Clues for the short form for "Illinois" usually refer to its neighboring states (Indiana, Iowa, Kentucky, Missouri, and Wisconsin), cities (such as Chicago), or its universities (such as Northwestern).

RAPPER'S DELIGHT

"Ill" means "excellent" in hip-hop slang, and appears in the titles of the Beastie Boys albums *Licensed to Ill* and *Ill Communication*.

▸•◆•◆•◆•◂ IMAGE ▸•◆•◆•◆•◂

THE NOUN
In the literal sense, commonly seen clues include "Likeness," "Picture," and "Reflection." Figuratively, there's "Candidate's concern," "Public persona," and "Spin doctor's crafting."

▸•◆•◆•◆•◂ IMP ▸•◆•◆•◆•◂

THINK SMALL
"Imp" is usually defined as a mischievous child, with clues like "Little rascal" and "Spoiled kid."

▸•◆•◆•◆•◂ INA ▸•◆•◆•◆•◂

BLANKETY-BLANKS
"___ nutshell," "Once ___ while," "One ___ million," "Pig ___ poke," "___ pig's eye!," and "Tempest ___ teapot" all clue IN A.

THE NAME
Ina Garten hosts the Food Network's *Barefoot Contessa*. Once in a while, you'll see clues that mention long-ago film actresses Ina Balin or Ina Claire.

▸•◆•◆•◆•◂ INANE ▸•◆•◆•◆•◂

THE ADJECTIVE
Commonly seen clues: "Absurd," "Nonsensical," "Pointless," "Preposterous," "Ridiculous," and "Silly."

▸•◆•◆•◆•◂ INC ▸•◆•◆•◆•◂

THE ABBREVIATION
Short for "incorporated," "Inc." clues will be variations of "Business abbr.," "Corp. designation," or references to its British equivalent, "Ltd." (short for "limited").

▶·◆·◆·◆·◀ INCA ▶·◆·◆·◆·◀

THE PEOPLE

The Inca empire flourished in what is today the area around Cuzco, Peru, from about 1200 to 1500. The ruins of the Inca city of Machu Picchu are a tourist attraction today. The Spanish, led by Francisco Pizarro, conquered the Incas, led by Emperor Atahualpa, in 1533. *Inca Gold* is a novel by Clive Cussler.

▶·◆·◆·◆·◀ INE ▶·◆·◆·◆·◀

THE SUFFIX

Besides being a chemical suffix, "-ine" is an adjective suffix meaning "resembling," and can be added to words like "labyrinth" and "serpent."

MUSICALLY SPEAKING

Tchaikovsky's Fifth Symphony and Beethoven's Seventh Symphony are just two of many famous works written in the key of E major, "in E" for short.

▶·◆·◆·◆·◀ INGE ▶·◆·◆·◆·◀

THE PLAYWRIGHT

The plays of William Inge include *Bus Stop*, *Picnic*, and *Come Back, Little Sheba*. He also wrote the screenplay for *Splendor in the Grass*.

▶·◆·◆·◆·◀ INIT ▶·◆·◆·◆·◀

THE ABBREVIATION

As a short form of "initial," commonly seen clues include "Handkerchief ltr." and "Monogram pt.," or, in the adjective sense, "Orig."

AS TWO WORDS

Colloquialisms like "___ for the long haul" and "What's ___ for me?" are some fill-in-the-blank clues for IN IT. As a standalone phrase, it can be clued as "Competing" or "Still having a chance to win."

▶•◆•◆•◆•◀ **INK** ▶•◆•◆•◆•◀

LITERAL

Commonly seen clues: "Calligrapher's need," "Pen filler," "Prepare, as a press," "Print shop purchase," and "Squid secretion."

FIGURATIVE

"Ink" is a slang term for publicity or press coverage. As a verb, it means to sign, as a contract.

▶•◆•◆•◆•◀ **INN** ▶•◆•◆•◆•◀

THE STOP

Commonly seen clues include "Bed-and-breakfast," "Roadhouse," "Rural hotel," "Travel guide listing," and references to the Holiday Inn and Ramada Inn lodging chains. The sitcom *Newhart* is set at a Vermont inn.

▶•◆•◆•◆•◀ **INON** ▶•◆•◆•◆•◀

THE PHRASE

Commonly seen clues for IN ON are variations of "Aware of" and "Privy to." To "barge in on" is to interrupt, and one can "get in on the ground floor."

▶•◆•◆•◆•◀ **INRE** ▶•◆•◆•◆•◀

IN LEGALESE

"In re" appears at the beginning of legal memos, where it is synonymous with "about," "as to," "concerning," "in the matter of," and "regarding."

147

▶·◆·◆·◆·◀ **INS** ▶·◆·◆·◆·◀

THE PLURAL

"Ins" are current holders of political offices, who may be helpful contacts to get something done. "Ins and outs" are the particular details of something.

THE ABBREVIATIONS

INS may be short for the Immigration and Naturalization Service (a defunct agency that issued Green Cards to noncitizen residents) or "insurance."

▶·◆·◆·◆·◀ **INT** ▶·◆·◆·◆·◀

FOR SHORT

In crosswords, "int." is usually short for "interest," and is clued in terms of bank accounts or bond income. It can also be short for "Internal" (as in the IRS), "interception" (as in football)—bad news for a quarterback (QB, for short).

▶·◆·◆·◆·◀ **INTO** ▶·◆·◆·◆·◀

THE PREPOSITION

Commonly seen clues are variations of "Division word," "Enthusiastic about," "Fascinated by," and "Fond of."

▶·◆·◆·◆·◀ **ION** ▶·◆·◆·◆·◀

IN SCIENCE

An ion is an electrically charged atom. Ions are propelled within a cyclotron, or in other kinds of particle accelerator. Lithium-ion is a type of battery.

ON THE ROAD

Ion is a formerly made model of the Saturn automobile.

▶•◆•◆•◆•◀ IOTA ▶•◆•◆•◆•◀

THE LETTER
Iota is the ninth letter of the Greek alphabet, following theta and preceding kappa.

THE BIT
As a very small quantity, commonly seen clues include "Scintilla," "Smidgen," "Tiny amount," and "Whit."

▶•◆•◆•◆•◀ IOU ▶•◆•◆•◆•◀

THE DEBT
Commonly seen clues: "Debtor's note," "Letters of credit," "Marker," and "Promise to pay."

▶•◆•◆•◆•◀ IOWA ▶•◆•◆•◆•◀

THE PLACE
Iowa is usually defined either by its neighbors (Wisconsin, Illinois, Nebraska, South Dakota, and Minnesota), its cities (Des Moines, Dubuque) its nickname (the Hawkeye State), or its region (the Midwest, the Corn Belt). Actor John Wayne was born there; the film *Field of Dreams*, the musical *The Music Man*, and the novel *The Bridges of Madison County* are set there.

▶•◆•◆•◆•◀ IPO ▶•◆•◆•◆•◀

IN THE NEWS
IPO is short for "initial public offering," the debut of the publicly traded stock of a company. You'll see clues such as "Wall St. launch" and "Stock mkt. milestone."

▶•◆•◆•◆•◀ **IRA** ▶•◆•◆•◆•◀

THE FUNDS
As an abbreviation for "individual retirement account," commonly seen clues include "Keogh or 401(k) alternative," "Kind of tax shelter," "Nest egg letters," and "S&L offering."

THE NAME
There's song lyricist Gershwin (a dedicated crossword fan himself, brother of George), novelist Levin, and public radio personality Glass.

THE ORGANIZATION
IRA may also be short for the Irish Republican Army, an Irish nationalist organization.

▶•◆•◆•◆•◀ **IRAN** ▶•◆•◆•◆•◀

THE MIDDLE EAST COUNTRY
Once known as Persia, Iran's neighboring countries are Armenia, Azerbaijan, Iraq, Pakistan, Turkey, and Turkmenistan. It lies on the Caspian Sea, the Gulf of Oman, and the Persian Gulf. The modern Persian language is known to natives as Farsi. Iran is a member of the oil cartel OPEC.

BLANKETY-BLANKS
If I Ran the Circus and *If I Ran the Zoo* are children's books by Dr. Seuss. "I Ran (So Far Away)" is a 1982 hit by A Flock of Seagulls.

NOT SO FAST!

"Middle East country": **I R A** ___

The answer can be IRAN or IRAQ.

▶•◆•◆•◆•◀ IRANI ▶•◆•◆•◆•◀

THE NATIVE

IRANI may be defined in terms of cities in clues like "Tehran resident" (other major cities are Qom, Shiraz, and Tabriz); by citing notable citizens (such as former president Bani-Sadr) or the titles of present or former rulers (shah and ayatollah, respectively); or by the currency used in Iran, rials.

▶•◆•◆•◆•◀ IRATE ▶•◆•◆•◆•◀

THE ADJECTIVE

Commonly seen clues: "Angry," "Furious," "Hopping mad," "Steaming," "Ticked off," and "Up in arms."

▶•◆•◆•◆•◀ IRE ▶•◆•◆•◆•◀

THE NOUN

As the noun form of "irate," commonly seen clues include "Anger," "Fury," "Infuriation," "Rage," and "Wrath." While the word will sometimes be clued as a verb meaning "to anger," this usage isn't very common in English today, and usually appears only in older unabridged dictionaries.

▶•◆•◆•◆•◀ IRENE ▶•◆•◆•◆•◀

THE GODDESS

Irene was the ancient Greek goddess of peace and one of the three Horae, the goddesses who controlled orderly life. Her Roman equivalent was Pax.

REAL PEOPLE

There's singer Cara, ballroom dancer Castle, actress Dunne, physicist Joliot-Curie, and actresses Papas and Ryan.

151

IN FICTION

Irene is a major character in John Galsworthy's series of novels known as *The Forsyte Saga*. *Me, Myself & Irene* is a 2000 film in which Renée Zellweger portrays Irene. The 1919 Broadway musical *Irene* was revived in 1973 with Debbie Reynolds in the title role. You may see the clue "Goodnight girl," a reference to the folk music standard "Goodnight, Irene."

IN THE AIR

Irene was the name of a destructive hurricane of 2011.

▶·◆·◆·◆·◀ IRIS ▶·◆·◆·◆·◀

IN THE SKY

"Iris" is another word for "rainbow." This sense is derived from Iris, the ancient Greek goddess of the rainbow.

IN YOUR EYE

The iris is the part of the eye that gives it its color, and is where the pupil is located.

THE FLOWER

The garden flower iris is known for its bearded blossoms. It is the state flower of Tennessee.

THE NAME

Iris Murdoch was an Irish novelist, who was portrayed in the 2001 film *Iris* by Judi Dench and Kate Winslet.

▶·◆·◆·◆·◀ IRK ▶·◆·◆·◆·◀

THE VERB

Commonly seen synonymous clues: "Irritate," "Nettle," "Tick off," "Perturb," "Bother," and "Pester."

▶•◆•◆•◆•◀ IRON ▶•◆•◆•◆•◀

THE ELEMENT
Iron is often an ingredient in multivitamin pills. The ores from which iron is obtained include hematite, magnetite, and siderite. Iron is "pumped" by bodybuilders.

THE APPLIANCES
As a clothes-pressing tool, IRON will often be clued as a verb, such as "Do a laundry job," "Remove wrinkles from," or, punnily, "Take care of a pressing task." An iron was formerly one of the playing pieces in the board game Monopoly. Branding irons are used by cowboys.

IN SPORTS
An iron is a type of golf club, used most often by players on the fairway.

THE ADJECTIVE
As an adjective, "iron" is synonymous with "inflexible" or "unyielding."

▶•◆•◆•◆•◀ IRS ▶•◆•◆•◆•◀

THE ABBREVIATION
The IRS, or Internal Revenue Service, is the agency of the U.S. Treasury Department responsible for collecting taxes and enforcing tax laws. Clues for IRS refer to the aforementioned facts, as well as the tax form for individuals (Form 1040), the April 15 annual filing deadline for tax returns, and the audits and auditors associated with it.

▶•◆•◆•◆•◀ ISAAC ▶•◆•◆•◆•◀

THE MEN
There are authors Asimov and Bashevis Singer, designer Mizrahi (a big crossword fan), scientist Newton, violinist Stern, and the Biblical patriarch (son of Abraham and Sarah, spouse of Rebecca, and father of Jacob and Esau).

153

▶•◆•◆•◆•◀ ISEE ▶•◆•◆•◆•◀

THE ACKNOWLEDGMENT

Common "I see" clues are variations of "Ah, yes," "Phrase of understanding," and "That's clear."

▶•◆•◆•◆•◀ ISLE ▶•◆•◆•◆•◀

IN GENERAL

Commonly seen nonspecific clues are variations of "Archipelago part" (an archipelago is a chain of islands), "Castaway's place," "Dot on a map," "Cruise destination," "Resort locale," and "Tropical spot."

SPECIFICALLY

Isles you're likely to encounter in crosswords include the major Hawaiian Islands (Hawaii, Kauai, Maui, and Oahu), England's Isle of Man and Isle of Wight, the Caribbean's Cuba and Aruba, and the Italian isle of Capri. You might also see "isle" clued as being part of an island group such as the Canaries or the Bahamas.

▶•◆•◆•◆•◀ ISNT ▶•◆•◆•◆•◀

THE CONTRACTION

The most common "isn't" clues include "Does not exist," "Ceases to be," and the blankety-blanks "Winning ___ everything" and "Money ___ everything."

▶•◆•◆•◆•◀ ITEM ▶•◆•◆•◆•◀

THE NOUN

Commonly seen clues are variations of "Agenda listing," "Checkout counter unit," and "Gossip column tidbit."

▶•◆•◆•◆•◀ **ITS** ▶•◆•◆•◆•◀

THE CONTRACTION

Colloquial quotes like "___ about time," "___ a deal!," and "For what ___ worth" can clue ITS. You'll also see references to the songs "It's De-Lovely," "It's Impossible," "It's Not Unusual," "It's Over," "It's So Easy," and the film *It's a Wonderful Life*. The most frequent clue by far for ITS that doesn't have a fill-in-the-blank refers to TGIF, short for "thank God it's Friday."

It's almost never defined as the possessive "its," because it's very difficult to write a brief clue for.

▶•◆•◆•◆•◀ **IVAN** ▶•◆•◆•◆•◀

THE NAME

Ivan, the Russian equivalent of John, was the name of several Russian czars, most notably Ivan IV, whose nickname was "the Terrible." There's also financier Boesky, tennis pro Lendl, Nobel physiologist Pavlov, director Reitman, and author Turgenev. Ivan is one of the three title characters (the others are Dmitri and Alexei) in Dostoyevsky's *The Brothers Karamazov*.

▶•◆•◆•◆•◀ **IVE** ▶•◆•◆•◆•◀

BLANKETY-BLANKS

Colloquial quotes like "___ been had!," "___ got it!," and "Now ___ seen everything!" may clue IVE. You'll also see references to song titles like "I've Got a Crush on You," "I've Gotta Be Me," and "I've Got You Under My Skin," as well as the old TV game show *I've Got a Secret*.

THE SUFFIX

The suffix "-ive" can be added to many words to form adjectives. A few of them are "combat," "distinct," "effect," and "secret."

K-L

Kilauea lava lake, Hawaii

▶•◈•◈•◈•◀ KNEE ▶•◈•◈•◈•◀

THE JOINT

Commonly seen clues: "Baby bouncing spot," "Leg joint," "Pants part," and "Patella place."

▶•◈•◈•◈•◀ LACE ▶•◈•◈•◈•◀

THE FABRIC

As a fabric, you'll often see veils, gowns, tablecloths, curtains, and valentines in the clue. The fabric also makes appearances in titles like *Arsenic and Old Lace* and the song "Chantilly Lace." Queen Anne's lace sounds like a fabric, but is a kind of flower.

ON YOUR FEET

"Shoestring" and "Sneaker part" are typical clues in this sense.

THE VERB

Besides its "interlace" meaning, to "lace" something is to add a small amount of liquor to it, as with a food or nonalcoholic drink.

▶•◈•◈•◈•◀ LAD ▶•◈•◈•◈•◀

THE KID

Commonly seen clues: "Little shaver," "Schoolboy," "Youngster," and "Youth."

▶•◈•◈•◈•◀ LAIR ▶•◈•◈•◈•◀

THE NOUN

A lair may be the den or resting place of a wild animal (such as a lion or a bear), or a person's secret retreat or hideout.

▶•◆•◆•◆•◀ LAME ▶•◆•◆•◆•◀

THE ADJECTIVE

As an adjective, "lame" is almost never clued in reference to walking, but rather in its figurative sense, as in a "lame excuse." Relevant clues include "Inadequate," "Ineffectual," and "Not at all convincing."

THE FABRIC

The two-syllable "lamé" is a gown fabric partially made of metallic threads such as gold or silver.

▶•◆•◆•◆•◀ LANE ▶•◆•◆•◆•◀

THE NOUN

A lane may be a narrow street, a highway division, a place to bowl, or a place to run a race.

THE NAME

In the Superman fictional universe, Lois Lane is a reporter for the *Daily Planet*, where she works with Clark Kent and Jimmy Olsen. She has been portrayed most recently on film by Kate Bosworth and Amy Adams. Actor Nathan Lane starred in the Broadway production of the Mel Brooks musical *The Producers*, as well as its film adaptation.

▶•◆•◆•◆•◀ LAP ▶•◆•◆•◆•◀

SITTING

Commonly seen clues in this sense: "Baby seat," "Santa's perch," and "Sitter's creation."

RACING

Athletic clues are similar to "NASCAR unit" and "Once around the track."

THE VERB

To "lap up" is either to drink up, or to receive enthusiastically.

▶•◆•◆•◆•◀ **LAS** ▶•◆•◆•◆•◀

THE SPANISH ARTICLE

"*Las*" is the Spanish feminine word for "the." City clue references include Las Cruces (in New Mexico), Las Palmas (in Spain's Canary Islands), and Las Vegas (in Nevada). The clue "Part of UNLV" refers to the University of Nevada at Las Vegas.

MUSICALLY SPEAKING

As the plural of the sixth note in a musical scale, las follow sols and precede tis. There's also "Singer's syllables" (as in "tra la la") and "'Deck the Halls' sounds" (as in "fa-la-la-la-la-la-la-la-la").

▶•◆•◆•◆•◀ **LASS** ▶•◆•◆•◆•◀

THE PERSON

Sometimes clued generically, such as "Young lady," sometimes referring to Scotland; as in "Highlands girl."

▶•◆•◆•◆•◀ **LAST** ▶•◆•◆•◆•◀

THE VERB

Verb clues include "Persevere," "Stand the test of time," and "Wear well."

THE ADJECTIVE

As an adjective, there's "Final," "Most recent," and "Ultimate."

THE ADVERB

This sense, related to the adjective, will have clues like "Finally" and "Behind everyone else."

THE NOUN

Unrelated to the above senses, a last is a form in the shape of a shoe that is used to shape or repair shoes.

▶·◆·◆·◆·◀ LATE ▶·◆·◆·◆·◀

THE ADJECTIVE
Commonly seen clues: "After the deadline," "Not on time," "Past due," "Recent," and "Tardy."

▶·◆·◆·◆·◀ LAVA ▶·◆·◆·◆·◀

HOT STUFF
Commonly seen clues include "Molten rock," "Volcanic output," and references to well-known volcanoes such as Etna, Kilauea, Stromboli, and Vesuvius.

OTHER STUFF
There's the soap brand, the material inside a lava lamp, and the decadent dessert of molten chocolate lava cake.

▶·◆·◆·◆·◀ LEA ▶·◆·◆·◆·◀

ON THE FARM
Commonly seen clues in the "pasture" sense: "Grassy area," "Grazing place," "Meadow," and "Rural expanse."

ON THE STAGE AND SCREEN
Actress Lea Michele starred in the musical TV series *Glee*. Lea Thompson starred in the *Back to the Future* film series and the sitcom *Caroline in the City*. Lea Salonga won a Tony Award for her role in the Broadway musical *Miss Saigon*.

NOT SO FAST!

"Meadow sound": ___ **A A**

The answer can be BAA (the sound sheep make) or MAA (the sound goats make).

161

▶•◆•◆•◆•◀ LEAN ▶•◆•◆•◆•◀

THE ADJECTIVE

Commonly seen clues: "Lanky," "Like Jack Sprat's diet," "Low in fat," and "Skinny." The word can also mean "low in fat" as in "economical."

THE VERB

Commonly seen verb clues: "Be partial," "Exert pressure (on)," and "Incline."

THE NAME

The films of British director David Lean include *The Bridge on the River Kwai*, *Doctor Zhivago*, and *Lawrence of Arabia*.

▶•◆•◆•◆•◀ LEAR ▶•◆•◆•◆•◀

THE PEOPLE

There are the Shakespearean king (father of Regan, Goneril, and Cordelia), sitcom producer Norman, business jet manufacturer William, and poet Edward (best known for his limericks).

▶•◆•◆•◆•◀ LEASE ▶•◆•◆•◆•◀

DON'T BUY IT

Commonly seen noun clues: "Apartment document," "Kind of auto contract," and "Rental agreement." As a verb: "Charter," "Pay rent on," and "Take temporarily."

▶•◆•◆•◆•◀ LED ▶•◆•◆•◆•◀

THE VERB

Commonly seen verb clues: "Headed," "Set the pace," "Took charge of," and "Was in first place."

IN MUSIC

Led Zeppelin was a 1970s British rock band.

THE ABBREVIATION
Short for "light-emitting diodes," LEDs are used in certain light bulbs, digital clocks, and watches.

▶•◆•◆•◆•◀ **LEE** ▶•◆•◆•◆•◀

LAST-NAME REGULARS
The films of director Ang Lee include *Brokeback Mountain*, *Life of Pi*, and *Crouching Tiger, Hidden Dragon*. Ann Lee founded the American Shakers religious sect. Author Harper Lee wrote *To Kill a Mockingbird*. General Robert E. Lee commanded Confederate forces at the battles of Antietam, Fredericksburg, and Manassas (a.k.a. Bull Run), and surrendered to Grant at Appomattox Court House, Virginia. The films of director Spike Lee include *Do the Right Thing, Crooklyn, Malcolm X*, and *BlacKkKlansman*. Stan Lee of Marvel Comics (and Marvel Cinematic Universe cameos) cocreated Spider-Man, the Hulk, the X-Men, the Fantastic Four, and many other superheroes.

LAST-NAME OCCASIONALS
Less frequently seen Lees include singer Brenda, entertainer Gypsy Rose, and singer Peggy.

FIRST NAME
There's actress Grant, former auto executive Iacocca, actors Majors and Marvin, actor/acting teacher Strasberg, and golfer Trevino.

MIDDLE NAME
There's attorney F. Lee Bailey, actor Tommy Lee Jones, rock singer Jerry Lee Lewis, and writer Edgar Lee Masters.

WITHOUT A CAPITAL
The lee side of a vessel or a mountain is the side that is sheltered or turned away from the wind.

CROSSWORDS 101
Lesson 6: Latin

These Latin words appear frequently
as crossword answers:

ALA, ALAE (wing, wings)	**DEO, DEUS** (god)
ALIA, ALII (others)	**DIEM** (day)
AMAS (you love)	**ECCE** (behold)
AMAT (he loves, she loves)	**ESSE** (to be)
AMO (I love)	**HIC** (here)
AMOR (love)	**ORA** (pray, mouths)
ARS (art)	**OVA** (eggs)
AVE (hello)	**RES** (thing)
AVIS, AVES (bird, birds)	**SIC** (thus)
DEI (gods)	**URSA** (bear)

▶•◆•◆•◆•◀ **LEER** ▶•◆•◆•◆•◀

THE NOUN/VERB

Commonly seen noun clues are variations of "Evil glance" and "Sly look." As a verb, there's "Eyeball," "Make eyes at," and "Ogle."

▶•◆•◆•◆•◀ **LEG** ▶•◆•◆•◆•◀

LITERAL

People and animals (especially chickens and turkeys, crossword-wise) have legs, as do chairs, tables, and trousers.

FIGURATIVE

A leg may be a part of a journey or a relay race, as well as either of the two nondiagonal sides of a right triangle.

▶•◆•◆•◆•◀ LEI ▶•◆•◆•◆•◀

IN HAWAII
Commonly seen clues are variations of "Luau neckwear," "Maui garland," "Oahu souvenir," and "Waikiki welcome."

▶•◆•◆•◆•◀ LEN ▶•◆•◆•◆•◀

THE NAME
There's sportscaster Berman, actor Cariou, pro football quarterback Dawson, author Deighton, and *Dancing With the Stars* judge Goodman.

▶•◆•◆•◆•◀ LENA ▶•◆•◆•◆•◀

THE NAME
Lena Dunham is best known for directing and starring in the HBO series *Girls*. Singer Lena Horne portrayed Glinda the Good Witch in the film version of *The Wiz*. Actress Lena Olin has appeared in such films as *Chocolat* and *Havana*.

ON THE MAP
Russia's Lena River flows through Siberia, including the city of Yakutsk.

▶•◆•◆•◆•◀ LENO ▶•◆•◆•◆•◀

THE NAME
Tonight Show host Jay Leno succeeded Johnny Carson in 1992, was (temporarily) succeeded by Conan O'Brien in 2009, and ultimately succeeded by Jimmy Fallon in 2014. His principal late-night TV rival was David Letterman. His autobiography is *Leading With My Chin*.

▶•◆•◆•◆•◀ LENS ▶•◆•◆•◆•◀

LOOK HERE
Things with lenses include eyes, cameras, periscopes, microscopes, and telescopes.

▶•◆•◆•◆•◀ LENT ▶•◆•◆•◆•◀

THE VERB
Commonly seen verb clues: "Advanced," "Allowed to use," "Gave for a while," and "Loaned."

ON THE CALENDAR
Pertaining to the Christian holiday, there's "Ash Wednesday begins it," "Easter preceder," "Mardi Gras follower," "Penitential period," "Spring season," and the wordplay clue "Fast time."

NOT SO FAST!

"Slow musical tempo": L __ __ __ O

The answer can be LENTO or LARGO.

▶•◆•◆•◆•◀ LEO ▶•◆•◆•◆•◀

THE SIGN
The summer zodiac sign of Leo (the Lion) covers the period from July 23 through August 22. It follows Cancer and precedes Virgo. It is named for the constellation Leo, whose best-known star is Regulus.

THE NAME
Famous Leos include author Buscaglia, baseball manager Durocher, and authors Rosten and Tolstoy. To date, 13 popes have been named Leo. It is also the tabloid nickname for actor Leonardo DiCaprio.

▶·◆·◆·◆·◀ LES ▶·◆·◆·◆·◀

IN FRANCE
"*Les*" is a plural form of "the" in French, usually clued in crosswords as part of the title of the Victor Hugo novel *Les Misérables,* or the Broadway musical adaptation commonly known as *Les Miz.*

THE NAME
There's bandleader Brown, TV executive Moonves, and guitarist Les Paul.

▶·◆·◆·◆·◀ LESS ▶·◆·◆·◆·◀

THE ADVERB
Commonly seen clues: "Discounted by," "Marked down," "Minus," and "Not so much."

▶·◆·◆·◆·◀ LET ▶·◆·◆·◆·◀

THE VERB
Commonly seen verb clues: "Allow," "Charter," "Permit," and "Rent out." To "let down" is to disappoint, to "let off" is to pardon, and to "let up" is to ease. The clue "Admit" can be answered both by LET IN and LET ON (in two difference senses of "admit").

THE NOUN
In tennis, a let is a play that is voided and must be redone.

▶·◆·◆·◆·◀ LIAR ▶·◆·◆·◆·◀

THE NOUN
You're likely to see "Fibber," "Deceitful one," "Storyteller," and "Untrustworthy sort."

▶•◆•◆•◆•◀ LIE ▶•◆•◆•◆•◀

THE UNTRUTH

Commonly seen noun clues in this sense: "False statement," "Fish story," "Prevarication," and "Whopper." As a verb: "Be deceitful," "Fudge facts," "Perjure oneself," and "Tell a fib."

OFF ONE'S FEET

Clues like "Recline" and "Sprawl" refer to the "relaxing" sense of "lie."

IN GOLF

On a golf fairway, a lie is the position of a ball.

▶•◆•◆•◆•◀ LIEN ▶•◆•◆•◆•◀

LEGALLY SPEAKING

A lien is a legal claim on property, as security for the payment of a debt. A mortgage is a type of lien, which a lending institution holds on a building.

▶•◆•◆•◆•◀ LIMO ▶•◆•◆•◆•◀

ON THE ROAD

Short for "limousine," a limo may be owned by a film star or other VIP, in which case it is probably driven by a chauffeur. It might also be rented by a promgoer or wedding party, or serve as a fancy taxi to the airport.

▶•◆•◆•◆•◀ LINE ▶•◆•◆•◆•◀

IN PRINT

A brief excerpt from a poem, film script, or most any type of printed work might define "line."

ON THE JOB

"Line" can be synonymous with "occupation" or a set of merchandise being offered for sale.

OTHER SENSES

A line can also be a transportation system (as in trains or buses), a short letter, a fishing cord, and a group of people waiting.

▶•◆•◆•◆•◀ **LION** ▶•◆•◆•◆•◀

THE BEAST

The "king of the jungle" wild feline is a summer sign of the zodiac (Leo) and the mascot of film studio MGM (also Leo). A group of lions is known as a "pride."

IN MYTH

In mythical multipart animals, a lion is a part of the griffin (part eagle also), the sphinx (part human also), the chimera (part goat and part serpent also), and manticore (part human and part dragon also). In Roman legend, the slave Androcles befriends a lion after removing a thorn from its paw; later he faces that same lion in the arena, and it is affectionate toward him rather than attacking him.

THE CHARACTERS

There's Simba in Disney's *The Lion King* (and other lion characters, like Mufasa, Scar, and Nala), the Cowardly Lion portrayed by Bert Lahr in *The Wizard of Oz*, and Aslan in C.S. Lewis's *Chronicles of Narnia*. The Detroit Lions are an NFL team, and the athletic teams of Columbia University are known as the Lions.

FIGURATIVELY SPEAKING

A lion may also be a person of great importance and/or influence, such as a "literary lion."

▶·◆·◆·◆·◀ **LIRA** ▶·◆·◆·◆·◀

THE MONEY

The lira is the current monetary unit of Turkey, and was formerly the currency of Italy and Malta, both of which have been replaced by the euro. The plural of the Turkish currency is "lira" or "liras"; the former Italian currency is pluralized "lire."

NOT SO FAST!

"Former Italian money": **L I R** ___

The answer can be LIRA or LIRE.

▶·◆·◆·◆·◀ **LIT** ▶·◆·◆·◆·◀

HOT STUFF

As the past tense of the verb "light," synonymous clues include "Ignited," "Illuminated," "Burning," and "Set ablaze."

IN BRIEF

Short for "literature," this sense of "lit" is often seen in phrases such as "kiddie lit" and "English Lit."

IN SLANG

In current parlance, a party that is lit is a very good party.

▶·◆·◆·◆·◀ **LLAMA** ▶·◆·◆·◆·◀

THE BEAST

Native to the Andes mountains of South America, the llama is a beast of burden and a source of wool. Its relatives include the camel, alpaca, and guanaco.

CROSSWORDS 101
Lesson 7: Spanish

These Spanish words appear frequently as crossword answers (accent and diacritical marks, if any, are omitted):

AMO (I love)	OLE (shout of	SER (to be)
CASA (house)	approval)	SOL (sun)
DOS (two)	ORO (gold)	SRA (Mrs.)
ELLA (she)	OTRO, OTRA	SUR (south)
ENERO (January)	(other)	TIA (aunt)
ESTA (is, this)	REY (king)	TIO (uncle)
ESTE (east)	RIO (river)	TORO (bull)
MAS (more)	SALA (room)	TRES (three)
NINO (boy)	SENOR (mister)	UNO, UNA (one)

▶•◆•◆•◆•◀ **LOA** ▶•◆•◆•◆•◀

THE SPEWER

Mauna Loa is a volcano on the island of Hawaii. "Loa" is the Hawaiian word for "long"; "mauna" means "mountain."

INSIDER'S TIP: Mauna Kea is also a volcano on the island of Hawaii, but KEA appears in crosswords far less often than LOA.

▶•◆•◆•◆•◀ **LONE** ▶•◆•◆•◆•◀

THE ADJECTIVE

Synonymous clues include "Unaccompanied," "Isolated," "Unrivaled," and "Sole." There is also the Lone Star State (a nickname of Texas) and Western hero the Lone Ranger.

171

▶•◆•◆•◆•◀ LORE ▶•◆•◆•◆•◀

THE NOUN

Commonly seen clues: "Folk wisdom," "Handed-down tales," "Oral history," and "Traditional knowledge."

▶•◆•◆•◆•◀ LOSE ▶•◆•◆•◆•◀

NO-WIN SITUATION

Clues in this sense include "Be defeated," "Come in second," and "Fall short."

OTHER SENSES

"Lose" is also synonymous with "misplace" or "squander," and (informally) to slip away from someone following you.

▶•◆•◆•◆•◀ LOT ▶•◆•◆•◆•◀

THE NOUN

A lot may be a piece of real estate, a place to park a car or buy a car, a group of items up for auction, a large quantity of anything, or one's destiny. *'Salem's Lot* is a Stephen King novel.

IN THE BIBLE

In the book of Genesis, Lot is the nephew of Abraham who escapes from the wicked city of Sodom.

▶•◆•◆•◆•◀ LOU ▶•◆•◆•◆•◀

THE NAME

There's comedian Costello (partner of Bud Abbott), TV journalist Dobbs, baseball greats Brock and Gehrig, football great Groza, singers Rawls and Reed, and gymnast Mary Lou Retton.

▶•◆•◆•◆•◀ **LPS** ▶•◆•◆•◆•◀

JUST LISTEN

LPs, short for "long-playing records," were the a major medium for recorded music in the 1950s and 1960s, now in something of a revival. Made of vinyl, LPs were largely supplanted by CDs, though hip-hop DJs often "spin" LPs today.

▶•◆•◆•◆•◀ **LSAT** ▶•◆•◆•◆•◀

THE EXAM

Short for "Law School Admission Test," the LSAT is taken by college seniors who are aspiring attorneys.

M

*New York City's Metropolitan Museum
of Art ("the Met," for short), c. 1905*

▶·◆·◆·◆·◀ MAD ▶·◆·◆·◆·◀

THE ADJECTIVE

In the "angry" sense, there's "Furious," "Ticked off," "Seething," and "Enraged." Though many crossword editors avoid any reference to mental illness, you'll sometimes see clues like "Cuckoo" and "Loony."

IN PRINT

The satire magazine *Mad* has been published since 1952, and might be clued with references to its mascot, Alfred E. Neuman, or the "Usual Gang of Idiots" who create the magazine.

▶·◆·◆·◆·◀ MAE ▶·◆·◆·◆·◀

THE NAME

Mae Clarke, Mae West, and Mae Murray were all actresses. Rita Mae Brown is an author. Dr. Mae Jemison was the first African-American woman in space. Daisy Mae Yokum is the wife of the title character in the comic strip "Li'l Abner."

THE PLANE

Winnie Mae was the airplane of aviator Wiley Post.

THE AGENCIES

"Mae" is part of the colloquial names of federal mortgage agencies, including Fannie Mae, Ginnie Mae, and Sallie Mae.

▶·◆·◆·◆·◀ MAMA ▶·◆·◆·◆·◀

ALL IN THE FAMILY

Commonly seen clues are usually variations of "Cry from a crib," "Doll's word," and "Papa's partner." There's also Mama Bear from the Goldilocks story and 1960s pop singer Mama Cass Elliot.

▶•◆•◆•◆•◀ MAP ▶•◆•◆•◆•◀

GEOGRAPHICALLY SPEAKING

Commonly seen clues: "GPS display," "Atlas page," "Former glove compartment item," "Navigator's need," and "Road guide."

▶•◆•◆•◆•◀ MAR ▶•◆•◆•◆•◀

THE VERB

Commonly seen verb clues: "Damage," "Scratch up," "Spoil," and "Tarnish."

THE ABBREVIATION

As a short form of the month of March, there's "Apr. preceder," "Feb. follower," "St. Patrick's Day mo.," and "When spring starts: Abbr."

▶•◆•◆•◆•◀ MAT ▶•◆•◆•◆•◀

THE NOUN

A mat may be a small rug by the front door or a bathtub, as well as a surface for gymnastics, wrestling, or yoga.

THE VERB

To mat is to become entangled.

▶•◆•◆•◆•◀ MBA ▶•◆•◆•◆•◀

IN SCHOOL

Short for "Master of Business Administration," the MBA degree is offered by business schools in specialty areas such as finance and marketing, and is often held by business executives such as CEOs. The University of Pennsylvania's Wharton School of business is frequently mentioned in clues for MBA.

▶·◆·◆·◆·◀ MEET ▶·◆·◆·◆·◀

THE VERB
Commonly seen clues: "Comply with" (as a demand), "Convene," "Encounter," and "Run into."

THE NOUN
In this sense, a meet is an athletic contest, usually of track-and-field or swimming events.

▶·◆·◆·◆·◀ MEN ▶·◆·◆·◆·◀

THE GUYS
Commonly seen clues: "Blokes," "Fellows," "Fraternity members," and "Gents."

THE TOKENS
Men may also be the playing pieces used in board games, particularly checkers and chess.

NOT SO FAST!

"Shopping center": **M A ___ ___**

The answer can be MALL or MART.

▶·◆·◆·◆·◀ MENU ▶·◆·◆·◆·◀

AT THE RESTAURANT
Commonly seen clues in this sense: "Bill of fare," "Course listing," "Restaurant reading," and "Waiter's handout."

ELSEWHERE
A menu can also be a list of items to choose from in other venues, particularly on a computer screen.

▶•◆•◆•◆•◀ MERE ▶•◆•◆•◆•◀

THE ADJECTIVE
Commonly seen clues: "Insignificant," "Nothing but," "Paltry," and "Simple."

IN PARIS
"*Mère*" is the French word for "mother," which you'll see as a clue now and then.

▶•◆•◆•◆•◀ MESA ▶•◆•◆•◆•◀

ON THE MAP
A mesa is a small plateau or tableland (similar to a butte), having steep walls and a relatively flat top, common in the Southwest. The city of Mesa, Arizona, is near Phoenix. Colorado's Mesa Verde National Park has ruins of prehistoric cliff dwellings.

▶•◆•◆•◆•◀ MESH ▶•◆•◆•◆•◀

THE NOUN
Mesh is a netlike fabric, often used for screens, nets, and hosiery.

THE VERB
In the verb sense, common clues include "Interlock," "Fit together," and "Intertwine."

▶•◆•◆•◆•◀ MESS ▶•◆•◆•◆•◀

THE DISORDER
Commonly seen clues in this sense: "Disarray," "Hodgepodge," "Pigsty," and "Predicament."

TO THE TROOPS
"Mess" is a military term for a meal taken as a group, in a mess hall.

▶·◆·◆·◆·◀ MET ▶·◆·◆·◆·◀

THE VERB

As the past tense of "meet," there's "Encountered," "Greeted," "Happened upon," and "Ran into."

IN THE BIG APPLE

The New York Mets are a National League baseball team, whose home games were played in Shea Stadium from 1964 to 2008, and the newly built Citi Field since 2009. "The Met" is a colloquial term for New York City's Metropolitan Opera House, part of the Lincoln Center complex, as well as for the Metropolitan Museum of Art.

▶·◆·◆·◆·◀ METE ▶·◆·◆·◆·◀

THE VERB

Commonly seen clues: "Allot," "Dole (out)," "Distribute," and "Parcel (out)."

▶·◆·◆·◆·◀ MOE ▶·◆·◆·◆·◀

THE PEOPLE

Moe Howard was the leader of the Three Stooges comedy team, brother of Curly. Moe is also the proprietor and bartender of the tavern frequented by Homer on *The Simpsons*.

▶·◆·◆·◆·◀ MOO ▶·◆·◆·◆·◀

IN THE FIELD

Clues will be variations of "Cow's call," "Bovine bellow," and "Meadow sound."

THE TITLE

Clues like "Bride's title" are on the wane these days. You're more likely to see a fictional Mrs. such as Doubtfire (Robin Williams role), Dalloway (Virginia Woolf character), or Miniver (Greer Garson role).

N

Scotland's Urquhart Castle, overlooking Loch Ness

▶•◆•◆•◆•◀ NAG ▶•◆•◆•◆•◀

THE VERB
Typical clues: "Pester persistently," "Annoy constantly," and "Badger."

THE PERSON
For a person who nags: "Faultfinder" and "Chronic critic."

THE BEAST
This nag is an inferior horse, or an informal term for any racehorse.

▶•◆•◆•◆•◀ NAME ▶•◆•◆•◆•◀

THE VERB
In the verbal sense, there's "Identify," "Appoint," "Mention," and "Christen."

THE PERSON
As in "big name," clues include "Celebrity" and "Big shot."
As a person's name in general, clues will often mention birth certificates, job applications, and drivers' licenses.

▶•◆•◆•◆•◀ NANA ▶•◆•◆•◆•◀

IN THE FAMILY
As a term for "grandmother," commonly seen clues include "Babysitter, at times," "Family nickname," and "Mom's mom."

IN LITERATURE
Nana is a novel by French author Émile Zola. Nana is the pet dog of the Darling family in J.M. Barrie's *Peter Pan*.

▶◆◆◆◆◀ NAP ▶◆◆◆◆◀

THE TIME-OUT
Commonly seen clues in this sense: "Afternoon break," "Catch some Z's," "Forty winks," "Short snooze," and "Siesta."

THE FUZZ
Nap is also the short fuzzy ends of fibers on the surface of fleece and fabric products such as flannel, towels, and carpets.

▶◆◆◆◆◀ NAPA ▶◆◆◆◆◀

ON THE MAP
Napa is a county and city in northern California (near Sacramento), well known for its wines.

ON THE ROAD
NAPA stores across the U.S. sell auto parts.

▶◆◆◆◆◀ NASA ▶◆◆◆◆◀

UP IN THE AIR
Clues about the National Aeronautics and Space Administrations are most likely to refer either to its spacecraft (such as space shuttles *Atlantis*, *Columbia*, *Discovery*, and *Endeavour*), its space projects (such as Mercury, Gemini, and Apollo), its best-known astronauts (such as Neil Armstrong, Buzz Aldrin, and John Glenn), or its Cape Canaveral location.

▶◆◆◆◆◀ NATO ▶◆◆◆◆◀

THE WESTERN DEFENSE FORCE
Founded in 1949, the North Atlantic Treaty Organization is headquartered in Brussels, Belgium. The Warsaw Pact was its former counterpart among European Communist states.

▷•◆•◆•◆•◁ **NAY** ▷•◆•◆•◆•◁

THE TURNDOWN

Commonly seen clues: "Thumbs-down vote," "Roll call response," and "Aye's opposite."

▷•◆•◆•◆•◁ **NBA** ▷•◆•◆•◆•◁

IN SPORTS

The National Basketball Association is usually clued either generically (such as "Cagers' gp.," "Court org.," or "Hoops gp.") or in reference to one of its teams, often in a casually shortened form (such as the Bucks, Bulls, Cavs, Hornets, Lakers, Magic, Mavs, Rockets, and Wizards).

NOT SO FAST!

"Pen point" or "Bird's beak": **N ___ B**

In both senses, the answer can be NIB or NEB.

▷•◆•◆•◆•◁ **NCAA** ▷•◆•◆•◆•◁

IN SPORTS

Short for "National Collegiate Athletic Association," the NCAA regulates athletes and competitions of many colleges and universities in the United States. NCAA games are frequently broadcast on ESPN. The annual NCAA Division I Men's Basketball Tournament is known as "March Madness," the semifinal round of which is called the "Final Four."

▶•◆•◆•◆•◀ NCO ▶•◆•◆•◆•◀

IN THE SERVICE

Short for "noncommissioned officer," NCOs in the U.S. military include the sergeant (sgt.) and corporal (cpl.).

▶•◆•◆•◆•◀ NEA ▶•◆•◆•◆•◀

THE UNION

The National Educational Association is a labor union that represents public school teachers.

THE AGENCY

The National Endowment for the Arts is a federal agency that funds artistic projects and public TV (PBS), for example.

▶•◆•◆•◆•◀ NEAR ▶•◆•◆•◆•◀

THE ADJECTIVE

Commonly seen adjective clues: "At hand," "Close by," "Imminent," and "Not far."

THE VERB

Commonly seen verb clues: "Approach," "Get close to," and "Move toward."

▶•◆•◆•◆•◀ NEAT ▶•◆•◆•◆•◀

THE ADJECTIVE

As a synonym for "orderly," there's "All in place," "Clean-cut," "Tidy," and "Uncluttered." Meaning "without ice" (as a drink), there's "Bar order," "Straight up," and "Undiluted."

THE EXCLAMATION

As a word of approval, commonly seen clues include "Cool!," "Nifty!," and "Swell!"

CROSSWORDS 101
Lesson 8: Nobel Prizes

These Nobel prize winners often appear as crossword answers:

Niels BOHR (physics)
Marie CURIE (chemistry, physics)
Bob DYLAN (literature)
ELIE Wiesel (peace)
Al GORE (peace)
LECH Walesa (peace)
Anwar SADAT (peace)
TONI Morrison (literature)
Desmond TUTU (peace)
Harold UREY (chemistry)

 **NEATO**

THE EXCLAMATION

A rather outdated variant of "Neat!," NEATO may be defined as other past expressions of approval, such as "Groovy!" and "Far out!," as well as any of the interjectional clues for NEAT.

NED

REAL

There's actor Beatty, composer Rorem, and Australian outlaw Kelly, who was sort of the Australian Jesse James.

FICTIONAL

Ned Flanders is the neighbor of the title family in the animated sitcom *The Simpsons*. *Waking Ned Devine* is a 1998 film. Ned Nickerson is the boyfriend of teenage sleuth Nancy Drew.

▶·◆·◆·◆·◀ NEE ▶·◆·◆·◆·◀

FROM PARIS

"*Née*," the French word for "born," is often seen on society pages and bridal notices before a woman's maiden name, as in "Jane Smith, *née* Jones."

▶·◆·◆·◆·◀ NEED ▶·◆·◆·◆·◀

THE VERB

Commonly seen verb clues: "Can't do without," "Call for," "Must have," and "Require."

THE NOUN

As a noun, there's "Necessity," "Requirement," "Scholarship criterion," and "Something essential."

▶·◆·◆·◆·◀ NEER ▶·◆·◆·◆·◀

THE CONTRACTION

"Ne'er" is a poetic form of the adverb "never." A ne'er-do-well is a good-for-nothing individual.

▶·◆·◆·◆·◀ NEMO ▶·◆·◆·◆·◀

THE NAME

Nemo is the captain of the submarine *Nautilus* in the Jules Verne novel *Twenty Thousand Leagues Under the Sea*. *Finding Nemo* is an animated film of 2003, whose title character is a clownfish. Nemo also appears in that movie's 2016 sequel, *Finding Dory*.

▶•◆•◆•◆•◀ NEO ▶•◆•◆•◆•◀

THE PREFIX

Meaning "new" or "recent," "neo-" can be added in front of words such as "classical," "colonial," and "natal." The prefix "paleo-" (meaning "ancient") is the opposite of "neo-."

IN THE MOVIES

In the 1999 film *The Matrix*, Keanu Reaves portrays the lead role of Neo.

▶•◆•◆•◆•◀ NEON ▶•◆•◆•◆•◀

THE GAS

The inert (a.k.a. "noble") gas neon is commonly used in advertising signs.

ON THE ROAD

The Dodge Neon is a formerly produced model of compact car.

▶•◆•◆•◆•◀ NERD ▶•◆•◆•◆•◀

THE NOUN

Commonly seen clues have historically included "Dweeb," "Geek," "Social outcast," and "Uncool one," though it has become more common to clue "nerd" less pejoratively, with clues such as "*The Big Bang Theory* type" or "Comic-Con attendee, probably."

▶•◆•◆•◆•◀ NERO ▶•◆•◆•◆•◀

LONG AGO

The infamous Roman emperor Nero, nephew of Caligula and husband of Octavia, was the successor of Claudius and the predecessor of Galba. Nero is portrayed by Peter Ustinov in the 1951 film *Quo Vadis*.

OF LATE

Franco Nero is an Italian actor, and Peter Nero is a pianist and conductor. Nero Wolfe is a fictional detective created by author Rex Stout. Nero is the antagonist in 2009's *Star Trek*, played by Eric Bana.

▶•◆•◆•◆•◀ **NESS** ▶•◆•◆•◆•◀

THE NAME

Federal agent Eliot Ness, adversary of Chicago gangster Al Capone, led the group of Prohibition agents known as "the Untouchables." He was portrayed in the 1960s TV series *The Untouchables* by Robert Stack, and in the 1987 film of the same name by Kevin Costner.

THE LAKE

Scotland's Loch Ness is the reputed home of a giant creature known as the Loch Ness monster.

IN LOWERCASE

A ness is a point of land that projects into the sea or other body of water. Clues in that sense are "Cape," "Headland," and "Promontory."

THE SUFFIX

A noun-forming suffix when appended to adjectives, "-ness" can be added to such words as sweet, kind, and glad.

▶•◆•◆•◆•◀ **NEST** ▶•◆•◆•◆•◀

THE RESIDENCE

A nest may be a home for insects (such as hornets) or birds, as well as a snug retreat for people.

THE VERB

In addition to the verb form of the sense above, items that fit together or within each other, such as Russian matryoshka dolls, are said to "nest."

▶•◆•◆•◆•◀ NET ▶•◆•◆•◆•◀

MONEYWISE

Commonly seen clues in this sense: "After taxes," "Bottom line," "End up with," and "Profit."

THE FABRIC

Nets are used by fishermen and lepidopterists (butterfly collectors), as a circus safety device, and in the sports of badminton, basketball, tennis, and volleyball.

IN CYBERSPACE

As a short form of "internet," you may see clues like "Something to surf." The internet suffix ".net" is a common one for websites.

▶•◆•◆•◆•◀ NEW ▶•◆•◆•◆•◀

THE ADJECTIVE

There's "Unused," "Unfamiliar," "Recent," "Cutting-edge," and "Still wrapped."

▶•◆•◆•◆•◀ NIECE ▶•◆•◆•◆•◀

IN GENERAL

Generically, you'll see "Family member," "Reunion attendee," "Sister's daughter," and "Brother's daughter."

SPECIFICALLY

Particular nieces often seen include actress Emma Roberts (to Julia), actress Bridget Fonda (to Jane), and Dorothy (to Em of *The Wizard of Oz*).

▶•◆•◆•◆•◀ NIL ▶•◆•◆•◆•◀

THE UN-QUANTITY

Commonly seen clues: "Goose egg," "Nothing," "Zero," and "Zilch." A score of zero in soccer is referred to as "nil."

▶·◆·◆·◆·◀ **NILE** ▶·◆·◆·◆·◀

ON THE MAP
One of the world's longest rivers, the Nile flows through the African nations of Egypt, Sudan, Uganda, Tanzania, and Rwanda, and the cities of Aswan, Cairo, Khartoum, and Luxor. Cleopatra sailed her royal barge on the Nile. Lake Victoria is part of the Nile's source. *Death on the Nile* is a novel by Agatha Christie.

THE COLOR
Nile is shade of bluish green or greenish blue.

▶·◆·◆·◆·◀ **NINA** ▶·◆·◆·◆·◀

IN MEXICO
"*Niña*" is the Spanish word for "girl."

IN HISTORY
The *Niña* was one of Columbus's three ships on his 1492 voyage to the New World.

THE PEOPLE
There are jazz singer Nina Simone, fashion designer Nina Ricci, and *Elle* editor and *Project Runway* judge Nina García.

▶·◆·◆·◆·◀ **NINE** ▶·◆·◆·◆·◀

THE COUNT
There are nine innings in a standard baseball game, nine defensive players on a baseball field, nine Muses in mythology, and nine Supreme Court justices. There are nine holes each on the "front nine" and "back nine" halves of a golf course.

THE NUMBER
Nine is the largest digit, the square of the number three, the standard number of different digits in sudoku, the emergency CB radio channel, and the lowest card in pinochle.

THE TIME

"Midmorning" or "Midevening" may define nine A.M. or P.M. The latter time is an hour for prime-time network TV broadcasts.

▶·◆·◆·◆·◀ **NIP** ▶·◆·◆·◆·◀

THE NOUN

A nip can be a small bite, a quick drink, or a small quantity of anything, as well as a chill in the air. It is also partnered with "tuck" in a common idiom.

THE VERB

Besides the "bite" meaning, "nip" as a verb is an informal term for "narrowly defeat."

▶·◆·◆·◆·◀ **NNE** ▶·◆·◆·◆·◀

THE ABBREVIATION

NNE stands for the direction of north-northeast, which is the point opposite south-southwest (SSW) on a compass. You'll often see city clues like "Dayton-to-Toledo dir.," where the second city is located north-northeast of the first. NNE and all the other compass points can be seen in weather reports (referring to wind direction) and on the screens of GPS devices.

▶·◆·◆·◆·◀ **NOAH** ▶·◆·◆·◆·◀

THE ANCIENT MARINER

The Genesis ark builder Noah had sons named Ham, Shem, and Japheth. He was portrayed by Russell Crowe in the 2014 film *Noah*.

OTHER FIRSTS

There's lexicographer Webster and actor Wyle.

AT LAST

Yannick Noah is a retired tennis pro. Trevor Noah succeeded Jon Stewart as host of *The Daily Show*.

▶·◆·◆·◆·◀ NOD ▶·◆·◆·◆·◀

THE VERB

"Nod" can mean "to doze" as well as to show approval by moving one's head up and down.

THE NOUN

In addition to the head motion, as a noun it's an informal term for "approval."

CAPITALIZED

In the Book of Genesis, Cain was exiled to the Land of Nod (east of Eden) after his murder of Abel. Informally, the "land of Nod" is the mythical land of sleep. The trio Wynken, Blynken, and Nod sail off in a wooden shoe in the children's poem by Eugene Field.

▶·◆·◆·◆·◀ NOEL ▶·◆·◆·◆·◀

THE NOUN

"Noel" may refer to a Christmas carol or the yuletide season.

THE NAME

Noël Coward was an actor, composer, and playwright.

NOT SO FAST!

"Mortgage, for example": **L ___ ___ N**

The answer can be LOAN or LIEN.

▶·◆·◆·◆·◀ NONO ▶·◆·◆·◆·◀

DON'T DO IT

Typical clues for "no-no": "Forbidden thing," "Taboo," and "Action to be avoided."

195

CROSSWORDS 101
Lesson 9: Popes

These papal names frequently appear as crossword answers, often followed by a Roman numeral. The names below are followed by the highest number associated with each.

ADRIAN VI (6)
LEO XIII (13)
PAUL VI (6)
PETER (1, the first pope)
PIUS XXIII (23)

▶•◆•◆•◆•◀ **NTH** ▶•◆•◆•◆•◀

TO THE MAX

Clues related to the phrase "to the nth degree" include "Ultimate degree" and "Utmost extent."

▶•◆•◆•◆•◀ **NOON** ▶•◆•◆•◆•◀

ON THE CLOCK

Commonly seen clues: "'High' time," "Lunch time for many," "Midday," and "When shadows are shortest."

▶·◆·◆·◆·◀ **NOR** ▶·◆·◆·◆·◀

THE CONJUNCTION

Commonly seen clues include "Common correlative," "Likewise not," "Negative connector," and "Neither's partner." Fill-in-the-blanks: "Hide ___ hair," "Neither fish ___ fowl," and "Neither here ___ there."

THE ABBREVIATION

As a short version of "Norway," there's "NATO member," "Neighbor of Swed.," and "Scand. nation."

▶·◆·◆·◆·◀ **NOS** ▶·◆·◆·◆·◀

THE PLURAL

Commonly seen clues in this sense: "Denials," "Negative votes," "Refusals," and "Turndowns."

THE ABBREVIATION

As a short version of "numbers," there's "CPA's expertise," "Figs.," "Lottery choices: Abbr.," and "Phone bk. listings."

▶·◆·◆·◆·◀ **NOSE** ▶·◆·◆·◆·◀

LITERALLY SPEAKING

Commonly seen clues: "Facial feature," "Scent sensor," "Sniffer," and "Smeller." Owners of famous noses include Cyrano de Bergerac, Jimmy Durante, Pinocchio, and flying reindeer Rudolph. Airplanes and rocket ships also have noses.

FIGURATIVELY SPEAKING

The "nose" of a wine is its aroma. As a verb, "nose" is synonymous with "snoop." To "nose out" is to defeat by a narrow margin.

▶•◆•◆•◆•◀ **NOT** ▶•◆•◆•◆•◀

THE EXCLAMATION

The 1992 film *Wayne's World* popularized the use of "Not!" at the end of a sentence to indicate what has just been stated isn't true. Clues like "Hardly!" and "Only kidding!" refer to this sense.

BLANKETY-BLANKS

"___ a chance!," "I should say ___!," "___ on your life!," and "___ to worry!" may also clue NOT.

THE ADVERB

NOT may also be clued how it's most used in English, such as "Negative word," "Ten Commandments word," and "Word of denial."

▶•◆•◆•◆•◀ **NOTE** ▶•◆•◆•◆•◀

THE MISSIVE

As a short letter, there's "Brief message" and "Memo."

THE VERB

Commonly seen verb clues include "Jot down" and "Observe."

OTHER NOUNS

A note can also be a piece of paper currency, an IOU, or a musical tone.

▶•◆•◆•◆•◀ **NOVA** ▶•◆•◆•◆•◀

IN THE SKY

A nova is a type of star whose brightness increases suddenly, then gradually fades.

ON THE TUBE

Nova is a TV science series seen on PBS.

ON THE MAP

Nova Scotia is an eastern province of Canada. Nova Scotia lox ("nova" for short) is a variety of smoked salmon.

ON THE ROAD

The Nova was a model of Chevrolet automobile manufactured from 1962 to 1979, and again from 1985 to 1988.

▶•◆•◆•◆•◀ **NRA** ▶•◆•◆•◆•◀

THE OLD AGENCY

The NRA, short for National Recovery Administration, was created in 1933, early in the first term of President Franklin Roosevelt, as part of his New Deal program. Its logo was a blue eagle.

TODAY

The National Rifle Association is a gun-advocacy group headed at one time by actor Charlton Heston. It publishes *American Hunter* magazine. Commonly seen clues in this sense with different references include "Influential D.C. lobby," "Marksman's org.," and "Second Amendment supporter: Abbr."

Okra pods

▶•◆•◆•◆•◀ OAF ▶•◆•◆•◆•◀

THE NOUN
Commonly seen clues: "Buffoon," "Clumsy one," "Lummox," and "Stumblebum."

▶•◆•◆•◆•◀ OAHU ▶•◆•◆•◆•◀

ON THE MAP
Oahu, the second largest of the Hawaiian Islands, is the home of Honolulu, Pearl Harbor, the volcanic peak Diamond Head, and Waikiki Beach. Nearby islands include Kauai, Maui, and Molokai. The TV series *Hawaii Five-O*, *Lost*, and *Magnum, P.I.* have been filmed there.

▶•◆•◆•◆•◀ OAK ▶•◆•◆•◆•◀

IN THE GROUND
Botanical clues include "Hardwood tree," "Source of acorns," and "Wine barrel wood."

ON THE MAP
There's Oak Ridge, Tennessee, hometown of the Oak Ridge Boys country music quartet.

▶•◆•◆•◆•◀ OAR ▶•◆•◆•◆•◀

THE IMPLEMENT
As a type of paddle, commonly seen clues include "Boathouse gear," "Dinghy implement," "Galley tool," and "Rower's need." An oar may also be a person who rows, especially as a member of a sculling or crew team. As a verb, to "oar" is to propel a vessel with oars.

▷•◆•◆•◆•◁ OAT ▷•◆•◆•◆•◁

THE EDIBLE

Commonly seen clues: "Bran source," "Cereal grain," "Feedbag morsel," and "Granola ingredient."

▷•◆•◆•◆•◁ OATH ▷•◆•◆•◆•◁

CALMLY

An oath is a formal promise, commonly spoken at swearing-in ceremonies in a courtroom or at a presidential inauguration.

ANGRILY

An oath can also be a profane outburst, usually clued in crosswords with mild examples such as "Drat!" or "Darn it!"

▷•◆•◆•◆•◁ OBESE ▷•◆•◆•◆•◁

SIZEWISE

Synonymous clues: "Portly," "Stout," and "Corpulent." Clues by example almost always mention fictional characters, such as Santa Claus, Humpty Dumpty, and Falstaff.

NOT SO FAST!

"Norwegian royal name": **O L A ___**

Both OLAV and OLAF are correct spellings.

▷•◆•◆•◆•◁ OBEY ▷•◆•◆•◆•◁

FOLLOW ME

You're likely to see clues such as "Follow instructions," "Do as told," and "Toe the line."

▶•◆•◆•◆•◀ **OBI** ▶•◆•◆•◆•◀

IN JAPAN

An obi is a broad sash worn as a belt with a kimono.

IN THE MOVIES

In the *Star Wars* film series, Obi-Wan Kenobi is a good-guy Jedi Knight. He is portrayed by Alec Guinness in the original trilogy, and by Ewan McGregor in the prequel trilogy.

▶•◆•◆•◆•◀ **OBOE** ▶•◆•◆•◆•◀

IN THE ORCHESTRA

The oboe is a double-reed woodwind instrument. Its woodwind "cousins" in the orchestra are the bassoon, clarinet, and flute. Other instruments in the oboe family include the English horn and heckelphone. In Sergei Prokofiev's *Peter and the Wolf*, an oboe plays the part of the duck.

▶•◆•◆•◆•◀ **OCEAN** ▶•◆•◆•◆•◀

ON THE GLOBE

The world's oceans include the Antarctic, Arctic, Atlantic, Indian, and Pacific. The ocean is the realm of the mythical gods Poseidon and Neptune. Generic clues include "Bounding main," "Liner's locale," and "Where the buoys are."

FIGURATIVELY SPEAKING

An ocean can also be a vast expanse or a large quantity of anything.

▶•◆•◆•◆•◀ **OCT** ▶•◆•◆•◆•◀

FOR SHORT

As an abbreviation for "October," "Oct." is usually clued in reference to autumn, Halloween, United Nations Day (Oct. 24), or the World Series of baseball.

▶·◆·◆·◆·◀ ODD ▶·◆·◆·◆·◀

UNEXPECTED

Commonly seen clues in this sense: "Eerie," "Peculiar," "Uncanny," and "Unusual."

UNMATCHED

In this sense, there's "Lacking a mate," "Left over," and "Unpaired."

UN-EVEN

An odd number (such as 37 or 101) is one that is not evenly divisible by two. A bet on all the odd numbers is often made in roulette.

▶·◆·◆·◆·◀ ODE ▶·◆·◆·◆·◀

THE POEM

An ode is a lyric poem often written to praise something or someone. Noted writers of odes include Samuel Taylor Coleridge, Thomas Gray, John Keats ("Ode to a Nightingale," "Ode on a Grecian Urn"), Percy Bysshe Shelley ("Ode to the West Wind"), William Wordsworth, the ancient Roman poet Horace, and the ancient Greek poet Pindar.

▶·◆·◆·◆·◀ ODIE ▶·◆·◆·◆·◀

IN THE COMICS

Odie is the dimwitted dog in Jim Davis's comic strip "Garfield." His owner is Jon Arbuckle.

▶·◆·◆·◆·◀ ODIN ▶·◆·◆·◆·◀

IN MYTH

Odin was the chief of the Aesir race of gods in Norse mythology, the husband of Frigg and the father of Thor. His hall is Valhalla, which is located in the land of Asgard. He rode an eight-legged horse named Sleipnir.

IN MOVIES

In Marvel's *Thor* movies, Odin is portrayed by Anthony Hopkins.

▶•◆•◆•◆•◀ **ODOR** ▶•◆•◆•◆•◀

WHAT THE NOSE KNOWS

Synonymous clues include "Aroma," "Bouquet," "Fragrance," and "Scent." More descriptive clues: "Air freshener target," "Fish market feature," and "Skunk's weapon." Although an odor may be any kind of scent, it is most often clued as an unpleasant scent, with "aroma" usually getting the association of a pleasant scent instead.

▶•◆•◆•◆•◀ **OER** ▶•◆•◆•◆•◀

IN VERSE

"O'er" is the poetic form of the preposition "over," the opposite of "'neath." The two best-known occurrences of the word are in "The Star-Spangled Banner" ("O'er the ramparts we watched ...") and "Jingle Bells" ("O'er the fields we go ...").

▶•◆•◆•◆•◀ **OGLE** ▶•◆•◆•◆•◀

THE VERB

Commonly seen clues: "Eye boldly," "Gawk at," "Look like a wolf," and "Stare at."

▶•◆•◆•◆•◀ **OGRE** ▶•◆•◆•◆•◀

THE MENACE

Commonly seen generic clues: "Cruel one," "Dictatorial boss," "Folklore villain," and "Meanie." The title character of the *Shrek* animated film series (voiced by Mike Myers) is an ogre.

►•◆•◆•◆•◄ OHARA ►•◆•◆•◆•◄

REAL

Author John O'Hara wrote *Pal Joey* and *BUtterfield 8*. Actress Maureen O'Hara's films include *Rio Grande, The Quiet Man*, and the original version of *The Parent Trap*.

FICTIONAL

Scarlett O'Hara is the heroine of the Margaret Mitchell novel *Gone With the Wind*, in which she marries Rhett Butler. Her Atlanta estate is called Tara. Actress Vivien Leigh won an Oscar for portraying her in the film version.

►•◆•◆•◆•◄ OHIO ►•◆•◆•◆•◄

THE BUCKEYE STATE

Clues for Ohio the state usually refer either to its major cities (Akron, Canton, Cincinnati, Cleveland, Columbus, Dayton, and Toledo), its neighboring states (Indiana, Kentucky, Michigan, Pennsylvania, and West Virginia) or its universities (Kent State and Oberlin). Seven U.S. presidents were born in Ohio, second only to Virginia.

THE RIVER

The Ohio River is formed at Pittsburgh from the Allegheny and Monongahela rivers. Other cities on the Ohio include Cincinnati, Louisville, and Wheeling.

►•◆•◆•◆•◄ OHM ►•◆•◆•◆•◄

THE UNIT

In science, an ohm is a measure of the electrical resistance of a circuit, named for German physicist Georg Ohm.

▶•◆•◆•◆•◀ OHNO ▶•◆•◆•◆•◀

THE SHOUT

OH NO is defined either descriptively (such as "Cry of distress") or with rather synonymous shouts (such as "Good heavens!").

THE SKATER

Once in a while you may see OHNO clued as the speed skater Apolo Anton Ohno, winner of eight Olympic medals.

▶•◆•◆•◆•◀ OIL ▶•◆•◆•◆•◀

IN AUTOS

There's "Black gold," "Friction reducer," "OPEC product," and "Texas tea."

IN ART

Many famous paintings are oils, such as Vincent van Gogh's *Starry Night*.

IN FOOD

Oil goes with vinegar in salad dressings. Sources of edible oil include corn, olives, peanuts, sesame, and sunflowers.

▶•◆•◆•◆•◀ OKRA ▶•◆•◆•◆•◀

THE VEGGIE

The pod vegetable is popular in Creole and Cajun cookery, where it is an ingredient of gumbo and jambalaya.

▶•◆•◆•◆•◀ OKS ▶•◆•◆•◆•◀

THE VERB

Commonly seen verb clues: "Authorizes," "Endorses," "Green-lights," and "Signs off on."

THE NOUN

Noun clues: "Agreements," "Approvals," and "Go-aheads."

▶·◆·◆·◆·◀ OLD ▶·◆·◆·◆·◀

THE ADJECTIVE
Commonly seen clues: "Ancient," "Antique," "Outdated," and "Stale."

▶·◆·◆·◆·◀ OLE ▶·◆·◆·◆·◀

THE CHEER
"*Olé*" is a Spanish shout of approval, frequently heard at a bullfight (a.k.a. a corrida).

THE MUSIC SHOW
Nashville's weekly *Grand Ole Opry*, which debuted in 1925, is America's oldest regularly scheduled radio program still airing.

▶·◆·◆·◆·◀ OLEO ▶·◆·◆·◆·◀

THE EDIBLE
Commonly seen clues include "Bread spread," "Butter alternative," "Margarine," and "Muffin topping."

OLEO is the only one of the 1,001 words profiled in this book that has essentially no contemporary usage beyond crosswords. It continues to proliferate in crosswords because of its convenient spelling.

▶·◆·◆·◆·◀ OLGA ▶·◆·◆·◆·◀

THE NAME
Most clues for OLGA refer to Russian gymnast Korbut, medal winner at the 1972 and 1976 Summer Olympics. Olga is also one of the title characters in the Anton Chekhov play *Three Sisters*, and a character in the Tchaikovsky opera *Eugene Onegin*. Actress Olga Kurylenko appeared in the James Bond movie *Quantum of Solace*.

▶•◆•◆•◆•◀ OLIVE ▶•◆•◆•◆•◀

THE FRUIT

Olives may be found in an antipasto or a Greek salad, and in martinis, sometimes with a pimiento inside. Named for the fruit is the color olive green.

THE TOON

The lanky Olive Oyl is the girlfriend of Popeye the Sailor.

▶•◆•◆•◆•◀ OMAHA ▶•◆•◆•◆•◀

IN THE U.S.

Omaha, on the Missouri River, is the largest city in Nebraska. The annual College World Series is played there, and Boys Town is nearby. Celebrities born there include actors Fred Astaire and Marlon Brando, and 1970s U.S. president Gerald Ford.

ACROSS THE SEA

Omaha Beach was the code name for one of the landing sites of the D-Day Normandy invasion during World War II.

▶•◆•◆•◆•◀ OMAN ▶•◆•◆•◆•◀

ON THE MAP

The Mideast nation of Oman is located on the Arabian peninsula, on the Arabian Sea, Persian Gulf, and the Gulf of Oman. Its capital is Muscat, and its neighbors are Saudi Arabia, the United Arab Emirates, and Yemen.

▶•◆•◆•◆•◀ OMAR ▶•◆•◆•◆•◀

THE NAME

There's World War II general Bradley, actor Epps, Persian poet Khayyám (a.k.a. "the Tentmaker," author of *The Rubáiyát*), actor Sharif, and baseball player Vizquel.

OMEGA

THE LETTER
Omega is the 24th and last letter of the Greek alphabet, immediately preceded by the letter psi.

THE BRAND
Omega is a brand of upscale watches, whose competitors include Rolex, Cartier, and Movado.

THE NUTRIENT
Omega-3 fatty acids are found in walnuts, flaxseed oil, and fish.

OMEN

THE NOUN
Commonly seen clues: "Augury," "Harbinger," "Portent," "Seer's sighting," and "Sign of the future."

OMIT

THE VERB
Commonly seen clues: "Exclude," "Leave out," "Pass over," and "Skip."

OMNI

THE PREFIX
Meaning "all," "omni-" can be added to words such as bus, potent, and present.

THE NAME
Omni Hotels is an upscale lodging chain. *Omni* was a science magazine, the Omni was an Atlanta sports arena, and the Dodge Omni automobile was manufactured from 1978 to 1990.

▶•◆•◆•◆•◀ ONAIR ▶•◆•◆•◆•◀

THE SIGN
"ON AIR" is seen outside radio and TV studios to indicate that they are currently broadcasting live.

THE IDIOM
"Walking on air" is synonymous with "elated" or "euphoric."

▶•◆•◆•◆•◀ ONCE ▶•◆•◆•◆•◀

THE ADVERB/NOUN
Commonly seen clues: "A single time," "Fairy tale starter" (as in "Once upon a time"), "Formerly," and "Years ago."

▶•◆•◆•◆•◀ ONE ▶•◆•◆•◆•◀

THE ADJECTIVE
Clock clues are variations of "Early afternoon time" and "Wee hour." Non-numerical clues include "Indivisible," "Like-minded," "Undivided," and "United." Numerical clues include "Bestseller's position," "Binary digit," "It's next to nothing," and "Low number."

THE MONEY
Commonly seen cash clues: "Buck," "Four quarters," "Single," and "Small bill."

THE PRONOUN
There's "A person," "Neuter pronoun," and "Nonspecific individual."

NOT SO FAST!

"Move smoothly": ___ L I D E

The answer can be SLIDE or GLIDE.

▶·◆·◆·◆·◀ ONEA ▶·◆·◆·◆·◀

THE RATING
1-A was the highest draft rating issued by the Selective Service System, indicating that a person was eligible for unrestricted military service.

THE BRAND
One A Day is a brand of vitamins.

▶·◆·◆·◆·◀ ONION ▶·◆·◆·◆·◀

THE EDIBLE
Common clues reference onions as a topping for burgers, pizza, and bagels, or as an ingredient in soups, omelets, and salsa. Varieties include the Vidalia and Bermuda. Its botanical relatives include garlic, scallions, and leeks.

THE NEWSPAPER
The Onion is a satirical online (and formerly print) newspaper that has published multiple books, including *Our Dumb Century* and *Our Dumb World*.

▶·◆·◆·◆·◀ ONO ▶·◆·◆·◆·◀

THE NAME
Yoko Ono, widow of ex-Beatle John Lennon, performed with him on the album *Double Fantasy*. The 1970s Plastic Ono Band consisted of Ono, Lennon, and other rock music notables. Lennon adopted Ono as his middle name.

▶·◆·◆·◆·◀ ONSET ▶·◆·◆·◆·◀

THE NOUN
Commonly seen clues: "Beginning," "Get-go," "Inception," "Square one," and "Start."

▸•◆•◆•◆•◂ ONT ▸•◆•◆•◆•◂

ON THE MAP

As an abbreviation for the Canadian province of Ontario, "Ont." can be clued by its neighboring states (Michigan, Minnesota, New York), neighbouring provinces (Manitoba and Quebec), and cities (such as Hamilton, Ottawa, Toronto, and Windsor).

▸•◆•◆•◆•◂ ONTO ▸•◆•◆•◆•◂

THE PREPOSITION

Commonly seen prepositional clues are variations of "Aware of" and "Not fooled by."

BLANKETY-BLANKS

Clued as two words, it may include a parenthetical synonym, as in "Catch ___ (figure out)" and "Hang ___ (retain)," or not, as in "Latch ___" and "Glom ___."

▸•◆•◆•◆•◂ ONUS ▸•◆•◆•◆•◂

THE NOUN

The three most frequent clues are "Burden," "Obligation," and "Responsibility."

▸•◆•◆•◆•◂ OOPS ▸•◆•◆•◆•◂

BY ACCIDENT

"Oops" is defined either descriptively (such as "Klutz's comment") or with rather synonymous cries (such as "Clumsy me!").

▸•◆•◆•◆•◂ OPAL ▸•◆•◆•◆•◂

THE GEM

The opal is a milky-white iridescent gemstone, the birthstone for October. Mexico is a source of the "fire opal," though most of the world's opals today come from Australia.

▶•◆•◆•◆•◀ **OPEC** ▶•◆•◆•◆•◀

THE OIL CARTEL

The members of the Vienna-based Organization of Petroleum Exporting Countries include Ecuador, Iraq, Qatar, and Venezuela.

▶•◆•◆•◆•◀ **OPEN** ▶•◆•◆•◆•◀

THE ADJECTIVE

Commonly seen adjective clues: "Amenable," "Candid," "Ready for business," and "Store sign."

THE VERB

Commonly seen verb clues: "Dentist's request," "Start the bidding," and "Unlock."

THE NOUN

An open is a type of tournament (such as in golf or tennis) in which professionals and amateurs may compete.

▶•◆•◆•◆•◀ **OPERA** ▶•◆•◆•◆•◀

IN MUSIC

You will usually see this defined either by well-known operas (such as *Carmen*, *Il Trovatore*, *La Bohème*, *La Traviata*, *The Magic Flute*, *Otello*, *Porgy and Bess*, and *Tosca*), operatic composers (such as Bizet, Mozart, Puccini, Verdi, and Wagner), or opera venues (such as the Met at New York City's Lincoln Center and Milan's La Scala).

▶•◆•◆•◆•◀ **OPT** ▶•◆•◆•◆•◀

THE VERB

Commonly seen clues include "Be decisive," "Get off the fence," and "Make a choice." To "opt for" is to choose, to "opt out" is to decline to participate.

▶·◆·◆·◆·◀ ORAL ▶·◆·◆·◆·◀

THE ADJECTIVE
Commonly seen adjective clues: "Spoken," "Verbal," and "Vocal." People and things that may be oral include history, hygiene, surgeons, thermometers, traditions, and vaccines.

THE NOUN
An oral (short for "oral examination") is often a requirement for a graduate school degree.

THE NAME
Tulsa's Oral Roberts University is named for the televangelist.

▶·◆·◆·◆·◀ ORATE ▶·◆·◆·◆·◀

THE VERB
Commonly seen clues: "Declaim," "Get on a soapbox," "Give a speech," "Make an address," and "Speak at length."

▶·◆·◆·◆·◀ ORB ▶·◆·◆·◆·◀

THE SHAPE
An orb can be a sphere, a globe, an eye, or a heavenly body. An orb atop a scepter is a symbol of royalty.

▶·◆·◆·◆·◀ ORCA ▶·◆·◆·◆·◀

THE MARINE MAMMAL
Also known as the killer whale, the black-and-white orca is the largest member of the dolphin family. The title character of the 1993 film *Free Willy* is an orca, and Shamu is the name used for many a performing orca at SeaWorld. In the film *Jaws*, *Orca* is the boat captained by Robert Shaw's character.

▶•◆•◆•◆•◀ ORE ▶•◆•◆•◆•◀

THE ROCK

Ores are metal-bearing rocks or minerals that are often mined. Commonly seen related clues include "Assay material," "Lode load," "Prospector's find," and "Refinery input." Types of ores include bauxite (aluminum), galena (lead), and hematite (iron).

THE ABBREVIATION

"Ore." is an abbreviation for Oregon, usually defined in this sense in terms of its neighbors (California, Idaho, Nevada, and Washington), cities (Eugene, Salem), or Mount Hood, its tallest peak.

▶•◆•◆•◆•◀ OREO ▶•◆•◆•◆•◀

THE MUNCHIE

About a half-trillion of Nabisco's cream-filled sandwich cookies have been sold since they were introduced in 1912. Double Stuf Oreos have more cream filling than the regulars. Oreos are often an ingredient in Cookies and Cream ice cream.

▶•◆•◆•◆•◀ ORION ▶•◆•◆•◆•◀

THE GUY IN THE SKY

Orion was a hunter in Greek mythology, placed by Zeus among the stars as the constellation of Orion. The best-known stars in Orion are Rigel and Betelgeuse. The group of three stars in a nearly straight line in the center of the constellation is known as Orion's Belt.

▶•◆•◆•◆•◀ ORO ▶•◆•◆•◆•◀

IN SPAIN

"*Oro*" is the Spanish word for "gold." *Oro y plata* ("gold and silver") is the state motto of Montana.

▶•◆•◆•◆•◀ ORS ▶•◆•◆•◆•◀

THE ABBREVIATION

Short for "operating rooms," clues will be variations on "Hosp. areas," "RN workplaces," "MD workplaces," and "Surgery sites, for short."

INSIDER'S TIP: All but the latter clue above can define ERS (short for "emergency rooms") as well as ORS. Both answers appear frequently in crosswords, so proceed with caution.

▶•◆•◆•◆•◀ ORSO ▶•◆•◆•◆•◀

NOT EXACTLY

Commonly seen clues for "or so": "About," "Approximately," "Roughly," and "Thereabouts."

▶•◆•◆•◆•◀ OSCAR ▶•◆•◆•◆•◀

THE PEOPLE

Famous Oscars include designer de la Renta, lyricist Hammerstein, pianist Levant, hot-dog merchant Mayer, pianist Peterson, basketball great Robertson, writer Wilde, and the grouchy *Sesame Street* muppet. Oscar Madison is the sloppy roommate of neatnik Felix Ungar in Neil Simon's *The Odd Couple* (Felix's last name in the TV series of the same name is "Unger").

THE TROPHY

The Academy Award statuette weighs 8½ pounds.

▶•◆•◆•◆•◀ OSHA ▶•◆•◆•◆•◀

THE ACRONYM

Short for the Occupational Safety and Health Administration, OSHA, an arm of the U.S. Department of Labor, regulates workplace health and safety.

▶•◈•◈•◈•◀ OSLO ▶•◈•◈•◈•◀

ON THE MAP

The Scandinavian city of Oslo (formerly known as Christiania) is the capital of Norway. The annual Nobel Peace Prize is awarded there, and the 1952 Winter Olympics were held there.

ON THE STAGE

Oslo by J.T. Rogers won the Tony Award for Best Play in 2017.

▶•◈•◈•◈•◀ OTIS ▶•◈•◈•◈•◀

THE NAME

Clues for Otis nearly always refer either to soul singer Otis Redding, elevator innovator Elisha Otis, the elevator company founded by Elisha, or the Cole Porter song "Miss Otis Regrets."

▶•◈•◈•◈•◀ OTTER ▶•◈•◈•◈•◀

IN THE WATER

Otters are web-footed aquatic mammals known for their playful behavior. Their relatives in the weasel family include the beaver, mink, and skunk.

▶•◈•◈•◈•◀ OTTO ▶•◈•◈•◈•◀

FICTIONAL

In the comic strip "Beetle Bailey," Otto is the pet bulldog of Sergeant Snorkel. The school bus driver in the animated sitcom *The Simpsons* is also named Otto.

REAL

Otto von Bismarck was a 19th-century German chancellor. Otto Klemperer was an orchestra conductor. Otto Preminger was a movie director.

▶•◆•◆•◆•◀ OUI ▶•◆•◆•◆•◀

IN PARIS

"*Oui*" is the French word for "yes." It is the opposite of "*non*," the French word for you-know-what.

▶•◆•◆•◆•◀ OUR ▶•◆•◆•◆•◀

THE PRONOUN

Commonly seen clues include "Not their," "Sharer's word," and "Your and my." "Our" is the first word of the Lord's Prayer. Titles with the word include the soap opera *Days of Our Lives*, the 1950s sitcom *Our Miss Brooks*, and the Thornton Wilder play *Our Town*. *Our Gang*, a.k.a. *The Little Rascals*, is the umbrella title of a series of short children's films of the 1930s, rerun endlessly on TV.

▶•◆•◆•◆•◀ OVAL ▶•◆•◆•◆•◀

THE SHAPE

The oval is usually defined by things of that shape, such as eggs, racetracks, cameos, faces, and the White House office. "Elliptical" and "Roundish shape" are more synonymous clues.

▶•◆•◆•◆•◀ OVEN ▶•◆•◆•◆•◀

THE HOT SPOT

There are microwave ovens, toaster ovens, Dutch ovens, and rotisserie ovens. Other types of ovens include the kiln (for pottery), oast (for hops or malt), and tandoor (in Indian cookery). Bakeries and pizzerias are the two types of establishments with ovens that are most often cited in clues.

CROSSWORDS 101
Lesson 10: Singers

Singers who often appear as crossword answers:

ADELE	**JONI** Mitchell
AIMEE Mann	**LANA** Del Rey
ALANIS Morissette	**LENA** Horne
Ed **AMES**	**LOU** Rawls or Reed
ANI DiFranco	**MEL** Tormé
ANITA Baker	**MIA**
Paul **ANKA**	**NEIL** Diamond or Sedaka
ARETHA Franklin	**NE-YO**
ARIANA (or **ARI**) Grande	**NICO**
India.**ARIE**	**NINA** Simone
ARLO Guthrie	**NORAH** Jones
BONO	Anita **O'DAY**
CHER	Yoko **ONO**
CLEO Laine	Rita **ORA**
DEMI Lovato	**OTIS** Redding
Celine **DION**	**PSY**
ELLA Fitzgerald	Carly **RAE** Jepsen
ELTON John	Bonnie **RAITT**
Brian **ENO**	**REBA** McEntire
ENYA	**SADE**
ETTA James or Jones	**SARA** Bareilles
Janis **IAN**	**SIA**
IDINA Menzel	**TONI** Braxton
Billy **IDOL**	**YMA** Sumac

... and **TORI AMOS** and **IRENE CARA**, each of whom have both first and last names that are crossword regulars.

▶•◆•◆•◆•◀ OVER ▶•◆•◆•◆•◀

THE PREPOSITION
Commonly seen prepositional clues: "Above," "Beyond," "More than," and "Throughout."

THE ADJECTIVE
Commonly seen adjective clues are variations of "Done" and "Ended."

THE INTERJECTION
"Over" is often used in radio communications to indicate that the speaker has finished and is waiting for a reply.

▶•◆•◆•◆•◀ OWE ▶•◆•◆•◆•◀

THE VERB
Commonly seen clues: "Be indebted to," "Be in the red," "Carry a balance," and "Have obligations."

▶•◆•◆•◆•◀ OWN ▶•◆•◆•◆•◀

THE VERB
"Own" is usually defined in the verbal sense, with clues like "Possess," "Hold," and "Have title to." In sports slang, it means to consistently dominate an opponent. To "own up" to something is to admit it. It's also part of the acronyms BYOB ("bring your own bottle") and MYOB ("mind your own business").

THE NETWORK
Shows aired on OWN, the Oprah Winfrey Network, include Ava DuVernay's *Queen Sugar* and Tyler Perry's *The Haves and the Have Nots*.

▶·◆·◆·◆·◀ **OXEN** ▶·◆·◆·◆·◀

THE BOVINES

Commonly seen clues: "Beasts of burden," "Farm animals," "Plow pullers," and "Yoked pair."

P

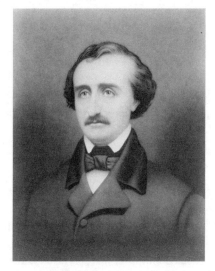

Portrait of Edgar Allan Poe, c. 1896,
by William Sartain

▶•◆•◆•◆•◀ **PAL** ▶•◆•◆•◆•◀

THE NOUN
Commonly seen clues: "Buddy," "Chum," "Crony," and "Sidekick."

▶•◆•◆•◆•◀ **PAN** ▶•◆•◆•◆•◀

THE COOKWARE
Skillets and woks are types of pans, often partnered with pots. Pizzas, desserts pies, and turkeys may be baked in pans.

IN THE PAPER
To "pan" a film is to give it a bad review. As a noun, it's the review itself.

THE NAME
Pan was the ancient Greek pipe-playing god of pastures and forests.

▶•◆•◆•◆•◀ **PAPA** ▶•◆•◆•◆•◀

THE PATRIARCH
Commonly seen generic clues are "Dad" and "Family man." Papa Bear was one of the three bears encountered by Goldilocks. "Papa" was the nickname of composer Joseph Haydn and author Ernest Hemingway. The song "Papa Loves Mambo" was popularized by Perry Como, "Papa Don't Preach" by Madonna.

▶•◆•◆•◆•◀ **PAR** ▶•◆•◆•◆•◀

ON THE COURSE
Par is the standard score for a hole, one lower than a bogey and one higher than a birdie. Par for an entire 18-hole golf course is usually around 72.

OFF THE COURSE
Commonly seen generic clues: "Average," "Norm," and "Standard."

226

▶•◆•◆•◆•◀ PASS ▶•◆•◆•◆•◀

THE VERB

As a verb, "pass" usually means "to go by" or "to complete successfully." In the former sense, there's "Skip over," "Disregard," and "Leave behind." In the latter, "Avoid an F" and "Make the grade." Bridge players pass when they don't want to make a bid.

THE NOUN

As a noun, a pass can be a free ticket, a throw made by a quarterback in football, or a route through a mountain range.

▶•◆•◆•◆•◀ PAT ▶•◆•◆•◆•◀

LOWERCASE

A pat may be a portion of butter or an encouraging touch. As an adjective/adverb, it can mean "exact" or "exactly."

UPPERCASE

Famous Pats include singer Benatar, TV commentator Buchanan, game show host Sajak, and 1970s first lady Nixon.

▶•◆•◆•◆•◀ PEA ▶•◆•◆•◆•◀

THE LEGUME

Peas are ingredients in stews, split-pea soup, and pot pies. Their color is "pea green." "The Princess and the Pea" is a fairy tale by Hans Christian Andersen.

▶•◆•◆•◆•◀ PEER ▶•◆•◆•◆•◀

THE NOUN

A peer may a social equal (as a member of a jury) or a British noble (such as earl or duke).

THE VERB

To "peer at" something is to look at it narrowly and/or searchingly.

227

▶•◆•◆•◆•◀ **PEN** ▶•◆•◆•◆•◀

FULL OF INK

You should know these manufacturers of pens: Bic, Cross, Mont Blanc, Paper Mate, and Parker. Clues like "Sword beater" refer to the old proverb "the pen is mightier than the sword." As a verb, to "pen" means to write or compose something.

FULL OF OINK

Other domesticated animals besides pigs may be kept in pens, such as horses and sheep.

IN THE CLINK

As a slang term for "prison," there's "Cooler," "Pokey," and "Slammer."

IN THE AIR

"Pen" is the term for a female swan. (The male is known as a "cob.")

▶•◆•◆•◆•◀ **PEP** ▶•◆•◆•◆•◀

THAT'S THE SPIRIT

Common clues include "Pizzazz," "Vivacity," "Liveliness," and "Vigor." To "pep up" is to animate.

▶•◆•◆•◆•◀ **PER** ▶•◆•◆•◆•◀

THE PREPOSITION

Commonly seen clues: "According to," "Apiece," "Each," and the slangy synonym "A pop." It is the "p" in the abbreviations mph (miles per hour) and rpm (revolutions per minute). In phrases from the Latin, "per capita" means "per person" and "per diem" means "per day."

▶·◆·◆·◆·◀ PERT ▶·◆·◆·◆·◀

THE ADJECTIVE

"Pert" is usually clued synonymously, as in "Impudent," "Smart-alecky," "Brash," and "Sassy."

IN YOUR HAIR

Pert is a brand of shampoo, whose competitors include Prell and Suave.

▶·◆·◆·◆·◀ PERU ▶·◆·◆·◆·◀

ON THE MAP

This South American nation is usually defined by one of its neighbors (Ecuador, Columbia, Brazil, Bolivia, and Chile), its capital (Lima), its mountain range (Andes), or the Inca Empire in its past.

NOT SO FAST!

"Flower part": ___ E ___ A L

The answer can be PETAL or SEPAL. (Sepals are the leafy parts on the outside of the flower.)

▶·◆·◆·◆·◀ PESO ▶·◆·◆·◆·◀

THE MONEY

The peso is the monetary unit of Argentina, Chile, Colombia, Cuba, the Dominican Republic, Mexico, the Philippines, and Uruguay. Crossword clues will often refer to cities in these countries, such as "Cancún cash."

►•◆•◆•◆•◄ PEST ►•◆•◆•◆•◄

THE NOUN

Commonly seen clues: "Annoyance," "Nudnik," "Nuisance," and "Pain in the neck."

►•◆•◆•◆•◄ PET ►•◆•◆•◆•◄

AROUND THE HOUSE

In this sense, PET may be clued either generically (such as "Furry friend" or "Household animal") or by example (such as "Parakeet or poodle").

THE ADJECTIVE

As an adjective, "pet" means "favorite," as in "pet peeve" and "pet project."

THE VERB

Synonym clues for the verb sense of "pet" include "Caress" and "Stroke."

►•◆•◆•◆•◄ PETE ►•◆•◆•◆•◄

THE NAME

Famous Petes include jazz clarinetist Fountain, Rose of baseball, tennis pro Sampras, folk singer Seeger, and the dog (a.k.a. Petey) in the *Little Rascals* (a.k.a. *Our Gang*) series of kids' short films.

►•◆•◆•◆•◄ PGA ►•◆•◆•◆•◄

ON THE COURSE

Short for the "Professional Golfers' Association," the PGA promotes the game of golf and sponsors several events with "PGA" in its name. The PGA Tour, the organization that runs professional tournaments, is a separate group.

▷•◆•◆•◆•◁ PIE ▷•◆•◆•◆•◁

IN YOUR MOUTH
In the edible sense, "pie" may be defined in terms of places they may be purchased (diners, bakeries, etc.) or their flavors (blueberry, coconut custard, etc.). There is, of course, also the pizza.

ON THE PAGE
A "pie chart" is often seen in print as a graphical representation of the components of a budget.

▷•◆•◆•◆•◁ PLEA ▷•◆•◆•◆•◁

THE NOUN
In court, a plea might be "guilty," "not guilty," "nolo contendere" (not contending the charge), or may be the result of plea bargaining. Generic clues include "Appeal," "Entreaty," and "Request."

▷•◆•◆•◆•◁ POE ▷•◆•◆•◆•◁

THE WRITER
You'll want to know these works written by Edgar Allan Poe: "Annabel Lee," "The Bells," "The Black Cat," "The Gold Bug," "The Purloined Letter," "The Raven," "The Tell-Tale Heart," and "Ulalume."

▷•◆•◆•◆•◁ POLO ▷•◆•◆•◆•◁

ON THE GROUND
The sport of polo is played on horseback, with mallets, in time periods called chukkers. Designer Ralph Lauren named one of his clothing lines after the sport.

ON YOUR SHOULDERS

The polo shirt (polo, for short), also named for the sport, is a short-sleeved pullover.

THE PEOPLE

Ancient Venetian explorer Marco Polo is remembered for his travels to China. There is also actress Teri Polo.

▶•◆•◆•◆•◀ PRO ▶•◆•◆•◆•◀

THE NOUN

As the short form of "professional," commonly seen clues include "Expert," "Golf teacher," "Money player," and "Veteran."

THE ADVERB

As a synonym for "in favor of," there's "Debate side," "Favoring," "For," and "Supporting."

▶•◆•◆•◆•◀ PSAT ▶•◆•◆•◆•◀

THE TEST

Previously short for the "Preliminary Scholastic Aptitude Test," the PSAT is taken by college-bound high school sophomores and juniors.

▶•◆•◆•◆•◀ PSI ▶•◆•◆•◆•◀

THE LETTER

Psi is the 23rd of 24 letters in the Greek alphabet, preceded by chi and followed by omega. Both an uppercase and lowercase psi resemble a trident or pitchfork.

THE ABBREVIATION

PSI can stand for "pounds per square inch," which is a measure of the pressure of things such as auto tires.

THE UNEXPLAINED

"Psi" is a term for any psychic phenomenon, such as ESP.

▶•◆•◆•◆•◀ **PSST** ▶•◆•◆•◆•◀

THE SOUND

Commonly seen clues are all variations of "Attention getter," "Hey, you!," and "Subtle signal."

▶•◆•◆•◆•◀ **PTA** ▶•◆•◆•◆•◀

THE ABBREVIATION

As a short form of parent-teacher association, commonly seen clues are usually variations of "Bake sale sponsor" and "Grade school org." "Harper Valley PTA" is a country music song of 1968.

R

French philosopher René Descartes;
engraving by W. Holl after a painting by Franz Hals

▶•◆•◆•◆•◀ RACE ▶•◆•◆•◆•◀

ON THE MOVE

As a verb, there are clues like "Hurry," "Zoom," and "Go quickly." As a noun, "Olympic event," "Speed contest," and "Sprint, for example."

▶•◆•◆•◆•◀ RAG ▶•◆•◆•◆•◀

THE NOUN

As a noun, a rag may be a dustcloth, a musical composition in ragtime (as popularized by composer Scott Joplin), or a disreputable newspaper.

THE VERB

As a verb, "rag" is synonymous with "scold" or "tease persistently."

NOT SO FAST!

"Fissure": R ___ ___ T

The answer can be RIFT or RENT.

▶•◆•◆•◆•◀ RAGE ▶•◆•◆•◆•◀

THE PASSION

As a noun, there's "Anger," "Frenzy," and "Fury." As a verb: "Blow up," "Fly off the handle," and "Go ballistic."

THE FASHION

A rage may also be something very popular or in fashion, often for just a short time.

236

▶·◆·◆·◆·◀ RAH ▶·◆·◆·◆·◀

THE EXCLAMATION
Commonly seen clues: "Cheer syllable," "Encouraging word,"
"Go, team!," and "Stadium shout."

▶·◆·◆·◆·◀ RAIL ▶·◆·◆·◆·◀

THE NOUN
A rail can be a part of a staircase or fence, a general term for train
transportation, or a marsh bird related to the crane.

THE VERB
As a verb, to "rail" is to complain bitterly.

▶·◆·◆·◆·◀ RAIN ▶·◆·◆·◆·◀

THE WEATHER
Commonly seen noun clues: "Desert rarity," "Drought relief,"
"Picnic spoiler," "Cause of a game delay," and "Wet forecast."
As a verb, there's "Come down," "Pour," "Precipitate," and
"Shower."

▶·◆·◆·◆·◀ RAISE ▶·◆·◆·◆·◀

THE NOUN
Commonly seen noun clues: "Poker ploy," "Salary increase,"
"Union demand," and "Worker's reward."

THE VERB
As a verb, there's "Boost," "Bring up," "Elevate," and "Lift." In the
sense of raising a child, there's "Rear."

▶·◆·◆·◆·◀ **RAM** ▶·◆·◆·◆·◀

THE BEAST

Generic clues that refer to the male sheep include "Ewe's mate," "Flock animal," and "Woolly male." The ram Aries is a spring sign of the zodiac. The Ram (formerly called the Dodge Ram), named for the beast, is a model of pickup truck. The Los Angeles Rams are an NFL team. The athletic teams of Fordham University are known as the Rams.

THE WEAPON

Noun clues in this sense: "Battering device" and "Door buster." As the related verb, there's "Bash," "Butt into," and "Hit broadside."

HIGH-TECH

RAM stands for "random access memory," an important part of computers.

▶·◆·◆·◆·◀ **RAN** ▶·◆·◆·◆·◀

THE VERB

In the speedy sense, there's "Jogged," "Raced," and "Took off." In the managerial sense, there's "Headed," "Managed," and "Operated." In the political sense, there's "Sought office" and "Was on the ticket."

THE MOVIE

You'll also sometimes see references to *Ran*, the Japanese adaptation of *King Lear* directed by Akira Kurosawa.

▶·◆·◆·◆·◀ **RANT** ▶·◆·◆·◆·◀

THE VERB

Commonly seen verb clues: "Carry on," "Go ballistic," and "Talk wildly."

THE NOUN

In the noun sense, there's "Angry speech," "Bluster," and "Tirade."

238

▶•◆•◆•◆•◀ RAP ▶•◆•◆•◆•◀

THE NOUN
The hip-hop music genre is often defined by its best-known performers, such as Eminem, Jay-Z, LL Cool J, Dr. Dre, Kanye West, Drake, Cardi B, and Kendrick Lamar. It is a category of the Grammy Awards. An older usage of "rap" is as a slang term for "punishment for a crime."

THE VERB
As a verb, "rap" can mean "to strike sharply," "to criticize," and, informally, "to converse."

▶•◆•◆•◆•◀ RAPT ▶•◆•◆•◆•◀

THE ADJECTIVE
"Rapt" is usually defined in its "engrossed" sense, with clues like "Entranced," "Spellbound," and "Fully attentive." It can also be synonymous with "ecstatic."

▶•◆•◆•◆•◀ RARE ▶•◆•◆•◆•◀

THE ADJECTIVE
In the "uncommon" sense, there's "Exceptional," "Hard to find," "Infrequent," and "Seldom seen." In the culinary sense, there's "Opposite of well-done," "Pink in the center," and "Steakhouse order."

NOT SO FAST!

"Less cooked": R A ___ E R

The answer can be either RAWER (food in general)
or RARER (steak in particular).

▶•◆•◆•◆•◀ RASH ▶•◆•◆•◆•◀

NOT SO FAST

As an adjective, you'll see clues like "Foolhardy," "Impulsive," and "Too hasty."

NOT SO NICE

As an allergic reaction, it's usually defined as a symptom of contact with poison ivy.

▶•◆•◆•◆•◀ RASP ▶•◆•◆•◆•◀

THE TOOL

A rasp is a coarse file that is used mainly on wood. The related verb means "scrape" or "grate."

THE SOUND

People who are hoarse speak with a rasp.

▶•◆•◆•◆•◀ RAT ▶•◆•◆•◆•◀

THE PERSON

Commonly seen "human" clues include "Snitch," "Scoundrel," "Tattletale," and "Turncoat." As a verb, there's "Spill the beans" and "Squeal."

THE BEAST

"Four-legged" clues include "Lab animal," "Mouse relative," and "Pied Piper follower." Remy from the Pixar film *Ratatouille* was a rat.

▶•◆•◆•◆•◀ RATE ▶•◆•◆•◆•◀

THE VERB

Commonly seen verb clues: "Appraise," "Assess," "Evaluate," "Have status," and "Size up."

THE NOUN
As a noun, there's "Bank posting," "Fixed charge," "Pace," and "Tempo."

▶•◆•◆•◆•◀ **RAVE** ▶•◆•◆•◆•◀

THE VERB
To rave is to speak angrily or enthusiastically.

THE NOUN
A rave may be an enthusiastic review, or, in slang, a large overnight dance party.

▶•◆•◆•◆•◀ **RAY** ▶•◆•◆•◆•◀

THE NAME
There's author Bradbury, actor Liotta, comedian Romano, boxer Sugar Ray Leonard, and singer Ray Charles, portrayed in the 2004 film *Ray* by Jamie Foxx.

OTHERWISE
A ray can also be a beam of light, a type of fish (such as the manta ray), or the arm of a starfish.

▶•◆•◆•◆•◀ **RBI** ▶•◆•◆•◆•◀

ON THE DIAMOND
In baseball, RBI is short for "run(s) batted in." Clues are variations on "Slugger's stat."

▶•◆•◆•◆•◀ **RCA** ▶•◆•◆•◆•◀

THE BRAND
The RCA brand of consumer electronics is often defined in terms of its competitors, which include Philips, Sharp, Sony, Toshiba, and Zenith. RCA's mascot is a dog named Nipper.

CROSSWORDS 101
Lesson 11: Roman Numerals

All the Roman numerals seen in crosswords are formed from these seven "basic" ones:

M = 1000; D = 500; C = 100; L = 50; X = 10; V = 5; I = 1

Form Roman numerals by following these rules:

1) Use the digits from left to right, and the list above as needed from largest to smallest. For example, 1551 = 1000 + 500 + 50 + 1, or **MDLI**.

2) I, X, **C** and **M** may be repeated up to three times consecutively. Thus, 2000 = MM, 30 = XXX, 75 = LXXV, and 323 = **CCC**XXIII.

3) Instead of using four of a particular symbol where needed, use:

IV = 4; IX = 9; XL = 40; XC = 90; CD = 400; CM = 900

In these cases, you can think of the first of the two numerals as a subtraction from the second (IV = V minus I).

▶·◆·◆·◆·◀ **REA** ▶·◆·◆·◆·◀

THE ACTOR

The films of Irish actor Stephen Rea include *The Crying Game*, *Michael Collins*, and *V for Vendetta*.

THE AGENCY

The New Deal–era Rural Electrification Administration was created in 1935 to provide electric power to rural areas.

▶·◆·◆·◆·◀ **READ** ▶·◆·◆·◆·◀

THE VERB

Commonly seen present-tense clues: "Interpret," "Leaf through," "Peruse," and "Pore over."

INSIDER'S TIP: Keep in mind that the past tense of "read" is also "read," though pronounced differently.

▶·◆·◆·◆·◀ **REAL** ▶·◆·◆·◆·◀

THE ADJECTIVE

Commonly seen clues: "Actual," "Authentic," "Bona fide," "Genuine," and "Sincere."

▶·◆·◆·◆·◀ **REAM** ▶·◆·◆·◆·◀

THE NOUN

A ream is 500-sheet package of paper.

THE VERB

As a verb, "ream" can mean "to enlarge a hole," "to reprimand," or "to cheat."

▶·◆·◆·◆·◀ REAP ▶·◆·◆·◆·◀

THE VERB

In the agricultural sense, there's "Bring in the sheaves," "Collect, as crops," "Harvest," and "Use a scythe." In the figurative sense, there's "Earn, as profits" and "Realize."

▶·◆·◆·◆·◀ REAR ▶·◆·◆·◆·◀

THE VERB

Commonly seen verb clues: "Bring up," "Elevate," and "Nurture."

THE NOUN

In a general sense, there's "Back" and "Tail end." In the "sitting" sense, there's "Caboose," "Posterior," "Rump," etc.

▶·◆·◆·◆·◀ REB ▶·◆·◆·◆·◀

AT WAR

A Reb (short for "Rebel") was a Confederate soldier during the Civil War, often under the command of General Robert E. Lee. Wearing a gray uniform, he was the adversary of a Yank.

▶·◆·◆·◆·◀ REBA ▶·◆·◆·◆·◀

THE NAME

Country singer Reba McEntire was the star of the sitcom *Reba*, which aired from 2001 to 2007.

▶·◆·◆·◆·◀ REC ▶·◆·◆·◆·◀

FOR SHORT

"Rec" may be short for "recreation," as in a "rec room" or "rec center." It may also be short for the verb "record," as these three letters are often seen on electronic devices that record (such as DVD players or DVRs), or on their accompanying remote controls.

▷•◆•◆•◆•◁ RED ▷•◆•◆•◆•◁

THE COLOR

Red things referred to in crossword clues include checkers, cherries, rubies, stop signs, traffic lights, and wines. Shades of red include carmine, crimson, and scarlet. Red is a sign of embarrassment or sunburn; red ink symbolizes a loss in business.

▷•◆•◆•◆•◁ REDO ▷•◆•◆•◆•◁

THE VERB

Commonly seen clues: "Decorate anew," "Fix up," "Make over," and "Overhaul."

▷•◆•◆•◆•◁ REED ▷•◆•◆•◆•◁

IN MUSIC

A reed is a part of various musical instruments, such as the clarinet, oboe, and saxophone, which are part of the "reed instrument" family.

THE PLANT

A reed is also the tall stalk of certain types of grass that typically grow in marshy areas.

▷•◆•◆•◆•◁ REEL ▷•◆•◆•◆•◁

THE NOUN

A reel may hold fishing line (accompanying a rod), or hold movie film in a projection booth. A reel is also a type of dance, specifically the country dance also known as the Virginia reel.

THE VERB

Commonly seen verb clues: "Stagger," "Walk unsteadily," and "Whirl."

▶•◆•◆•◆•◀ REESE ▶•◆•◆•◆•◀

THE NAME

There's singer/actress Della Reese, Baseball Hall of Famer Pee Wee Reese, and actress Reese Witherspoon, plus the candy maker of Reese's Pieces fame.

▶•◆•◆•◆•◀ REF ▶•◆•◆•◆•◀

IN SPORTS

Refs (short for "referees") are officials in boxing, football, hockey, and tennis. Football refs are called "zebras," for the black-and-white striped shirts they wear.

▶•◆•◆•◆•◀ REIN ▶•◆•◆•◆•◀

THE NOUN

Commonly seen noun clues: "Bridle attachment," "Harness part," "Horse stopper," and "Jockey's brake."

THE VERB

As a verb, there's "Check," "Hold back," and "Restrain."

▶•◆•◆•◆•◀ RELY ▶•◆•◆•◆•◀

THE VERB

Typical synonym clues: "Depend (on)," "Count (on)," and "Bank (on)."

▶•◆•◆•◆•◀ RENE ▶•◆•◆•◆•◀

THE NAME

There's philosopher René Descartes, tennis pro René Lacoste, artist René Magritte, actor René Auberjonois, and actress Rene Russo.

▶•◆•◆•◆•◀ RENEE ▶•◆•◆•◆•◀

THE NAME

The most frequently seen clues for "Renée" refer to actresses Zellweger and Taylor, soprano Fleming, and the 1966 song "Walk Away Renée" (by the Left Banke).

▶•◆•◆•◆•◀ RENO ▶•◆•◆•◆•◀

THE CITY

Reno, Nevada, located near Lake Tahoe on the Truckee River, is the seat of Washoe County. It's nicknamed "The Biggest Little City in the World" and is home to numerous gambling casinos.

THE NAME

Janet Reno served as Bill Clinton's attorney general, succeeding William Barr and preceding John Ashcroft.

▶•◆•◆•◆•◀ RENT ▶•◆•◆•◆•◀

FOR TENANTS

Commonly seen noun clues in this sense: "Apartment payment," "Budget expense," "Housing cost," and "Monopoly payment" (as in the board game). Verb clues: "Charter," "Lease," and "Pay for the use of."

THE OTHER VERB

"Rent" is also the past tense of "rend," meaning to split or tear.

THE SHOW

The Broadway show *Rent*, based on the opera *La Bohème*, won the Best Musical Tony Award in 1996.

▶•◆•◆•◆•◀ REP ▶•◆•◆•◆•◀

THE PEOPLE

As a short form of (a generic) "representative," there's "Account exec," "Agent, for short," and "Salesperson." Short for "representative" (as in a member of Congress), there's "D.C. VIP" and "One of 435." Short for "Republican," there's "Dem. rival" and "GOP member."

THE THINGS

Short for "reputation," there's "One's good name" and "Public image." Short for "repetition" (used especially in exercise), there's "Gym unit," "Iron-pumping unit," and "Workout unit."

▶•◆•◆•◆•◀ REPO ▶•◆•◆•◆•◀

FOR SHORT

Short for "repossession," "repo" is most often defined in terms of an auto being forfeited because of lack of repayment on a loan. The 1984 cult movie *Repo Man* stars Emilio Estevez and Harry Dean Stanton.

▶•◆•◆•◆•◀ RESET ▶•◆•◆•◆•◀

THE VERB

Commonly seen verb clues include "Adjust, as a clock," "Put back to zero," and references to various devices that have a reset button, such as bowling alley pinsetters, furnaces, pedometers, and stopwatches.

▶•◆•◆•◆•◀ REST ▶•◆•◆•◆•◀

THE BREAK

As a verb, there's "Kick back," "Relax," "Take five," and "Unwind." As a noun: "Breather" and "Time off." On a piece of music, a rest is a marking that indicates an interval of silence between notes.

LEGALLY SPEAKING

You may also see clues for REST such as "Conclude an argument, in court" or "I ___ my case."

WHAT'S LEFT

In this sense, there's "Balance" and "Remainder."

▶•◆•◆•◆•◀ REV ▶•◆•◆•◆•◀

FOR SHORT

"Rev" can be short for "revolution" (as of a car engine); in this sense the verb to "rev" or "rev up" means "to accelerate sharply." "Rev" is also an informal term for "reverend."

▶•◆•◆•◆•◀ RHO ▶•◆•◆•◆•◀

THE LETTER

Rho is the seventeenth letter of the Greek alphabet, coming after pi and before sigma.

▶•◆•◆•◆•◀ RIB ▶•◆•◆•◆•◀

ON YOUR PLATE

Beef and pork ribs are often barbecued or roasted.

IN YOUR BODY

The human bone is often clued as "Part of a cage" or "Chest protector."

ON YOUR CASE

"Rib" is an informal term for "tease."

▶·◆·◆·◆·◀ RICE ▶·◆·◆·◆·◀

THE CROP

The starchy cereal grain is found in sushi, paella, and jambalaya. As a side dish it is an alternative to pasta or potatoes. Rice is traditionally thrown at the couple after a wedding ceremony.

THE PEOPLE

Novelist Anne Rice is the creator of the vampire Lestat. Condoleezza Rice served as secretary of state for George W. Bush. Lyricist Tim Rice has collaborated with Elton John and Andrew Lloyd Webber.

▶·◆·◆·◆·◀ RID ▶·◆·◆·◆·◀

THE VERB

Commonly seen clues: "Clear (of)," "Disencumber," "Free (of)," and "Purge." Note that the past tense of "rid" is also "rid."

▶·◆·◆·◆·◀ RIDE ▶·◆·◆·◆·◀

ON THE MOVE

Any travel on something, be it a horse, vehicle, or Ferris wheel, can be a ride (as a noun or verb). From this sense is derived the informal term for "tease."

IN SPACE

Astronaut Sally Ride was the first American woman in space.

▶·◆·◆·◆·◀ RILE ▶·◆·◆·◆·◀

THE VERB

Commonly seen clues: "Agitate," "Rub the wrong way," "Tee off," "Tick off," and "Vex."

▸•◆•◆•◆◄ RIM ▸•◆•◆•◆◄

THE NOUN

A rim can be the outer edge of anything, from basketball hoops to cups to canyons to craters. Rims can also hold tire hubcaps.

▸•◆•◆•◆◄ RINSE ▸•◆•◆•◆◄

THE VERB

Besides the "remove suds from" and "wash lightly" meanings, one may be instructed by a dentist to "rinse" in the middle of a dental procedure.

THE NOUN

The noun sense of RINSE is usually defined either as a cycle of a washing machine or dishwasher, or a hair salon preparation used for dyeing.

▸•◆•◆•◆◄ RIO ▸•◆•◆•◆◄

IN SOUTH AMERICA

"*Río*" is the Spanish word for "river" (in Portuguese it has no accent). Rio de Janeiro is the former capital of Brazil. "Rio" for short, it's a popular cruise port and site of an annual Carnival festival just before Lent. Rio is the home of Sugar Loaf Mountain, as well as Copacabana and Ipanema beaches.

IN NORTH AMERICA

The Rio Grande forms the border between Texas and Mexico, and flows through New Mexico and Colorado.

IN THE MOVIES

Blame It on Rio is a Michael Caine film. *Rio Bravo* and *Rio Lobo* are John Wayne films. *Road to Rio* is a Bob Hope/Bing Crosby film, one of their famous "Road" movies. The 2011 animated film *Rio* follows the adventures of a macaw named Blu.

IN THE GARAGE

Rio is a model of Kia automobile.

▶•◆•◆•◆•◀ RIOT ▶•◆•◆•◆•◀

THE NOUN

In the "disorder" sense, there's "Mob scene," "Public disturbance," and "Uproar." In the humorous sense, there's "Barrel of laughs," "Hilarious one," and "Knee-slapper."

THE VERB

Commonly seen verb clues are similar to "Go hog-wild" and "Run amok."

NOT SO FAST!

"Something funny": ___ ___ O T

The answer can be RIOT or HOOT.

▶•◆•◆•◆•◀ RIP ▶•◆•◆•◆•◀

THE VERB

"Rip" can mean "to tear," "to criticize," "to move quickly," or "to copy, as data from a CD to a computer."

THE PEOPLE

There's actor Rip Torn and fictional snoozer Rip Van Winkle.

THE INSCRIPTION

On a gravestone, "RIP" means "rest in peace," which conveniently has the same initials as the original Latin phrase that RIP is an abbreviation of, "*requiescat in pace.*"

▶•◆•◆•◆•◀ RIPE ▶•◆•◆•◆•◀

THE ADJECTIVE

Commonly seen clues: "Mature," "Pickable," and "Ready for harvest."

▶•◆•◆•◆•◀ RISE ▶•◆•◆•◆•◀

THE VERB

Commonly seen verb clues: "Ascend," "Get out of bed," "Go up," and "Stand." Clues also often reference the command "All rise," spoken when a judge enters a courtroom. "Rise" might also be referred to as part of the phrase "rise up," as in "Rebel, with 'up.'"

THE NOUN

As a noun, there's "Ascent," "Slope," and "Upswing." In the sense used in "get a rise out of," there's "Angry reaction."

▶•◆•◆•◆•◀ RITE ▶•◆•◆•◆•◀

THE NOUN

A rite is a solemn ceremony, often of a religious nature. Rites mentioned in crossword clues: baptism, bar mitzvah, communion, confirmation, and marriage.

▶•◆•◆•◆•◀ RNS ▶•◆•◆•◆•◀

THE ABBREVIATION

As a short form for "registered nurses," there's "ER workers," "Hosp. employees," "ICU staffers," and "IV monitors."

INSIDER'S TIP: Keep in mind that many of the clues for RNS are also used to clue MDS.

▶•◆•◆•◆•◀ ROAR ▶•◆•◆•◆•◀

FOR CRYING OUT LOUD

As a noun or verb, a roar can come from a lion, a crowd, or by one person in reaction to a funny joke.

FOR SINGING OUT LOUD

"Roar" was a #1 hit single for Katy Perry in 2013.

▶·◆·◆·◆·◀ ROB ▶·◆·◆·◆·◀

THE VERB

Commonly seen verb clues: "Hold up," "Rip off," "Steal from," and "Stick up."

THE NAME

The best-known Robs are actor Lowe, director Reiner, and Scottish folk hero Rob Roy.

▶·◆·◆·◆·◀ ROD ▶·◆·◆·◆·◀

THE NOUN

Things with rods include curtains, fishing gear, rotisseries, nuclear reactors, and the rods (groups of rodlike cells) in the retina of the eye.

THE NAME

There's tennis pro Laver, sci-fi writer and TV host Serling, and singer Stewart.

▶·◆·◆·◆·◀ ROE ▶·◆·◆·◆·◀

IN THE SEA

Roe are fish eggs, certain types of which are used for caviar.

IN THE WOODS

A roe is also a type of small deer.

IN THE COURT

The names Richard Roe and Jane Roe are often used for anonymous parties in court proceedings, such as in the landmark Supreme Court decision *Roe v. Wade*.

▶•◆•◆•◆•◀ ROLE ▶•◆•◆•◆•◀

THE NOUN

Commonly seen generic clues include "Auditioner's goal," "Casting slot," "Function," and "Part to play." You'll also see references to numerous specific roles in well-known works, and roles played by specific well-known performers.

▶•◆•◆•◆•◀ ROLL ▶•◆•◆•◆•◀

THE NOUN

"Roll" is clued most often as a noun, either as an edible (as in bread or sushi), a roster, a dice throw, a drum sound, or a package of coins.

THE VERB

As a verb, you're likely to see clues such as "Get moving" or "Toss the dice."

▶•◆•◆•◆•◀ RON ▶•◆•◆•◆•◀

THE NAME

There's Tarzan portrayer Ely, director Howard, presidential son Reagan, politican Ron Paul (father of Rand Paul), and Ron Weasley, friend of Harry Potter in the J.K. Rowling novels.

▶•◆•◆•◆•◀ ROO ▶•◆•◆•◆•◀

UP IN THE AIR

Short for "kangaroo," "roo" may refer to any kangaroo (with generic clues such as "Aussie hopper" or "Critter with a pouch") or, from the Winnie-the Pooh stories of A.A. Milne, the character Roo, whose mother is Kanga and whose oft-mentioned other friends include Piglet, Tigger, and Eeyore.

CROSSWORDS 101
Lesson 12: The Greek Alphabet

It will be very useful for you to know all 24 letters in the Greek alphabet, in order. Not only do most of these appear frequently in crosswords, but the letters that precede and follow them are often used as clues, such as "Sigma preceder" for RHO. The shortest answers in standard crosswords are 3 letters, so the 2-letter ones appear only as plurals.

alpha	nu
beta	xi
gamma	omicron
delta	pi
epsilon	rho
zeta	sigma
eta	tau
theta	upsilon
iota	phi
kappa	chi
lambda	psi
mu	omega

▷•◈•◈•◈•◁ **ROOT** ▷•◈•◈•◈•◁

THE NOUN

As a noun, a root may be the underlying part of a plant, tooth, or hair, or the underlying cause of something.

THE VERB

As a verb, "root" is usually clued as its "encourage a team" meaning.

ROPE

THE NOUN

Typical clues include "Lariat," "Lasso," and "Rodeo gear." A rope is also one of the weapons in the whodunit board game Clue. Alfred Hitchcock's 1948 film *Rope* is notable for having been edited to appear as if it were filmed in one continuous take.

ROSE

THE FLOWER

There's "American Beauty, for example," "Thorny bloom," and "Valentine's Day gift." Roses are handed out at the end of an episode of *The Bachelor*. The British royal houses of Lancaster and York are symbolized by red and white roses, respectively; they vied for control of the throne in the Wars of the Roses.

THE DRINK

Rosé is a variety of pink wine.

THE VERB

As the past tense of "rise," there's "Ascended" and "Got up."

THE NAME

Rose Kennedy was the mother of JFK, Betty White portrayed Rose Nylund on the sitcom *The Golden Girls*, and Pete Rose is a retired baseball player. Actress Rose Byrne appeared on the television show *Damages*, and Rose Marie played Sally Rogers on *The Dick Van Dyke Show*. Rose and Jack were the ill-fated lovers in *Titanic*, played by Kate Winslet and Leonardo DiCaprio.

▶•◆•◆•◆•◀ ROT ▶•◆•◆•◆•◀

THE VERB
Commonly seen verb clues: "Deteriorate," "Go bad," and "Spoil."

THE NOUN
Any synonym for "nonsense" may be seen in this sense, such as "Baloney," "Claptrap," "Hogwash," and "Malarkey."

▶•◆•◆•◆•◀ ROTE ▶•◆•◆•◆•◀

THE NOUN
Commonly seen clues: "Dull routine," "Learning method," and "Repetitive process."

▶•◆•◆•◆•◀ RTE ▶•◆•◆•◆•◀

THE ABBREVIATION
As a short form of "route," there's "AAA suggestion," "GPS creation," "Hwy.," and "Numbered rd."

▶•◆•◆•◆•◀ RUE ▶•◆•◆•◆•◀

THE VERB
You'll see clues like "Be sorry about," "Regret," and "Wish undone."

IN PARIS
"*Rue*" is the French word for "street."

ON TELEVISION
Actress Rue McClanahan was a regular on *Maude*, but is best known for playing Blanche Devereaux on *The Golden Girls*.

►•◆•◆•◆•◄ **RYE** ►•◆•◆•◆•◄

WHAT TO EAT

Rye is a delicatessen sandwich bread, an alternative to white or pumpernickel. It is an essential ingredient of a Reuben sandwich (with corned beef, Swiss cheese, and sauerkraut).

WHAT TO DRINK

Rye is also a type of whiskey, an essential ingredient of a Manhattan cocktail (with vermouth) and a highball (with club soda or ginger ale).

S

Sloe berries on a blackthorn hedge

▶•◈•◈•◈•◀ **SAD** ▶•◈•◈•◈•◀

THE ADJECTIVE

Commonly seen clues: "Downcast," "Feeling blue," "Melancholy," "Unfortunate," and "Woebegone."

▶•◈•◈•◈•◀ **SAFE** ▶•◈•◈•◈•◀

THE NOUN

When referring to the noun, crossword clues are most likely to mention either banks or hotels.

THE ADJECTIVE

For the adjective sense, you're likely to see clues like "Out of danger," "Trustworthy," and "Not harmful."

THE YELL

"Safe!" may be shouted by a baseball umpire, ruling on a close play on the basepaths.

▶•◈•◈•◈•◀ **SAG** ▶•◈•◈•◈•◀

THE VERB

Common clues include "Droop," "Yield to gravity," and "Lose energy."

THE NOUN

Once in a while "sag" will be defined as an instance of sagging, as in "Mattress problem."

THE UNION

Clues for SAG will sometimes refer to the Screen Actors Guild, though it is now part of SAG-AFTRA (as of their merger in 2012). The yearly awards are still called the Screen Actors Guild Awards, or SAG Awards for short.

▶·◆·◆·◆·◆·◀ SAGA ▶·◆·◆·◆·◆·◀

DO TELL

Originally a medieval Icelandic or Norse historical tale, a saga today is any grand or heroic story.

▶·◆·◆·◆·◆·◀ SAGE ▶·◆·◆·◆·◆·◀

THE PERSON

Commonly seen noun clues in this sense: "Philosopher," "Pundit," and "Wise one." As an adjective, there's "Learned," "Prudent," and "Wise."

THE HERB

Sage is used in turkey stuffing, sausages, and meat marinades.

▶·◆·◆·◆·◆·◀ SAL ▶·◆·◆·◆·◆·◀

THE NAME

In real life, there's baseball players Bando and Maglie, and actor Mineo. Sal Paradise is the narrator of Jack Kerouac's novel *On the Road*. Sal is the pizzeria owner portrayed by Danny Aiello in the Spike Lee film *Do the Right Thing*. And there are two relevant old songs: "My Gal Sal" (for obvious reasons) and "Fifteen Miles on the Erie Canal" (which features a mule named Sal).

▶·◆·◆·◆·◆·◀ SALAD ▶·◆·◆·◆·◆·◀

ON YOUR PLATE

The course of greens is often "tossed" and eaten by the health-conscious, served in restaurants as an alternative to soup. There are Caesar salads, Waldorf salads, Cobb salads, chef's salads, and potato salads.

▶•◆•◆•◆•◀ SALE ▶•◆•◆•◆•◀

THE NOUN

Commonly seen clues: "Ad headline," "Auction, for example," "Shopper's incentive," and "Store event."

▶•◆•◆•◆•◀ SALT ▶•◆•◆•◆•◀

THE SEASONING

Table salt is known to chemists as sodium chloride, NaCl symbolically. It may top a bagel or pretzel, garnish a margarita, or be used to cure meat. In larger crystals, salt is used to deice winter roads.

THE PERSON

Informally, a salt (or, often, "old salt") is an experienced sailor.

THE VERB

To salt something away is to save it up.

▶•◆•◆•◆•◀ SAM ▶•◆•◆•◆•◀

REAL

Noted Sams include TV journalist Donaldson, statesman Houston, playwright Shepard, golfer Snead, retail mogul Walton, director Mendes, and actors Neill, Elliott, and Waterston.

FICTIONAL

There's the piano player in the film *Casablanca*, Tolkien character Sam Gamgee from *The Lord of the Rings*, fictional sleuth Sam Spade, Warner Bros. toon Yosemite Sam, and red-white-and-blue Uncle Sam.

▶•◆•◆•◆•◀ SAME ▶•◆•◆•◆•◀

THE ADJECTIVE

Commonly seen clues: "Ditto," "Identical," "Just the ___," and "Unchanged."

▶•◆•◆•◆•◀ SAN ▶•◆•◆•◆•◀

ON THE MAP

Most of the relevant place names are in California: San Clemente, San Diego, San Francisco, San Jose, San Mateo, and the San Andreas fault. The most notable exceptions: San Antonio, Texas; San Juan, Puerto Rico; and San Remo, Italy.

IN TOKYO

"*San*" is a Japanese term of respect, added as a suffix after a person's name or title.

▶•◆•◆•◆•◀ SANE ▶•◆•◆•◆•◀

THE ADJECTIVE

Commonly seen clues: "Levelheaded," "Lucid," "Rational," and "Sensible." Since mental health is a taboo subject for many crossword editors, you generally won't see clues like "Not batty."

NOT SO FAST!

"Clean thoroughly": **S C ___ U ___**

The answer can be SCOUR as well as the nearly synonymous SCRUB.

▶•◆•◆•◆•◀ SAO ▶•◆•◆•◆•◀

ON THE MAP

This Portuguese word for "saint" is clued most of the time by Brazil's largest city of São Paulo. There's also São Tomé and Príncipe (an island nation off the west coast of Africa), and São Miguel, the largest island of the Azores in the eastern Atlantic.

▶•◆•◆•◆•◀ SAP ▶•◆•◆•◆•◀

THE PERSON
Commonly seen clues in this sense: "Chump," "Dupe," "Easy mark," and "Patsy."

THE FLUID
From trees, there's "Maple product" and "Syrup source."

THE VERB
Commonly seen verb clues: "Drain," "Undermine," and "Weaken."

▶•◆•◆•◆•◀ SARA ▶•◆•◆•◆•◀

THE NAME
Famous Saras include Delano (mother of president Franklin Roosevelt), actress Gilbert, novelist Paretsky, poet Teasdale, and the Sara Lee brand of frozen foods.

▶•◆•◆•◆•◀ SARI ▶•◆•◆•◆•◀

WHAT TO WEAR
The sari is the traditional garment worn by Hindu women, especially in India. It is a long piece of fabric that is wrapped around the body.

▶•◆•◆•◆•◀ SAS ▶•◆•◆•◆•◀

IN THE AIR
Originally short for "Scandinavian Airlines System," SAS is the national airline of Sweden, Norway, and Denmark. Not surprisingly, its principal destinations include Stockholm, Oslo, and Copenhagen. Its competitors include Finnair and KLM.

▶•◆•◆•◆•◀ **SASE** ▶•◆•◆•◆•◀

THE ABBREVIATION
SASE is short for "self-addressed stamped envelope," often enclosed with a letter for the postpaid return of a manuscript (abbreviated "MS.") to an editor.

▶•◆•◆•◆•◀ **SASH** ▶•◆•◆•◆•◀

WHAT TO WEAR
A sash is a decorative band, belt, or scarf. Sashes are worn by Scouts, beauty pageant contestants, and military band marchers. The sash on a Japanese kimono is called an "obi."

WHAT NOT TO WEAR
A sash is the framework of a door or window, into which panes of glass are set.

▶•◆•◆•◆•◀ **SASS** ▶•◆•◆•◆•◀

THE NOUN/VERB
Commonly seen noun clues: "Back talk," "Guff," and "Lip." As a verb, there's "Disrespect," "Get fresh with," and "Talk back to."

▶•◆•◆•◆•◀ **SAT** ▶•◆•◆•◆•◀

THE VERB
Commonly seen verb clues: "Convened," "Formed a lap," "Posed for a photo," "Rested," and "Took a chair."

THE ABBREVIATIONS, CURRENT AND FORMER
"Sat." is short for Saturday. The SAT is the test taken by high-school seniors as a requirement for admission to college; it was once an abbreviation for "Scholastic Aptitude Test" (and, later, "Scholastic Assessment Test"), but since 1997 it has simply been SAT.

▶•◆•◆•◆•◀ **SATE** ▶•◆•◆•◆•◀

THE VERB

To "sate" is to satisfy something fully, as one's appetite. It can also mean to fill to excess. Commonly seen clues in these senses include "Glut," "Gorge," "Overfill," and "Stuff."

▶•◆•◆•◆•◀ **SAW** ▶•◆•◆•◆•◀

THE NOUN

As a noun, a saw may be a wood-cutting tool or a wise old saying.

THE VERB

As the past tense of "see," common clues include "Noticed," "Glimpsed," "Understood," and "Went out with."

▶•◆•◆•◆•◀ **SCAM** ▶•◆•◆•◆•◀

THE NOUN/VERB

Commonly seen noun clues: "Con game," "Fraud," and "Ripoff." As a verb, there's "Fleece" and "Hoodwink." Clues that work as both a noun and a verb: "Con," "Flimflam," "Hustle," and "Swindle."

▶•◆•◆•◆•◀ **SCAN** ▶•◆•◆•◆•◀

THE VERB

As a verb, "scan" has two opposite meanings: to examine hastily, or to examine with great care. It can also mean to read electronically (as a bar code at a checkout counter, or during a medical test such as a CAT scan), or to digitize (as a document converted by a scanner to a PDF).

►•◆•◆•◆•◄ SCAR ►•◆•◆•◆•◄

THE MARK

Commonly seen noun clues: "Duel mark," "Fight memento," and "Lasting impression." As a verb, there's "Mark permanently" and "Traumatize." Fictional wizard Harry Potter has a forehead scar in the shape of a lightning bolt.

THE NAME

Scar is the villainous lion in the Disney animated film *The Lion King*.

►•◆•◆•◆•◄ SCENE ►•◆•◆•◆•◄

THE NOUN

A scene may be the place where something happens, an excerpt of a film or play, or an embarrassing emotional episode.

►•◆•◆•◆•◄ SCI ►•◆•◆•◆•◄

THE ABBREVIATION

Short for "science," "sci." may be clued by any science, abbreviated or not, such as biology, chemistry, and anatomy. You may also see "___ -fi."

►•◆•◆•◆•◄ SEA ►•◆•◆•◆•◄

LITERALLY

The world's seas include the Adriatic, Aegean, Baltic, Bering, Black, Caribbean, Caspian, and Red. The sea was the domain of the Greek god Poseidon and his Roman equivalent, Neptune. There are also generic clues such as "Cruise locale" and "Ocean."

FIGURATIVELY

"Sea" can also mean a large quantity of anything.

269

►•◆•◆•◆•◄ SEAL ►•◆•◆•◆•◄

THE NOUN AND VERB

A seal can be an aquatic mammal, an official stamp of authenticity, the device used to make such a stamp, or (in all caps) a commando in the U.S. Navy SEALs. It can also be a tight closure; as a verb, it means to make such a closure.

►•◆•◆•◆•◄ SEAT ►•◆•◆•◆•◄

THE NOUN

In addition to a place to sit, a seat can be an elected office (such as a Senate seat), a government center (such as a county seat), or a membership in a stock exchange.

►•◆•◆•◆•◄ SEC ►•◆•◆•◆•◄

FOR SHORT

As a shortened form of "second," clues include "Brief moment" and "Short time." SEC is also an abbreviation for the Securities and Exchange Commission, a U.S. Government agency that regulates stock markets.

FOR DRINKING

In the wine industry, "sec" means "dry," as in "not sweet." Triple sec is an orange-flavored liqueur.

►•◆•◆•◆•◄ SECT ►•◆•◆•◆•◄

THE GROUP

Though the dictionary tells us that a sect can be any group of people united by a specific doctrine, in crosswords it's almost always defined as a religious group, often a faction or offshoot of a larger one.

▶·◆·◈·◆·◀ SEE ▶·◆·◈·◆·◀

THE VERB

In the visual sense, there's "Look at," "Notice," "Observe," and "Spot." In the "comprehend" sense, there's "Catch on," "Get the point," and "Understand." In the social sense, there's "Date," "Drop in on," "Go out with," and "Visit." In the card game poker, to "see" a bet is to match the bet just made.

THE QUESTION

Colloquial phrases that clue the one-word sentence "See?" are similar to "Get it?" and "Didn't I tell you?"

THE NOUN

A see is the jurisdiction of a bishop, a.k.a. "diocese."

▶·◆·◈·◆·◀ SEED ▶·◆·◈·◆·◀

THE NOUN

Plants and trees have seeds, and tennis tournaments have seeds (player rankings). Edible seeds include caraway, nutmeg, sesame, and sunflower. A seed may also be the beginning or source of anything, such as an idea.

THE VERB

"To seed" may mean to plant seeds, or to provide the initial capital for a startup business.

▶·◆·◈·◆·◀ SEEP ▶·◆·◈·◆·◀

THE VERB

Commonly seen clues: "Flow slowly," "Ooze," "Percolate," and "Trickle."

►·◆·◆·◆·◄ SEER ►·◆·◆·◆·◄

THE PERSON

Commonly seen clues: "Clairvoyant," "Crystal ball user," "Fortune teller," "Soothsayer," and "Visionary."

►·◆·◆·◆·◄ SELL ►·◆·◆·◆·◄

THE VERB

Commonly seen clues: "Auction off," "Deal in," "Peddle," and "Unload." In Wall Street lingo, a bear is a pessimistic investor who is likely to place a sell order with a broker.

►·◆·◆·◆·◄ SEMI ►·◆·◆·◆·◄

THE NOUN

A "semi," short for "semitrailer," is a detachable trailer for hauling freight, to which a tractor is attached. Commonly seen clues in this sense: "18-wheeler," "Big rig," "Highway hauler," and "Teamster vehicle." It is also short for "semifinal," the next-to-last round of a tournament.

THE PREFIX

"Semi-" (meaning "half") can be placed in front of many words, such as circle, conductor, precious, and private.

►·◆·◆·◆·◄ SEN ►·◆·◆·◆·◄

THE ABBREVIATION

As a short form for "senator," there's "Capitol Hill VIP," "One of a D.C. 100," or any well-known senator's surname, followed by "for one: Abbr."

▶·◆·◆·◆·◀ SENSE ▶·◆·◆·◆·◀

THE NOUN

Thinking "smart," there's "Brains," "Good judgment," and "Logical thinking." As used throughout this book, "sense" is also the meaning of a word in context. And don't forget the five senses (hearing, sight, smell, taste, and touch).

THE VERB

Commonly seen verb clues: "Detect," "Have a feeling," "Perceive," and "Pick up on."

▶·◆·◆·◆·◀ SENT ▶·◆·◆·◆·◀

THE VERB

Commonly seen clues in the literal sense: "Dispatched," "Mailed," "Shipped out," and "Transmitted." In a slangy sense, there's "Delighted," "Elated," and "Thrilled." Change any of these to the present tense, and you'll have the usual clues for "send," which appears in crosswords somewhat less often than "sent."

▶·◆·◆·◆·◀ SERA ▶·◆·◆·◆·◀

THE NOUN

As the plural of "serum," commonly seen clues include "Antitoxins," "Blood fluids," and "Vaccines."

IN SPAIN

"*Será*" with an accent on the "a" is Spanish for "will be," although the accent was left out of the title of the 1956 Doris Day tune "Que Sera, Sera."

IN ROME

"*Sera*" is the Italian word for "evening," as in the greeting "*Buona sera*" ("Good evening").

273

▶·◆·◆·◆·◀ SET ▶·◆·◆·◆·◀

THE NOUN

A set can be a collection of anything, a part of a tennis match, the location where a movie shoot takes place, or the arrangement of hair as styled in a salon.

THE VERB

Commonly seen verb clues: "Arrange," "Determine," "Establish," "Harden," and "Prepare." The past tense of all these clues are often seen also, since the past tense of "set" is "set."

THE ADJECTIVE

"All in place," "Prepared," and "Ready" clue the adjective sense of "set."

▶·◆·◆·◆·◀ SETH ▶·◆·◆·◆·◀

THE GUYS

First of all, Seth was the third son of Adam and Eve, brother of Cain and Abel. There's also clockmaker Thomas, actor Rogen, actor/filmmaker MacFarlane, and TV host Meyers.

NOT SO FAST!

"Piece of leather": **S T R ___ P**

The answer can be STRAP or STROP.

▶·◆·◆·◆·◀ SEW ▶·◆·◆·◆·◀

THE VERB

Commonly seen clues: "Baste," "Do darning," "Use a needle," and "Work as a tailor." Colloquially speaking, to "sew up" is to finalize, complete, or control exclusively.

▸•◂•▸•◂•▸◂ **SGT** ▸•◂•▸•◂•▸◂

THE ABBREVIATION

"Sgt." is short for "sergeant," a noncommissioned officer (NCO for short) in the U.S. Army, Marines, and Air Force; in the Army and Marines, it's one step up from a corporal (cpl.). It's also a rank in a police department (P.D.). Sergeants often mentioned in clues: Snorkel (from the "Beetle Bailey" comic strip), Friday (from the *Dragnet* TV series), Pepper (from the Beatles album), and York (hero from World War I).

▸•◂•▸•◂•▸◂ **SHE** ▸•◂•▸•◂•▸◂

THE PRONOUN

Women, ships, and half of the currently named hurricanes are called "she." And there's the "she" who "sells seashells by the seashore" in an old tongue twister.

BLANKETY-BLANKS

She Stoops to Conquer is a play by Oliver Goldsmith, and then there are the songs "She Bop" (Cyndi Lauper), "And She Was" (Talking Heads), "She Loves You" (the Beatles), "She Bangs" (Ricky Martin), and the Tin Pan Alley standard "Ain't She Sweet." Relevant colloquial phrases include "That's all she wrote," "That's what she said!," and the nautical "Steady as she goes" and "Thar she blows!"

▸•◂•▸•◂•▸◂ **SHED** ▸•◂•▸•◂•▸◂

THE NOUN

A shed is a storage building, often used to store firewood, tools, or farm machinery. A "lean-to" is a type of shed.

THE VERB

"Shed" can mean "to lose feathers or fur," or, clued figuratively, "Discard," "Cast off," and "Abandon."

▶·◆·◆·◆·◀ SHOE ▶·◆·◆·◆·◀

ON YOUR FEET

Types of shoes seen in crosswords include sneakers, loafers, moccasins, wingtips, and oxfords. A "cobbler" is a repairer of shoes.

FIGURATIVELY SPEAKING

Named for its resemblance to a shoe, it's also the box in a casino that holds the cards for dealing blackjack. It's also a rigid plate of a vehicle brake that produces the braking action.

▶·◆·◆·◆·◀ SHOO ▶·◆·◆·◆·◀

THE SHOUT

Similar shouts seen in clues include "Scram!," "Scat!," "Get lost!," and "Beat it!"

INSIDER'S TIP: SHOO and SCAT are synonymous, though SHOO appears in crosswords more often.

▶·◆·◆·◆·◀ SHY ▶·◆·◆·◆·◀

THE ADJECTIVE

In the usual sense, synonym clues include "Timid," "Bashful," and "Skittish." It can also mean "deficient," especially of cash.

▶·◆·◆·◆·◀ SILO ▶·◆·◆·◆·◀

ON THE FARM

A silo is an often-cylindrical structure on a farm in which grain is stored.

ON THE BASE

A silo is also a military structure in which a ballistic missile (such a Minuteman or Titan) is stored.

CROSSWORDS 101
Lesson 13: OPEC Members

OPEC, founded in 1960, is often clued by its member countries, which currently include the following. (The years they joined are also indicated.)

Algeria (1969)
Angola (2007)
Ecuador (1973-92, rejoined 2007)
Equatorial Guinea (2017)
Gabon (1975-1995, rejoined 2016)
Iran (1960)
Iraq (1960)
Kuwait (1960)
Libya (1962)
Nigeria (1971)
Qatar (1961)
Republic of the Congo (2018)
Saudi Arabia (1960)
United Arab Emirates (UAE for short; 1967)
Venezuela (1960)

▷•◆•◆•◆•◁ SIN ▷•◆•◆•◆•◁

THE NOUN AND VERB

Commonly seen noun clues: "Trangression," "Moral wrong," and "Sermon subject." Also often seen in clues are one or more of the seven deadly sins: pride, covetousness, lust, envy, gluttony, anger, and sloth. As the related verb, there's "Do wrong" and "Transgress."

►·◆·◆·◆·◄ **SIP** ►·◆·◆·◆·◄

THE NOUN AND VERB

Either way, SIP involves ingesting a small sample of a liquid.

NOT SO FAST!

"Small drink": ___ I P

The answer can be SIP or NIP.

►·◆·◆·◆·◄ **SIR** ►·◆·◆·◆·◄

HERE

Commonly seen "domestic" clues are "Military address" and "Polite title."

IN ENGLAND

"Sir" is the title given to a British man who has been knighted by the reigning monarch. Any well-known knighted Brit of past or present may be seen in a clue, such as actor Michael Caine, statesman Winston Churchill, singer Elton John, and scientist Isaac Newton.

►·◆·◆·◆·◄ **SIRE** ►·◆·◆·◆·◄

TO A FARMER

A sire is the male parent of any four-legged animal, but most often clued in terms of horses. Synonyms of the verb form include "Beget" and "Father."

TO A ROYAL

"Sire" is a respectful term of address to a king or emperor.

▸•◆•◆•◆•◂ **SIS** ▸•◆•◆•◆•◂

THE RELATIVE

As a short form of "sister," commonly seen clues include "Bro's close relative," "Certain sibling," and "Family nickname."

THE EXCLAMATION

"Sis boom bah" is a cheer at high-school and college sports events.

NOT SO FAST!

"Family member, for short": S I ___

The answer can be SIB or SIS.

▸•◆•◆•◆•◂ **SITE** ▸•◆•◆•◆•◂

THIS IS THE PLACE

A site is the location where something takes place, often clued specifically in terms of building construction or internet surfing.

▸•◆•◆•◆•◂ **SKI** ▸•◆•◆•◆•◂

THE VERB

Commonly seen verb clues: "Hit the slopes," "Schuss," "Slalom," "Travel on snow," and references to ski resorts (such as Aspen, Stowe, and Vail). The word is infrequently defined as the sporting-equipment noun.

▸•◆•◆•◆•◂ **SLAM** ▸•◆•◆•◆•◂

THE DOOR

In the "door" sense, there's "Close loudly" and "Shut forcefully."

279

THE DIS

In the sense of "criticize," there's "Castigate," "Criticize," and "Lambaste." "Slam" may also be a noun in this sense, meaning "criticism."

IN BRIDGE

A slam is an achievement for a player in the card game.

 **SLAP**

THE NOUN AND VERB

Literally, it's an open-handed blow (such as a "high-five"), or to deliver one. Figuratively, it's an unkind comment.

NOT SO FAST!

"Put-down": **S L A ___**

The answer can be SLAM or SLAP.

SLAT

THE NOUN

A slat is a narrow strip of wood or metal. Slats can be found in beds, benches, and Venetian blinds.

SLED

THE GLIDER

Sleds are pulled by dogs in Alaska, in the annual Iditarod race in particular. A sled named Rosebud is a key prop in the film *Citizen Kane*. Luges and toboggans are types of sleds used in the Winter Olympics.

▶•◆•◆•◆•◀ SLEET ▶•◆•◆•◆•◀

DOWN TO EARTH
Sleet is frozen rain, and, as a verb, the falling of same.

▶•◆•◆•◆•◀ SLEW ▶•◆•◆•◆•◀

THE NOUN
As a large quantity of anything, clues include "Whole bunch," "Multitude," and "Abundance."

THE VERB
As the past tense of "slay," clues are most likely to refer to the figurative sense (as in "overwhelming with jokes"), or the "doing in" of a dragon.

BLANKETY-BLANK
Thoroughbred racehorse Seattle Slew won the Triple Crown in 1977.

▶•◆•◆•◆•◀ SLO ▶•◆•◆•◆•◀

TAKING IT EASY
The letters "SLO" are often seen on road pavement, as a warning for drivers to slow down. There's also the slo-mo (slow motion) replay on sports telecasts, and slo-pitch softball.

▶•◆•◆•◆•◀ SLOE ▶•◆•◆•◆•◀

THE FRUIT
The sloe is the plumlike fruit of the blackthorn tree. The liqueur sloe gin is flavored with it.

▶•◀•◀•◀•◀ **SLOT** ▶•◀•◀•◀•◀ .

THE NOUN
Things with slots include parking meters, piggy banks, and vending machines. Figuratively, a slot can be a place in a schedule or a job opening.

NOT SO FAST!

"Thin opening": **S L ___ T**

The answer can be SLOT or SLIT.

▶•◀•◀•◀•◀ **SLY** ▶•◀•◀•◀•◀

THE ADJECTIVE
Commonly seen clues: "Crafty," "Cunning," "Foxy," "Shrewd," "Sneaky," and "Wily."

THE PEOPLE
Sly Stone was the bandleader of Sly and the Family Stone, and Sylvester Stallone's nickname is Sly.

▶•◀•◀•◀•◀ **SMEE** ▶•◀•◀•◀•◀

THE NAME
Smee is the villainous pirate associate of Captain Hook in J.M. Barrie's *Peter Pan*.

▶•◀•◀•◀•◀ **SMOG** ▶•◀•◀•◀•◀

OVER YOUR HEAD
Commonly seen clues: "Air pollution," "Urban woe," and "EPA concern."

282

▶·◆·◆·◆·◀ SNAG ▶·◆·◆·◆·◀

THE NOUN

Commonly seen clues: "Catch," "Complication," "Fly in the ointment," "Glitch," "Impediment," and "Hose woe." "Snag" is also a verb, but it's rarely clued that way in crosswords.

▶·◆·◆·◆·◀ SNAP ▶·◆·◆·◆·◀

THE NOUN

In the "simple" sense, there's "Breeze," "Cinch," and "Something easy." A snap can also be a clothes fastener, a ginger cookie, a photograph, the action taken by the center at the start of a football play, and one of the three sounds (snap, crackle, and pop) made by Rice Krispies cereal.

THE VERB

Commonly seen verb clues: "Break sharply," "Go ballistic," "Lose it," and "Flip out."

▶·◆·◆·◆·◀ SNARE ▶·◆·◆·◆·◀

THE VERB

As a verb, there's "Entrap," "Entangle," and "Defraud."

THE NOUN

As a noun, a snare can be something that traps, or one of the tightly stretched strings on a snare drum (or the drum itself).

▶·◆·◆·◆·◀ SNEER ▶·◆·◆·◆·◀

THE LOOK

As a noun, there's "Scornful expression," "Sinister smile," and "Villainous glance." As a verb: "Curl the lip," "Scoff," and "Show disdain."

283

▶·◆·◆·◆·◀ **SNIP** ▶·◆·◆·◆·◀

THE VERB/NOUN

Commonly seen "action" clues: "Quick cut," "Salon sound," and "Use scissors." A snip is also an insignificant or impertinent person.

▶·◆·◆·◆·◀ **SNIT** ▶·◆·◆·◆·◀

THE NOUN

Commonly seen clues: "Agitated state," "Huff," "Peeved mood," and "Tizzy."

▶·◆·◆·◆·◀ **SNL** ▶·◆·◆·◆·◀

ON TV

Short for *Saturday Night Live*, SNL has been an NBC weekend staple since 1975. Its recurring sketches are often cited, including "Weekend Update," "Celebrity Jeopardy!," the Coneheads, Mr. Bill, and the Blues Brothers.

▶·◆·◆·◆·◀ **SNO** ▶·◆·◆·◆·◀

FOR SHORT

As a short form of "snow," there are the edible sno-cones, Sno-Caps, and Sno Balls, as well as the Sno-Cat winter vehicle.

▶·◆·◆·◆·◀ **SNOB** ▶·◆·◆·◆·◀

THE NOUN

Typical clues: "Stuffed shirt," "Snooty one," and "Stuck-up person."

▶•◆•◆•◆•◀ SNOW ▶•◆•◆•◆•◀

DOWN TO EARTH

As a noun or verb, "snow" might be clued with references to flurries, blizzards, shoveling, or skiing. More trickily, it might also be the material in a bank, fort, ball, or blanket.

FIGURATIVELY

In an informal sense, "snow" is synonymous with "deceive."

▶•◆•◆•◆•◀ SOAP ▶•◆•◆•◆•◀

IN THE WASH

In addition to the noun and verb "clean up" meaning, clues often reference brands of soap, such as Dove and Dial.

ON THE AIR

Short for "soap opera," afternoon TV programs of this genre were once much more plentiful than they are today. Soaps often seen in crosswords include *All My Children* and *General Hospital*.

▶•◆•◆•◆•◀ SOAR ▶•◆•◆•◆•◀

IN THE AIR

Commonly seen clues: "Fly high," "Take wing," and "Reach new heights."

▶•◆•◆•◆•◀ SOD ▶•◆•◆•◆•◀

IN THE GROUND

In the noun or verb sense, "sod" refers to the pregrown grass that landscapers install as a lawn.

▶•◆•◆•◆•◀ SODA ▶•◆•◆•◆•◀

THE DRINK

Commonly seen clues: "Carbonated beverage," "Fizzy drink," "Pop," and "Scotch partner."

▶•◆•◆•◆•◀ SOFA ▶•◆•◆•◆•◀

BE SEATED

As placed in a living room, types of sofas include love seats, settees, davenports, and chesterfields.

▶•◆•◆•◆•◀ SOL ▶•◆•◆•◆•◀

IN THE SKY

Sol is the astronomer's name for our sun.

IN THE SCALE

Sol (a.k.a. "so") is the fifth note of the musical scale, after fa and before la.

IN SPANISH

"*Sol*" is the Spanish word for "sun." The Costa del Sol ("sun coast") is a resort region of Spain on the Mediterranean. Peru's primary currency is the sol.

▶•◆•◆•◆•◀ SOLE ▶•◆•◆•◆•◀

THE ADJECTIVE

Commonly seen adjective clues: "Exclusive," "Only," and "Unique."

THE NOUN

As a noun, a sole may be a food fish or the bottom of a shoe.

▶•◆•◆•◆•◀ SOLO ▶•◆•◆•◆•◀

HELPLESS
Commonly seen adverb clues: "By oneself," "Stag," and "Unaccompanied." As a noun, "Pilot's test" and "Recital piece." As a verb, "Fly alone" and "Perform an aria."

HEROIC
Harrison Ford originated the part of Han Solo in the *Star Wars* films. Alden Ehrenreich played the role in 2018's prequel *Solo*.

HANDY
Solo is also a brand of drinking cup.

NOT SO FAST!

"Aria, for one": **S O __ __**

The answer can be SOLO or SONG.

▶•◆•◆•◆•◀ SOME ▶•◆•◆•◆•◀

THE ADJECTIVE
As an adjective, there's "A few," "Unspecified number," and "A handful of."

THE PRONOUN
As a pronoun, "some" means "some people."

THE ADVERB
"Some" can also mean "approximately," as in "Some 25,000 were in the stands."

ALL IN THE FAMILY

Commonly seen clues: "Heir, often," "Junior," "One of the Trinity," and "Young fellow." Also popular are references to well-known father-son pairs, such as Abel and Adam, Bob Cratchit and Tiny Tim, Kirk and Michael Douglas, and Homer and Bart Simpson.

▶•◆•◆•◆•◆◀ **SORE** ▶•◆•◆•◆•◆◀

THE ADJECTIVE

In the "angry" sense, there's "Miffed," "Peeved," "Steamed," and "Ticked off." In the "discomfort" sense, there's "Achy," "Painful," and "Tender."

▶•◆•◆•◆•◆◀ **SORT** ▶•◆•◆•◆•◆◀

THE VERB

As a verb, there's "Alphabetize," "Put in order," and "Do postal work."

THE NOUN

As a noun: "Type," "Variety," and "Kind."

▶•◆•◆•◆•◆◀ **SOS** ▶•◆•◆•◆•◆◀

AT SEA

As a maritime distress signal in Morse code, commonly seen clues include "Call for help," "Coast Guard alert," "Mayday!," and "Sea plea."

AT THE SUPERMARKET

S.O.S (correctly spelled without a period at the end) is a brand of steel-wool soap pads, whose best-known competitor is Brillo.

▶•◆•◆•◆•◀ SOSO ▶•◆•◆•◆•◀

NOT BAD

Commonly seen clues for "so-so": "Fair," "Just OK," "Mediocre," and "Passable."

▶•◆•◆•◆•◀ SPA ▶•◆•◆•◆•◀

THE NOUN

A spa may be a mineral spring, a health resort with a spring, a fitness center, or a hot tub.

▶•◆•◆•◆•◀ SPAM ▶•◆•◆•◆•◀

EAT IT OR NOT

Originally a Hormel brand of luncheon meat (short for "spiced ham"), SPAM is almost always clued these days in the "unwanted email" sense.

▶•◆•◆•◆•◀ SPAN ▶•◆•◆•◆•◀

THE NOUN/VERB

As a noun, there's "Bridge length," "Duration," "Period of time," and "Wing measurement." Commonly seen verb clues are variations of "Extend over" and "Reach across."

▶•◆•◆•◆•◀ SPAR ▶•◆•◆•◆•◀

IN A FIGHT

Commonly seen clues in this sense: "Exchange words," "Practice punching," "Train for a bout," and "Wrangle."

ON A SHIP

A spar is also a nautical pole that is used as a mast or boom to hold sails or handle cargo.

▶•◆•◆•◆•◀ **SPAT** ▶•◆•◆•◆•◀

CROSS WORDS

Commonly seen clues: "Disagreement," "Minor quarrel," "Petty argument," and "Tiff."

> ### NOT SO FAST!
>
> "Quarrel": **S P A** ___
>
> The answer can be SPAR or SPAT.

▶•◆•◆•◆•◀ **SPED** ▶•◆•◆•◆•◀

THE VERB

Commonly seen clues: "Exceeded the limit," "Rushed," "Stepped on it," and "Zoomed."

▶•◆•◆•◆•◀ **SPOT** ▶•◆•◆•◆•◀

THE VERB

Commonly seen verb clues: "Catch sight of," "Detect," and "Notice."

THE NOUN

A spot can be the location of something, a place to park, or a predicament. In the sense of a stain or mark, it might be clued as a problem for a dry cleaner or for Lady Macbeth.

THE NAME

Spot is a traditional name for a pet dog. The line "See Spot run," from the famous reading primer featuring Dick and Jane, is sometimes cited.

▶•◆•◆•◆•◀ SPY ▶•◆•◆•◆•◀

THE PERSON
In addition to generic clues like "Secret agent," you may see spies of fact and fiction such as Mata Hari, James Bond (007), and Austin Powers.

THE VERB
As a verb, "spy" can mean "observe secretly" or just "observe."

▶•◆•◆•◆•◀ SRA ▶•◆•◆•◆•◀

THE TITLE
"*Sra.*" is the abbreviation for "*señora*," the Spanish word for "Mrs." The equivalent abbreviation in French (also seen in crosswords, though less often) is "*Mme.*," short for "Madame."

▶•◆•◆•◆•◀ SRI ▶•◆•◆•◆•◀

THE TITLE
"Sri" is a respectful title of address in India, equivalent to "Mr."

ON THE MAP
The island nation of Sri Lanka (formerly called Ceylon) is located in the Indian Ocean, southeast of India.

▶•◆•◆•◆•◀ SRO ▶•◆•◆•◆•◀

THE ABBREVIATION
SRO is short for "standing room only," once regularly seen posted at theater box offices when all seats for that day's performance had been sold. Less commonly, SRO also stands for "single-room occupancy," a kind of low-income housing.

▶•◆•◆•◆•◄ **SRS** ▶•◆•◆•◆•◄

THE ABBREVIATION

"Srs." is short for "seniors." In crosswords, the seniors referred to are usually in school, with clues like "Grads-to-be: Abbr.," "SAT takers: Abbr.," and "Yearbook gp." Sometimes the reference is to senior citizens, with clues like "AARP members: Abbr."

▶•◆•◆•◆•◄ **SSE** ▶•◆•◆•◆•◄

THE ABBREVIATION

SSE stands for the direction of south-southeast, which is the point opposite north-northwest (NNW) on a compass. You'll often see city clues like "Dallas-to-Houston dir.," where the second city is located south-southeast of the first. SSE and all the other compass points can be seen in weather reports (referring to wind direction) and on the screens of GPS devices.

▶•◆•◆•◆•◄ **SSN** ▶•◆•◆•◆•◄

THE ABBREVIATION

Clues for one's nine-digit SSN (short for "Social Security number") usually have "ID" somewhere, with a reference to the IRS or its Form 1040, a bank account, or a job application.

▶•◆•◆•◆•◄ **SSS** ▶•◆•◆•◆•◄

THE ABBREVIATION

SSS stands for "Selective Service System," the federal agency that was once responsible for administering the military draft.

THE SOUND

"Sss" can also be clued as the sound of a tire leak, a radiator, a snake, or a barbecue.

▶•◆•◆•◆•◀ SST ▶•◆•◆•◆•◀

THE ABBREVIATION
SST stands for "supersonic transport," the class of passenger airplanes (no longer active) that flew faster than the speed of sound (a.k.a. Mach 1). Only two SSTs saw passenger service: the Concorde (flown by Air France and British Airways between Europe and the United States) and the USSR's Tupolev Tu-144.

▶•◆•◆•◆•◀ STAB ▶•◆•◆•◆•◀

THE NOUN
Noun clues are usually in the figurative sense, such as "Attempt," "Try," and "Wild guess."

THE VERB
Verb clues are always in the literal sense, such as "Pierce," "Puncture," and "Skewer."

▶•◆•◆•◆•◀ STAG ▶•◆•◆•◆•◀

THE PARTY
A stag is a party attended by men only. By extension, it can also mean a male who attends a party unaccompanied by a woman.

THE BEAST
A stag is also a male deer, the mate of a doe.

▶•◆•◆•◆•◀ STAN ▶•◆•◆•◆•◀

THE NAME
Famous Stans include satirist Freberg, jazz saxophonist Getz, film comedian Laurel (partner of Oliver Hardy), comic-book character creator Lee, baseball great Musial, and one of the juvenile characters in the animated sitcom *South Park*.

GEOGRAPHICALLY SPEAKING
The suffix "-stan" ends the names of seven countries, all in Asia.

▶•◆•◆•◆•◀ **STAR** ▶•◆•◆•◆•◀

IN PERFORMANCE
As a noun, there's "Celebrity," "Headliner," and "Top banana." As a verb, "Get top billing," "Head the cast," and "Take the lead."

THE SHAPE
Things shaped like a star include a sheriff's badge, an asterisk, the symbol on the flag of Texas, and the stars awarded by film reviewers.

IN THE SKY
Commonly seen astronomical clues: "Constellation component," "Milky Way part," or references to well-known stars such as Antares, Polaris, and Rigel.

▶•◆•◆•◆•◀ **STAT** ▶•◆•◆•◆•◀

THE NUMBER
As a short form of "statistic," clues may refer to statistics in baseball (such as RBIs and HRs), football (such as TDs), or economics (such as GNP).

THE ORDER
"Stat," when spoken by a physician, means "immediately," sort of the medical equivalent of "ASAP" or "PDQ."

▶•◆•◆•◆•◀ **STAY** ▶•◆•◆•◆•◀

DON'T GO
Commonly seen verb clues: "Command to a canine," "Hang around," and "Remain." Clues for the related noun: "Hotel visit," "Legal delay," and "Postponement."

THE SUPPORT
A stay is a flat strip used for stiffening shirt collars and corsets.

▶·●·◆·●·◆·◀ **STE** ▶·●·◆·●·◆·●·◀

THE ABBREVIATION
"Ste." is the short form of "*sainte*," the French word for a female saint, Joan of Arc (*Jeanne d'Arc* in French) being the most notable. It is usually clued geographically, most often by the Michigan city of Sault Ste. Marie.

▶·●·◆·●·◆·◀ **STEAM** ▶·●·◆·●·◆·◀

THE NOUN
Typical clues may mention kettles, irons, radiators, saunas, or geysers, as well as the source of power for old-time engines or locomotives.

THE VERB
As a verb, "steam" can mean "to cook with steam" or "to make angry."

▶·●·◆·●·◆·◀ **STEER** ▶·●·◆·●·◆·●·◀

ON THE ROAD
Commonly seen clues in this sense: "Direct," "Navigate," and "Take the wheel."

ON THE RANCH
A steer is a type of bull that is raised for beef.

▶·●·◆·●·◆·◀ **STEM** ▶·●·◆·●·◆·◀

THE NOUN
Things with stems include flowers, mushrooms, pipes, wineglasses, and wristwatches.

THE VERB
As a verb, "stem" can mean to stop or to dam up.

▶◆◆◆◆ STENO ▶◆◆◆◆

ON THE JOB
A steno, short for "stenographer," takes dictation in shorthand, or takes down the proceedings in a courtroom.

▶◆◆◆◆ STEP ▶◆◆◆◆

THE NOUN
Commonly seen literal noun clues: "Dance move" and "Footfall." More figuratively, there's "Ladder rung," "Part of a plan," and "Short distance"

THE VERB
Commonly seen verb clues: "Stride" and "Walk."

▶◆◆◆◆ STERN ▶◆◆◆◆

THE ADJECTIVE
Adjective clues include "Harsh," "Uncompromising," and "Hard-nosed."

THE NOUN
As a noun, it's the rear part of a ship.

THE PEOPLE
Howard Stern is a radio talk-show host. Isaac Stern was an eminent violinist.

▶◆◆◆◆ STET ▶◆◆◆◆

ON A MANUSCRIPT
The word "stet" is written on a manuscript by an editor or proofreader, to indicate that certain text previously marked for deletion should be retained. It is the opposite of the editorial term "dele."

▶•◆•◆•◆•◀ STEW ▶•◆•◆•◆•◀

THE NOUN

Commonly seen culinary clues: "Crockpot creation," "Meat-and-potatoes dish," and references to particular types of stews, such as bouillabaisse, goulash, and hasenpfeffer.

THE VERB

Verb clues are usually in the figurative sense, such as "Fret," "Fume," and "Worry."

▶•◆•◆•◆•◀ STIR ▶•◆•◆•◆•◀

THE VERB

Commonly seen culinary clues: "Agitate," "Mix," and "Recipe direction." In the sense of "start to wake up," there's "Begin to awaken" and "Move slightly."

THE NOUN

As a synonym for "commotion," there's "Ado," "Fuss," "Hubbub," and "Tumult." As a slang term for a prison, there's "Hoosegow," "Poky," and "Slammer."

▶•◆•◆•◆•◀ STL ▶•◆•◆•◆•◀

ON THE MAP

This abbreviation for Saint Louis is usually defined using either Missouri (Mo.) or the National League (N.L.) Central Division Cardinals (or the logo on their caps).

▶•◆•◆•◆•◀ STONE ▶•◆•◆•◆•◀

THE NOUN

A stone can be a rock (large or small), a precious gem, a fruit pit, or a British unit of weight equal to 14 pounds.

THE PEOPLE

There are actresses Emma and Sharon, and director Oliver (of such films as *JFK*, *Platoon*, and *Wall Street*).

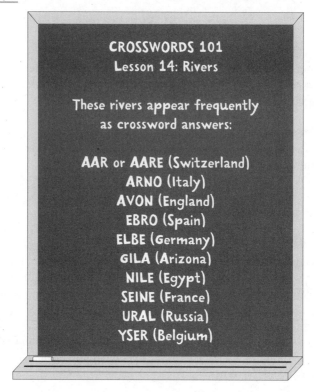

CROSSWORDS 101
Lesson 14: Rivers

These rivers appear frequently
as crossword answers:

AAR or **AARE** (Switzerland)
ARNO (Italy)
AVON (England)
EBRO (Spain)
ELBE (Germany)
GILA (Arizona)
NILE (Egypt)
SEINE (France)
URAL (Russia)
YSER (Belgium)

▶·◆·◆·◆·◀ **STOP** ▶·◆·◆·◆·◀

THE VERB

Commonly seen synonym clues: "Cease," "Discontinue," "Halt,"
and "Quit." In the imperative, there's "Cut that out!" and "Enough!"

THE NOUN

Buses and trains have stops, telegrams use STOP to end a sentence
instead of a periods, and a church organ's stops are the devices that
admit air to its pipes.

▶·◆·◆·◆·◀ **STOW** ▶·◆·◆·◆·◀

THE VERB

Typical clues: "Stash away" and "Put in storage," often mentioning
the overhead storage bin of a passenger plane.

▶·◆·◆·◆·◀ STP ▶·◆·◆·◆·◀

THE BRAND NAME

Originally short for "Scientifically Treated Petroleum," STP is a brand of auto products, particularly fuel and oil additives. STP is a longtime sponsor of auto races and auto racers. Its longtime slogan is "The Racer's Edge."

▶·◆·◆·◆·◀ STS ▶·◆·◆·◆·◀

THE ABBREVIATION

As a short form of "streets," there's "Ave. crossers," "GPS readings," and "Urban rds." As a short form of "saints," you'll see well-known saints given as examples, such as Peter, Paul, and Mary.

▶·◆·◆·◆·◀ STU ▶·◆·◆·◆·◀

THE NAME

Real people named Stu include actor Erwin and original Beatle Sutcliffe. There is also Disco Stu on the animated sitcom *The Simpsons*.

ALPHABETICALLY SPEAKING

Referring to the three consecutive letters, there's "Alphabetic trio" and "R-V connection."

▶·◆·◆·◆·◀ STY ▶·◆·◆·◆·◀

THE MESS

"On the farm" clues include "Hog's home," "Pigpen," and "Place for a trough." Figuratively, a sty is any filthy place. While the word can also mean a type of eye irritation, it's not clued that way very often in crosswords (that definition is generally reserved for the spelling STYE, which can only mean the eye irritation).

▶•◆•◆•◆•◀ **SUE** ▶•◆•◆•◆•◀

THE VERB

Commonly seen verb clues: "Attorney's advice," "Seek damages from," and "Take to court."

THE NAME

The best-known Sue is mystery author Grafton. In song titles, there's "A Boy Named Sue" (Johnny Cash), "Peggy Sue" (Buddy Holly), and "Runaround Sue" (Dion).

T

Czarina Alexandra of Russia wearing a tiara, c. 1910–15

▶•◆•◆•◆•◀ TAB ▶•◆•◆•◆•◀

THE NOUN

In the "amount owed" sense, there's "Bar bill" and "Check." Tabs are also the projections on file folders, while pull tabs are used to open soda cans, and don't forget about the Tab key on computer keyboards.

THE SODA

Tab was Coca-Cola's first diet soda (but not the first diet soda ever; that was Diet Rite). It's still around, though not as ubiquitous as it once was.

NOT SO FAST!

"Coke product": **T A ___**

The answer can be TAB (the diet soft drink made by Coca-Cola), or TAR (which can be made from coke, the solid obtained by distilling coal).

▶•◆•◆•◆•◀ TACO ▶•◆•◆•◆•◀

ON YOUR PLATE

In Tex-Mex cuisine, a taco is a fried tortilla that is folded over and filled with ingredients such as chopped beef, lettuce, tomatoes, and cheese.

▶•◆•◆•◆•◀ TAD ▶•◆•◆•◆•◀

THE NOUN

Commonly seen clues: "Little bit," "Smidgen," and "Tiny amount."

THE NAME

Thomas "Tad" Lincoln was the youngest son of Abraham Lincoln.

▶•◆•◆•◆•◀ TADA ▶•◆•◆•◆•◀

THE EXCLAMATION
"Ta-da!" is an informal shout of triumph, often clued by other such shouts, such as "Look what I did!" and "And here it is!"

▶•◆•◆•◆•◀ TAG ▶•◆•◆•◆•◀

THE NOUN AND VERB
Tag can be a kids' game, a luggage or pet ID, a merchandise attachment indicating its price, or a touch made by an infielder to a base runner in baseball.

▶•◆•◆•◆•◀ TAI ▶•◆•◆•◆•◀

BLANKETY-BLANKS
A mai tai is a type of rum cocktail. Tai chi is a Chinese martial art.

THE NAME
Tai Babilonia is an American former figure skater, the partner of Randy Gardner.

▶•◆•◆•◆•◀ TALC ▶•◆•◆•◆•◀

THE NOUN
Talc is a soft mineral used in making talcum powder.

▶•◆•◆•◆•◀ TALE ▶•◆•◆•◆•◀

THE NOUN
In the "story" sense, there's "Narrative," "Saga," and "Yarn." In the "untrue" sense, there's "Falsehood," "Lie," and "Whopper."

▶•◆•◆•◆•◀ **TAN** ▶•◆•◆•◆•◀

THE NOUN/VERB

Colors close to tan include almond, bronze, and caramel. Noun clues in the "beach" sense: "Basker's quest" and "Sunbather's goal." As a verb, there's "Catch some rays" and "Do leather work."

THE NAME

The books of novelist Amy Tan include *The Joy Luck Club* and *The Kitchen God's Wife*.

NOT SO FAST!

"Parlor product": **T A** ___

The answer can be TAN or TAT (short for "tattoo").

▶•◆•◆•◆•◀ **TAP** ▶•◆•◆•◆•◀

THE NOUN AND VERB

A tap can be a light touch, a spigot for water or alcohol, an attachment to a dancing shoe, or a hidden listening device. Verb clues are based on the noun meanings, including the figurative meaning "gain access to."

▶•◆•◆•◆•◀ **TAR** ▶•◆•◆•◆•◀

ON THE ROAD

Commonly seen clues in this sense: "Coal product," "Pavement goo," and "Roofing material."

ON THE OCEAN

"Tar" is an informal term for a sailor, with synonyms "Gob," "Salt," and "Sea dog."

▶•◆•◆•◆•◀ TARA ▶•◆•◆•◆•◀

THE PLACE
Tara is the Atlanta plantation that is the home of Scarlett O'Hara and her family in the Margaret Mitchell novel *Gone With the Wind* and the film based on it.

THE NAME
Tara Lipinski is a figure skater. Tara Reid is an actress.

▶•◆•◆•◆•◀ TASTE ▶•◆•◆•◆•◀

THE NOUN AND VERB
Taste can be one of the five senses, artistic/fashion discernment, or a sample of food or drink. Verb clues are based on the latter meaning.

▶•◆•◆•◆•◀ TATA ▶•◆•◆•◆•◀

ON THE WAY OUT
"Ta-ta," a word of farewell, is usually defined by other parting words and phrases, such as "So long," "Bye," and "See ya."

▶•◆•◆•◆•◀ TAU ▶•◆•◆•◆•◀

THE LETTER
Tau is the 19th letter of the Greek alphabet. Sigma precedes it; upsilon follows it.

▶•◆•◆•◆•◀ TAXI ▶•◆•◆•◆•◀

THE NOUN, ETC.
Typical clues: "Cab," "Car for hire," "Metered vehicle," "Curbside cry," and references to the competitive car-for-hire companies Uber and Lyft.

THE VERB

Airplanes taxi on the ground before taking off and after landing.

▶•◆•◆•◆•◀ **TDS** ▶•◆•◆•◆•◀

IN FOOTBALL

As a short form of "touchdowns," commonly seen clues include "NFL scores," "QB's successes" (QB is short for "quarterback"), and "Six-pt. plays."

▶•◆•◆•◆•◀ **TEA** ▶•◆•◆•◆•◀

THE DRINK

Commonly seen clues include "British beverage," "Coffee alternative," and "Herbal brew," plus references to tea varieties (such as Earl Grey, oolong, and pekoe) and tea brands (such as Lipton and Tetley). A tea is an afternoon reception at which tea is served.

▶•◆•◆•◆•◀ **TEAR** ▶•◆•◆•◆•◀

THE VERB

As a verb, "tear" can mean to move quickly or to rip.

THE NOUNS

Pronounced "*teer*," it's a drop from the eye. Pronounced "*tare*," it's either a rip or a spree.

▶•◆•◆•◆•◀ **TEASE** ▶•◆•◆•◆•◀

JUST KIDDING

Commonly seen verb clues: "Make fun of," "Needle," "Taunt," and "Twit." As a noun, there's "Coquette" and "Flirt."

▶•◆•◆•◆•◀ TED ▶•◆•◆•◆•◀

THE NAME

Famous Teds include actor Danson, British poet Hughes, senator Kennedy, TV newsman Koppel, and media mogul Turner.
TED Talks are a popular lecture series.

▶•◆•◆•◆•◀ TEE ▶•◆•◆•◆•◀

THE NOUN

A tee may be a collarless shirt, a small platform for a golf ball or football, the golf area where a ball is teed up, or a T-shaped pipe.

▶•◆•◆•◆•◀ TEEM ▶•◆•◆•◆•◀

THE VERB

Commonly seen clues: "Abound," "Overflow," "Rain hard," and "Swarm."

▶•◆•◆•◆•◀ TEEN ▶•◆•◆•◆•◀

THE PERSON

Commonly seen clues: "Adolescent," "High-schooler," and "New driver, often."

▶•◆•◆•◆•◀ TEL ▶•◆•◆•◆•◀

ON THE MAP

Tel Aviv is the second-largest city in Israel.

THE ABBREVIATION

As a short form for "telephone," there's "Addr. book entry," "Business card no.," and "Letterhead abbr."

▶•◆•◆•◆•◀ TEN ▶•◆•◆•◆•◀

NUMERICALLY SPEAKING

Ten is a perfect score in many ranking systems (though not gymnastics anymore), the end of a knockout count in a boxing match, the number of pins in a bowling alley, and the number of players on a lacrosse team. It's the lowest playing card in a royal flush. A portrait of Alexander Hamilton is on a $10 bill (a.k.a. sawbuck). The Roman numeral X is equivalent to 10.

▶•◆•◆•◆•◀ TENET ▶•◆•◆•◆•◀

THE NOUN

A tenet is a principle or doctrine of a group. Synonymous clues include "Belief," "Credo," and "Dogma."

▶•◆•◆•◆•◀ TENOR ▶•◆•◆•◆•◀

IN MUSIC

Tenor is a singing range for male voices, and a range for certain musical instruments, such as the saxophone.

OTHERWISE

Tenor can also be the general tone of a speech or piece of writing.

▶•◆•◆•◆•◀ TENSE ▶•◆•◆•◆•◀

THE ADJECTIVE

Commonly seen adjective clues: "Edgy," "High-strung," "Nervous," and "Uptight."

THE NOUN

Verb tenses include past, present, future, and perfect.

▶•◆•◆•◆•◀ TENT ▶•◆•◆•◆•◀

THE NOUN

Commonly seen clues: "Camping gear," "Circus structure," "Loose-fitting dress," and "Portable shelter."

▶•◆•◆•◆•◀ TERI ▶•◆•◆•◆•◀

THE NAME

Actresses Garr, Hatcher, and Polo are the best-known people named Teri.

▶•◆•◆•◆•◀ TERSE ▶•◆•◆•◆•◀

THE ADJECTIVE

Typical clues: "To the point," "Curt," "Not wordy," and "Brief in speech."

NOT SO FAST!

"You, old-style": **T H __ __**

The answer can be THEE or THOU.

▶•◆•◆•◆•◀ TESLA ▶•◆•◆•◆•◀

THE MAN

Serbian inventor Nikola Tesla is remembered for his contributions to the modern alternating-current electricity supply system. In that endeavor, he was a business rival of Thomas Edison.

THE COMPANY

Named for Nikola, Tesla, Inc., is an electric car company based in Silicon Valley, headed by PayPal cofounder Elon Musk.

▶·◆·◆·◆·◀ TESS ▶·◆·◆·◆·◀

MRS. DICK TRACY

The lantern-jawed police detective in the Chester Gould comic strip wed Tess Trueheart on Christmas Eve, 1949. She is portrayed by Glenne Headly in the 1990 film *Dick Tracy*, starring Warren Beatty.

THE "HARDY" GIRL

Tess Durbeyfield is the title character of the 1891 Thomas Hardy novel *Tess of the d'Urbervilles*. The 1979 film *Tess*, directed by Roman Polanski, is based on the Hardy novel; Nastassja Kinski has the title role.

OTHER TESSES, OTHER FILMS

Joanne Dru portrays Tess Millay, love interest of Montgomery Clift in the 1948 John Ford film *Red River*. Melanie Griffith portrays ambitious secretary Tess McGill in the 1988 film *Working Girl*. More recently, Julia Roberts is Tess Ocean, ex-wife of Danny Ocean (George Clooney), in the 2001 film *Ocean's Eleven* and its 2004 sequel *Ocean's Twelve*.

▶·◆·◆·◆·◀ TEST ▶·◆·◆·◆·◀

THE VERB/NOUN

Commonly seen noun clues: "Dry run," "Exam," "Midterm or final," and "Trial." As a verb, there's "Evaluate" and "Try out." Many of the clues for TEST work as both a noun and a verb, such as "Assay," "Audition," "Experiment," "Quiz," and "Sample."

▶·◆·◆·◆·◀ THAI ▶·◆·◆·◆·◀

IN THE COUNTRY

Thai can be a native of Thailand, the language of Thailand, or an adjective meaning "of Thailand," as the spicy cuisine of that country. In crossword clues, a Thai may be the "neighbor" of a Laotian, a Cambodian, or a Malaysian.

▶•◆•◆•◆•◀ THE ▶•◆•◆•◆•◀

THE ARTICLE

In English grammar, "the" is called the definite article (as opposed to "a" and "an," which are indefinite articles), which is usually ignored in alphabetization. "The" is the most commonly written word in English.

IN FRANCE

"*Thé*" is the French word for "tea," for which it may be clued as "Café alternative."

▶•◆•◆•◆•◀ TIARA ▶•◆•◆•◆•◀

THE NOUN

Commonly seen clues: "Beauty pageant headgear," "Papal wear," "Princess topper," and "Small crown."

▶•◆•◆•◆•◀ TIC ▶•◆•◆•◆•◀

THE NOUN

A tic may be a muscle spasm or a personal quirk. And, of course, there is the game tic-tac-toe.

▶•◆•◆•◆•◀ TIE ▶•◆•◆•◆•◀

WHAT TO WEAR (OR NOT)

Commonly seen clues in this sense: "Cravat," "Haberdashery buy," "Neckwear," and "Suit accessory." Figuratively, there's "Attachment" and "Connection."

THE NO-WIN SITUATION

In this sense, there's "Deadlock," "Overtime cause," "Stalemate," and "Standoff."

THE VERB

Verb clues may be related to either of the above senses, as in "Even the score" and "Make a knot."

311

▶•◆•◆•◆•◀ TIER ▶•◆•◆•◆•◀

THE NOUN

Synonym clues include "Echelon," "Level," and "Rank." Stadiums, theaters, and wedding cakes all have tiers.

NOT SO FAST!

"Ripped off": **T O** ___ ___

In the literal sense, the answer can TORE or TORN; in the slang sense, it can also be TOOK.

▶•◆•◆•◆•◀ TILE ▶•◆•◆•◆•◀

IN THE HOUSE

A tile may be a piece of mosaic, linoleum, or ceramic, etc., found on the floor, wall, or ceiling of a home.

IN THE GAME

Games that use tiles include mah-jongg and Scrabble.

▶•◆•◆•◆•◀ TIN ▶•◆•◆•◆•◀

THE NOUN

As the element (with chemical symbol Sn), commonly seen clues include "Pewter component," "Soft metal," "10th anniversary gift," and references to the countries that are major producers of tin, including Bolivia, Indonesia, and Malaysia. As a container, there's "Baking pan" and "Sardine holder."

▶•◆•◆•◆•◀ TINA ▶•◆•◆•◆•◀

THE NAME

The two best-known Tinas are actress Fey and singer Turner.

312

▶•◈•◈•◈•◀ TIRE ▶•◈•◈•◈•◀

THE VERB

Commonly seen verb clues: "Fatigue," "Grow weary," "Lose energy," and "Tucker out."

THE NOUN

As a noun, you'll see "Bicycle part," "Trunk item," and references to types of tires (such as spare and radial) and tire manufacturers (such as Bridgestone, Goodrich, Goodyear, and Michelin).

▶•◈•◈•◈•◀ TIS ▶•◈•◈•◈•◀

THE CONTRACTION

The poetic form of "it is," usually clued either as part of the songs "Deck the Halls" ("'Tis the season to be jolly") or "America" ("My country, 'tis of thee"), or as the title of the Frank McCourt memoir.

▶•◈•◈•◈•◀ TKO ▶•◈•◈•◈•◀

IT'S OVER

Short for "technical knockout," a TKO is declared when a boxing referee or ring physician decides during a round that a fighter cannot safely continue a match.

▶•◈•◈•◈•◀ TLC ▶•◈•◈•◈•◀

THE TREATMENT

Short for "tender loving care," synonymous clues include "Pampering" and "Special attention," followed by "briefly" or "for short."

ON TV

Originally short for "The Learning Channel," the TLC cable channel currently specializes in reality programming, including the series *Cake Boss* and *Say Yes to the Dress*.

313

THE BAND

Hits by the R&B trio TLC include "Creep," "Waterfalls," "No Scrubs," and "Unpretty."

▶•◆•◆•◆•◀ **TNT** ▶•◆•◆•◆•◀

THE CHEMICAL

TNT, short for "trinitrotoluene," is used as an explosive.

ON THE TUBE

TNT, short for Turner Network Television, is a cable TV channel founded by Ted Turner. Past and current TNT shows include *Claws*, *Rizzoli & Isles*, and *The Closer*.

▶•◆•◆•◆•◀ **TOAD** ▶•◆•◆•◆•◀

THE ANIMAL

The small hopping amphibian, relative of the frog, may be found in ponds or marshes, and is known for its warty skin. Mr. Toad is the main character in Kenneth Grahame's children's novel *The Wind in the Willows*; his friends are Mole, Rat, and Mr. Badger.

THE PERSON

Figuratively speaking, a toad can also be a contemptible person.

▶•◆•◆•◆•◀ **TOE** ▶•◆•◆•◆•◀

ON YOUR FEET

In addition to feet, toes are parts of boots, shoes, socks, and stockings. Toes are the "little piggies" in the kids' nursery rhyme, and what ballet dancers pivot on when performing pirouettes. To "toe the line" is to follow the rules (a figurative extension of runners getting into the correct position before a race, with their toes at the starting line).

▶·◆·◆·◆·◀ **TOGA** ▶·◆·◆·◆·◀

WHAT TO WEAR

In ancient Rome, a loose outer garment worn by citizens, as at the Roman Forum (public square). A "toga party" is a college fraternity event where such garments are worn.

▶·◆·◆·◆·◀ **TON** ▶·◆·◆·◆·◀

THE MEASURE

As 2,000 pounds, commonly seen clues are variations of "Freight weight" and "Trucking unit." Figuratively speaking, a ton can also be a large quantity of anything.

▶·◆·◆·◆·◀ **TONE** ▶·◆·◆·◆·◀

THE NOUN/VERB

In the "hue" sense, there's "Coloring" and "Shade." In the audible sense, there's "Inflection," "Musical signal," "Pitch," and "Vocal quality." "Tone" can also refer to the resiliency of one's muscles, and, as a verb, to improve those muscles.

▶·◆·◆·◆·◀ **TOO** ▶·◆·◆·◆·◀

THE ADVERB

In the "ditto" sense, there's "Also," "As well," "In addition," and "Moreover." In the "excessive" sense, there's "Overly" and "Unduly."

▶·◆·◆·◆·◀ **TOP** ▶·◆·◆·◆·◀

THE NOUN

A top can be the highest point or best part of anything, a lid, a blouse/shirt, or a spinning toy.

THE VERB
As a verb, there's "Beat," "Surpass," and "Outdo."

THE ADJECTIVE
Adjectivally, "top" is synonymous with "foremost" or "highest."

▶•◆•◆•◆•◀ TORE ▶•◆•◆•◆•◀

THE VERB
As the past tense of "tear," "tore" can mean "moved quickly" or "ripped."

▶•◆•◆•◆•◀ TOSS ▶•◆•◆•◆•◀

THE VERB AND NOUN
"Toss" can mean "light throw" (or the throw itself) or, informally, "to throw away."

▶•◆•◆•◆•◀ TOT ▶•◆•◆•◆•◀

THE KID
Commonly seen "juvenile" clues: "Moppet," "Preschooler," "Rug rat," and "Tyke."

THE VERB
To "tot up" means to calculate or to add.

▶•◆•◆•◆•◀ TOTE ▶•◆•◆•◆•◀

THE VERB/NOUN
Commonly seen verb clues: "Carry," "Lug," and "Schlep." As a noun, it's a bag with a handle.

CROSSWORDS 101
Lesson 15: Greek Goddesses

These Greek goddesses appear frequently in crosswords (their Roman equivalents are in parentheses).

APHRODITE (Venus): goddess of Beauty, daughter of Zeus, mother of **Ares**

ARTEMIS (Diana): goddess of the Hunt, daughter of Zeus, twin sister of **Apollo**

ATHENA (Minerva): goddess of Wisdom, daughter of Zeus

DEMETER (Ceres): goddess of **Agriculture**, sister of Zeus and Hera

EOS (Aurora): goddess of the Dawn, sister of Selene

ERIS: goddess of Discord

HERA (Juno): Queen of the gods, sister and wife of Zeus

HESTIA (Vesta): goddess of the Hearth, sister of Zeus and Hades

IRENE (Pax): goddess of Peace, daughter of Zeus

IRIS: goddess of the Rainbow

RHEA (Ops): Mother of the gods, mother of Zeus, Hera, and Hades

SELENE (Luna): goddess of the Moon, sister of Eos

317

▶•◆•◆•◆•◀ TOTO ▶•◆•◆•◆•◀

THE POOCH

Toto is Dorothy's dog in the Oz stories of L. Frank Baum and the film *The Wizard of Oz*.

THE BAND

The band Toto's hits include "Hold the Line," "Rosanna," and "Africa."

FROM THE LATIN

The phrase "*in toto*" means "completely."

▶•◆•◆•◆•◀ TRA ▶•◆•◆•◆•◀

IN MUSIC

"Tra" is sung as part of the filler syllables "tra-la-la."

▶•◆•◆•◆•◀ TRAP ▶•◆•◆•◆•◀

THE VERB

Common verb clues include "Ensnare," "Capture," and "Corner."

THE NOUN

As a noun, a trap can be something that ensnares, a sandy golf hazard, or a slang term for "mouth."

▶•◆•◆•◆•◀ TREE ▶•◆•◆•◆•◀

LITERALLY SPEAKING

Commonly seen clues include "Arbor Day planting," "Fruit bearer," "Hammock holder," "Shade source," and references to many common types of trees, such as apple, maple, peach, sequoia, walnut, etc.

FIGURATIVELY SPEAKING

A tree is also a genealogy diagram and a device for preserving the shape of a shoe.

THE VERB

To "tree" someone or something is to corner them, or put them in a difficult position.

►•◆•◆•◆•◄ **TREK** ►•◆•◆•◆•◄

THE NOUN AND VERB

A trek is a difficult journey, or to make such a journey. And there is the *Star Trek* franchise of TV series and films.

►•◆•◆•◆•◄ **TRI** ►•◆•◆•◆•◄

THE PREFIX

Meaning "three," "tri-" can be added to words such as "angle" and "cycle." It is also what the first T stands for in TNT.

►•◆•◆•◆•◄ **TRIO** ►•◆•◆•◆•◄

THE NOUN

A trio is any group of three persons or things, but is most commonly clued as a small group of musicians, either generically (such as "Quartet minus one" or "Small combo") or with specific examples (such as the singing groups the Dixie Chicks and the Supremes).

►•◆•◆•◆•◄ **TROT** ►•◆•◆•◆•◄

THE NOUN AND VERB

A trot is a slow running gait, applied to people or horses. Specifically for horses, it's also a harness race.

►•◆•◆•◆•◄ **TRUE** ►•◆•◆•◆•◄

THE ADJECTIVE

Commonly seen clues: "Factual," "Faithful," "Loyal," and "Undeniable."

▶·◆·◆·◆·◀ **TRY** ▶·◆·◆·◆·◀

THE VERB AND NOUN

In addition to its "attempt" or "test" meaning (as either a verb or noun), a court case is tried, and one's patience may be tried.

▶·◆·◆·◆·◀ **TSE** ▶·◆·◆·◆·◀

IN CHINA

Mao Tse-tung (a.k.a. Mao Zedong) was the Communist leader of the People's Republic of China from 1949 into the 1970s. Lao-tse was an ancient Chinese philosopher.

THE INITIALS

TSE is the monogram of poet T.S. Eliot, whose works include *Ash Wednesday*, *The Waste Land*, "The Love Song of J. Alfred Prufrock," and a collection of light verse that was the basis for the Andrew Lloyd Webber musical *Cats*.

▶·◆·◆·◆·◀ **TSK** ▶·◆·◆·◆·◀

THE SOUND

"Tsk" may be defined generically, such as "Sound of disapproval," or by phrases expressing disapproval, such as "Shame on you!"

▶·◆·◆·◆·◀ **TSP** ▶·◆·◆·◆·◀

FOR SHORT

An abbreviation for "teaspoon," "tsp." is often seen in recipes and dosages of liquid medicines. It's a measure of volume equivalent to ⅙ of a fluid ounce.

▶·◆·◆·◆·◀ **TUNA** ▶·◆·◆·◆·◀

AT SEA

Tuna may be found in a sandwich or in sushi. Tuna varieties include albacore and bluefin. Popular brands of tuna: Chicken of the Sea, Bumble Bee and Star-Kist, the latter promoted in ads by cartoon character Charlie the Tuna.

▶·◆·◆·◆·◀ **TWO** ▶·◆·◆·◆·◀

NUMERICALLY SPEAKING

Two is an early afternoon hour, and a "wee hour" in the A.M. In games, it's a playing card also called a "deuce" and a dice roll of "snake eyes." Two are needed to perform a duet, to ride on a seesaw, and (as the old saying goes) to tango.

U-Z

Ute chief Sevara and family, c. 1899

►◆·◆·◆·◆·◄ UBOAT ►◆·◆·◆·◆·◄

AT SEA

A U-boat was a German submarine of World War II. The "U" was short for *Untersee*, German for "undersea."

►◆·◆·◆·◄ UCLA ►◆·◆·◆·◄

THE ABBREVIATION

The University of California–Los Angeles is a member of the Pac-12 sports conference. Its teams are called the Bruins, whose rivals are the Trojans of USC. Celebrities who attended UCLA include Arthur Ashe, Carol Burnett, and Jackie Robinson.

►◆·◆·◆·◄ UFO ►◆·◆·◆·◄

IN THE SKY

Common clues: "Sci-fi vehicle," "E.T.'s craft" and "Space alien's ship."

NOT SO FAST!

"Exited": ___ E ___ T

The answer can be LEFT or the nearly synonymous WENT.

►◆·◆·◆·◄ UMA ►◆·◆·◆·◄

THE ACTRESS

Uma Thurman has appeared in such films as *Pulp Fiction*, *The Producers*, and *Kill Bill*.

▶·◆·◆·◆·◀ UNE ▶·◆·◆·◆·◀

IN PARIS

"*Une*" is the French word for "one" (half of *deux*) or the article "a."

▶·◆·◆·◆·◀ UNI ▶·◆·◆·◆·◀

THE PREFIX

"Uni-" can be added to words such as "cycle," "form," "lateral," and "verse." Meaning "one," it is similar to "mono-."

▶·◆·◆·◆·◀ UNIT ▶·◆·◆·◆·◀

THE NOUN

Commonly seen clues: "Army group," "Condo division," "Curriculum section," and references to common units of measure such as the foot and the gallon.

▶·◆·◆·◆·◀ UNITE ▶·◆·◆·◆·◀

THE VERB

Commonly seen clues: "Bring together," "Fuse," "Join forces," and "Merge."

▶·◆·◆·◆·◀ UNO ▶·◆·◆·◆·◀

IN SPAIN

"*Uno*" is the Spanish word for "one." It's Italian for "one" too, but it's seldom clued that way.

THE GAME

Uno is a brand name for a card game with rules similar to crazy eights.

▶▪◆▪◆▪◆▪◀ UNTO ▶▪◆▪◆▪◆▪◀

THE PREPOSITION

The old-style preposition, frequently used in the Bible, is part of the golden rule ("Do unto others ...")

▶▪◆▪◆▪◆▪◀ UPON ▶▪◆▪◆▪◆▪◀

TWO WORDS

Commonly seen clues for UP ON include "Familiar with" and "Versed in."

THE PREPOSITION

The preposition "upon" is the second word of Edgar Allan Poe's "The Raven" ("Once upon a midnight dreary ...") and many fairy tales ("Once upon a time ..."). There's also Stratford-Upon-Avon, Shakespeare's hometown, as well as the colloquial "Upon my word!" A common synonym clue for this sense of the word is "Atop."

▶▪◆▪◆▪◆▪◀ URAL ▶▪◆▪◆▪◆▪◀

ON THE MAP

Russia's Ural Mountains form part of the border between Europe and Asia. The Ural River originates in the Ural Mountains and flows into the Caspian Sea.

▶▪◆▪◆▪◆▪◀ URGE ▶▪◆▪◆▪◆▪◀

THE VERB

Commonly seen verb clues: "Advocate," "Egg on," "Lobby for," and "Press."

THE NOUN

Commonly seen noun clues: "Craving," "Desire," "Hankering," and "Impulse."

▶•◆•◆•◆•◀ URIS ▶•◆•◆•◆•◀

THE NAME
The novels of author Leon Uris include *Battle Cry*, *Exodus*, *The Haj*, *Mila 18*, *Topaz*, and *Trinity*.

▶•◆•◆•◆•◀ URN ▶•◆•◆•◆•◀

THE CONTAINER
An urn may be a type of vase, or a large machine that brews coffee or tea.

▶•◆•◆•◆•◀ URSA ▶•◆•◆•◆•◀

UP IN THE SKY
"*Ursa*" is the Latin word for "bear," seen in crosswords solely as part of the constellations Ursa Minor (which contains the Big Dipper) and Ursa Minor (which contains the Little Dipper).

▶•◆•◆•◆•◀ USA ▶•◆•◆•◆•◀

ON THE MAP
In this sense, USA is often defined either in terms of the treaties or organizations that it's a member of (such as NAFTA, NATO, and OAS), recent Olympic games it has hosted (1996 Summer and 2002 Winter), its geographic neighbors (Mexico and Canada), or the patriotic cheer for American teams at international athletic competitions.

ON TV
The USA cable network broadcasts much "second run" programming, plus the (former and current) original series *Monk*, *Burn Notice*, *Suits*, and *Mr. Robot*.

▸·◆·◆·◆·◀ **USE** ▸·◆·◆·◆·◀

THE VERB

Commonly seen verb clues: "Consume," "Employ," "Put to work," and "Take advantage of."

THE NOUN

As a noun, there's "Application," "Function," "Purpose," and "Wear and tear."

▸·◆·◆·◆·◀ **USER** ▸·◆·◆·◆·◀

THE PERSON

"User" is most often defined as the user of a computer, with clues such as "___-friendly," "PC owner," "Software buyer," and "Web surfer."

▸·◆·◆·◆·◀ **USO** ▸·◆·◆·◆·◀

R&R

Short for "United Service Organizations," the USO provides recreation centers and live entertainment to members of the Armed Forces and their families. Bob Hope performed in USO shows for many years and is still strongly associated with them, so you may see him referenced in clues for USO.

▸·◆·◆·◆·◀ **USSR** ▸·◆·◆·◆·◀

ON THE MAP

Short for "Union of Soviet Socialist Republics" (a.k.a. the former Soviet Union), commonly seen clues include "Cold War letters," "Former U.N. member," and references to its onetime leaders (such as Lenin, Stalin, Khrushchev, and Gorbachev).

▶•◆•◆•◆•◀ UTAH ▶•◆•◆•◆•◀

ON THE MAP

Utah is usually defined in terms of its cities (such as Provo and Salt Lake City), its neighboring states (Arizona, Colorado, Idaho, Nevada, and Wyoming, and with New Mexico at a single point at the Four Corners border), its National Parks (such as Bryce Canyon and Zion), or the Utah Jazz pro basketball team. Its nickname is the Beehive State. Utah's borders are six straight lines, so it will sometimes be clued as "Six-sided state" or "Hexagon on the map."

▶•◆•◆•◆•◀ UTE ▶•◆•◆•◆•◀

THE PEOPLE

The Utes are a Shoshonean Native American group now living primarily in Utah and Colorado. "Utes" is the nickname of the sports teams of the University of Utah at Salt Lake City.

ON THE ROAD

"Ute" is short for "utility" in the phrase "sport ute," another way to say "SUV."

▶•◆•◆•◆•◀ VIA ▶•◆•◆•◆•◀

THE PREPOSITION

Often seen on travel itineraries, "via" is synonymous with "by way of" or "passing through."

IN ROME

"*Via*" is also the Latin word for "way" (as in "road"), in such Latin routes as Via Appia (Appian Way). The word has the same meaning in modern Italian; the Via Veneto is a street in Rome known for its upscale hotels and restaurants.

▶•◆•◆•◆•◀ WAR ▶•◆•◆•◆•◀

THE NOUN

Commonly seen clues include "Armed conflict" and "Combat." There is also the children's card game.

▶•◆•◆•◆•◀ WAS ▶•◆•◆•◆•◀

THE VERB

Clues will usually be similar to "Existed," "Used to be," and "Took place."

▶•◆•◆•◆•◀ WEE ▶•◆•◆•◆•◀

THE ADJECTIVE

Most any synonym of "little" may be seen as a clue for WEE, including "Tiny," "Very small," and "Diminutive."

▶•◆•◆•◆•◀ WET ▶•◆•◆•◆•◀

THE ADJECTIVE AND VERB

You're likely to see clues like "Drenched," "Damp" (or "Dampen"), or "Freshly painted." Referring to weather, you may see "Rainy."

IN HISTORY

During prohibition, a "wet" was someone opposed to prohibition (unlike a "dry," who was in favor of it), and who might have been seen at a speakeasy.

NOT SO FAST!

"Family member": ___ A ___ A

This may be either MAMA, PAPA, or NANA (grandmother).

CROSSWORDS 101
Lesson 16: Mythical Gods

These male gods appear frequently
in crosswords.

Greek (and Roman equivalents):

APOLLO: god of music and poetry, son of
Zeus and Leto, twin of Artemis

ARES (Mars): god of war, son of Zeus and Hera

EROS (Cupid, Amor): god of love, son
of Aphrodite

HADES (Pluto): god of the underworld, son of
Cronus and Rhea, brother of Zeus, Hera, and
Poseidon

HERMES (Mercury): messenger of the gods,
son of Zeus and Maia

PAN: god of forests and pastures

ZEUS (Jupiter): supreme god, son of Cronus
and Rhea, brother of Hades, Hera, and
Poseidon, father of Ares, Apollo, Artemis,
Athena, Hermes, and the Muses

Norse:

LOKI: trickster god

ODIN: supreme god and god of war, husband
of Frigg, father of Thor

THOR: god of thunder, son of Odin and Frigg

▶•◈•◈•◈•◀ **YALE** ▶•◈•◈•◈•◀

THE SCHOOL

Located in New Haven, Connecticut, Yale University is a member of the Ivy League group of schools. Thus its athletic rivals include Harvard and Brown. You'll often seen Yale clued with its most famous alumni, such as actresses Meryl Streep and Jodie Foster, Nathan Hale, Noah Webster, both presidents Bush, and Bill and Hillary Clinton. Its students are called Elis, and its mascot is a bulldog.

▶•◈•◈•◈•◀ **YDS** ▶•◈•◈•◈•◀

THE ABBREVIATION

Yds. (short for "yards") are usually clued in terms of distances and lengths usually measured in yards, such as in sports (football and golf) and fabrics.

NOT SO FAST!

"Football stats: Abbr.": ___ **D S**

The answer can be TDS (short for "touchdowns") or YDS (short for "yards").

▶•◈•◈•◈•◀ **YEA** ▶•◈•◈•◈•◀

THAT'S O.K.

"Yea" is an affirmative vote, often spoken by legislators in parliamentary roll calls, for whom "nay" is the opposite.

INSIDER'S TIP: Many clues for YEA are also applicable to AYE and YES, and all three words are regularly seen in crosswords.

▶•◈•◈•◈•◀ YEAR ▶•◈•◈•◈•◀

THE TIME

Commonly seen clues: "Calendar capacity," "Fiscal period,"
"Once around the sun," and "Wine label info." Clues may also
reference class years, as in freshmen, sophomores, juniors,
and seniors.

▶•◈•◈•◈•◀ YEN ▶•◈•◈•◈•◀

INTANGIBLE

Synonymous clues include "Craving," "Yearning," and "Longing."

TANGIBLE

Yen is the monetary unit of Japan, where its plural is also yen. In
harder puzzles, it is sometimes clued with a reference to the Tokyo
Stock Exchange's Nikkei index, such as "Nikkei unit."

▶•◈•◈•◈•◀ YES ▶•◈•◈•◈•◀

THE INTERJECTION

In this sense, the clue is usually a colloquial expression, such as
"I do," "Of course!," "Okay!," and "You bet!"

THE VOTE

Commonly seen clues in this sense: "Affirmative response,"
"Assent," and "Thumbs-up vote."

THE BAND

The rock band Yes is known for their songs "Roundabout" and
"Owner of a Lonely Heart."

INSIDER'S TIP: Many clues for YES are also applicable to
AYE and YEA, and all three words are regularly seen in
crosswords.

▶·◆·◆·◆·◆·◀ **YET** ▶·◆·◆·◆·◆·◀

THE ADVERB

Common crossword synonyms: "So far," "Up to now," and "To date."

THE CONJUNCTION

As a conjunction, "yet" is synonymous with "nevertheless" and "though."

▶·◆·◆·◆·◆·◀ **ZERO** ▶·◆·◆·◆·◆·◀

THE ROUND NUMBER

Typical clues include "Zilch," "Nothing," and "Not any."

ACKNOWLEDGMENTS

For their help in making this book possible, the author would like to thank:

- Kevin McCann, proprietor of the "Crossword Community Center" website www.cruciverb.com. Cruciverb includes a database of clues and answers for many of America's best-known crosswords, which I consulted frequently as a check on and a supplement to my own puzzle database and less-than-perfect memory.
- At Puzzlewright Press: Peter Gordon and Francis Heaney, for their considerable assistance and good counsel.
- And a special thanks to Michael Owen, Archivist for the Ira and Leonore Gershwin Trusts, who kindly supplied a photo of Mr. Gershwin, and revealed that Ira was a crossword solver of long standing.

PHOTO CREDITS

Denver Public Library: 323
Ira and Leonore Gershwin Trusts: 139
fotolia.com: 87, 183, 201, 261
Library of Congress: 9, 175, 225, 235, 301
National Human Genome Research Institute: 79
U.S. Fish and Wildlife Service: 67, 129
U.S. Geological Survey: 157